The War of the Realms
Journey Into Mystery

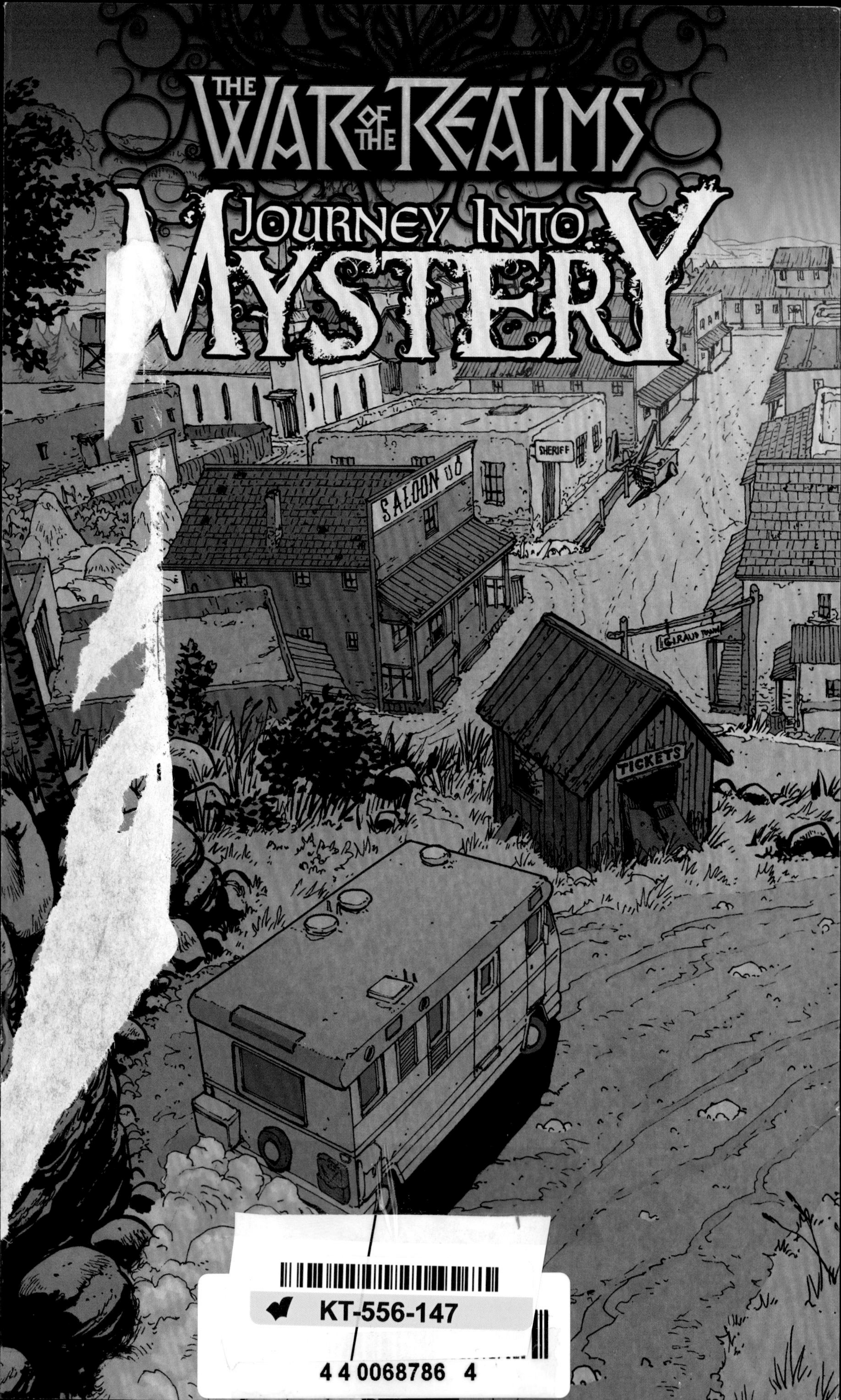
SHERIFF
SALOON
TICKETS

THE WAR OF THE REALMS

After laying waste to nine of the Ten Realms, the Dark Elf king
Malekith and his powerful allies have finally brought the
War of the Realms to Midgard — the last realm standing!

The gods of Asgard, who have been living as refugees on Earth after
Malekith sieged the Mangog on their home, have united with the heroes
of Earth to defend their adopted realm. Thor himself is trapped in the Frost
Giant's realm, leaving his mother, Lady Freyja, to command Asgard's forces.
Among the Asgardians fights Balder, Thor's recently resurrected brother.

And they're all about to meet the devil. Malekith's ally Sindr,
queen of fiery Muspelheim and daughter of Surtur, one of Asgard's
greatest enemies, has her hell-fired heart set on revenge. The Asgardians
have fouled her and her father's plans for the last time...

COLLECTION EDITOR **JENNIFER GRÜNWALD**   **CAITLIN O'CONNELL** ASSISTANT EDITOR
ASSOCIATE MANAGING EDITOR **KATERI WOODY**   **MARK D. BEAZLEY** EDITOR, SPECIAL PROJECTS
VP PRODUCTION & SPECIAL PROJECTS **JEFF YOUNGQUIST**   **JAY BOWEN** BOOK DESIGNER

SVP PRINT, SALES & MARKETING **DAVID GABRIEL**   **SVEN LARSEN** DIRECTOR, LICENSED PUBLISHING
EDITOR IN CHIEF **C.B. CEBULSKI**   **JOE QUESADA** CHIEF CREATIVE OFFICER
PRESIDENT **DAN BUCKLEY**   **ALAN FINE** EXECUTIVE PRODUCER

WAR OF THE REALMS: JOURNEY INTO MYSTERY. Contains material originally published in magazine form as WAR OF THE REALMS: JOURNEY INTO MYSTERY #1-5. First printing 2019. ISBN 978-1-302-91834-7. Published by MARVEL WORLDWIDE, INC., a subsidiary of MARVEL ENTERTAINMENT, LLC. OFFICE OF PUBLICATION: 135 West 50th Street, New York, NY 10020. © 2019 MARVEL No similarity between any of the names, characters, persons, and/or institutions in this magazine with those of any living or dead person or institution is intended, and any such similarity which may exist is purely coincidental. **Printed in Canada.** DAN BUCKLEY, President, Marvel Entertainment; JOHN NEE, Publisher; JOE QUESADA, Chief Creative Officer; TOM BREVOORT, SVP of Publishing; DAVID BOGART, Associate Publisher & SVP of Talent Affairs; DAVID GABRIEL, SVP of Sales & Marketing, Publishing; JEFF YOUNGQUIST, VP of Production & Special Projects; DAN CARR, Executive Director of Publishing Technology; ALEX MORALES, Director of Publishing Operations; DAN EDINGTON, Managing Editor; SUSAN CRESPI, Production Manager; STAN LEE, Chairman Emeritus. For information regarding advertising in Marvel Comics or on Marvel.com, please contact Vit DeBellis, Custom Solutions & Integrated Advertising Manager, at vdebellis@marvel.com. For Marvel subscription inquiries, please call 888-511-5480. **Manufactured between 7/5/2019 and 8/6/2019 by SOLISCO PRINTERS, SCOTT, QC, CANADA.**

10 9 8 7 6 5 4 3 2 1

JOURNEY INTO MYSTERY

The
McElroys
WRITERS

André Lima
Araújo
ARTIST

Chris
O'Halloran
COLOR ARTIST

VC's Clayton
Cowles
LETTERER

Valerio Schiti & David Curiel
COVER ART

Sarah Brunstad
ASSOCIATE EDITOR

Wil Moss
EDITOR

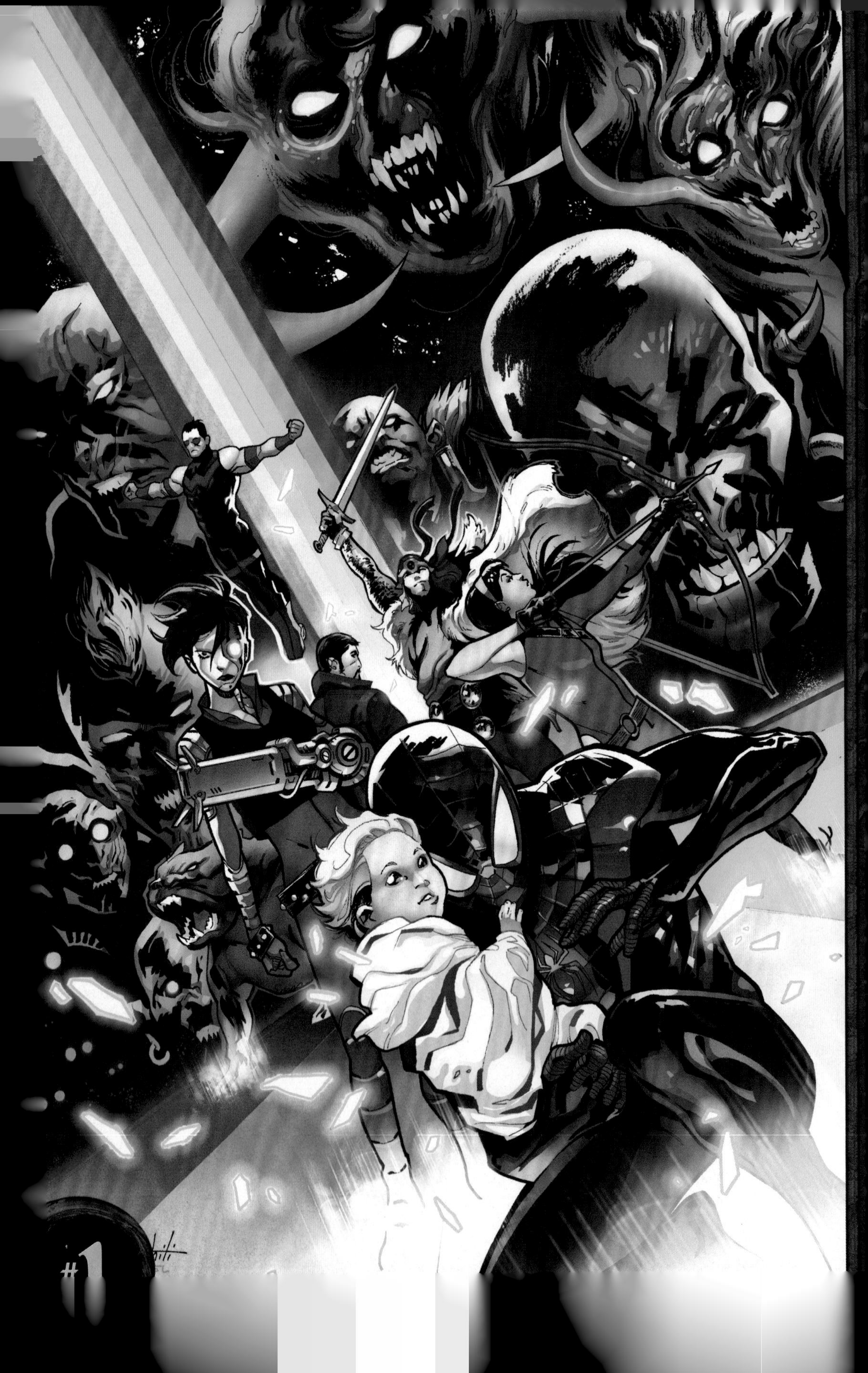
#1

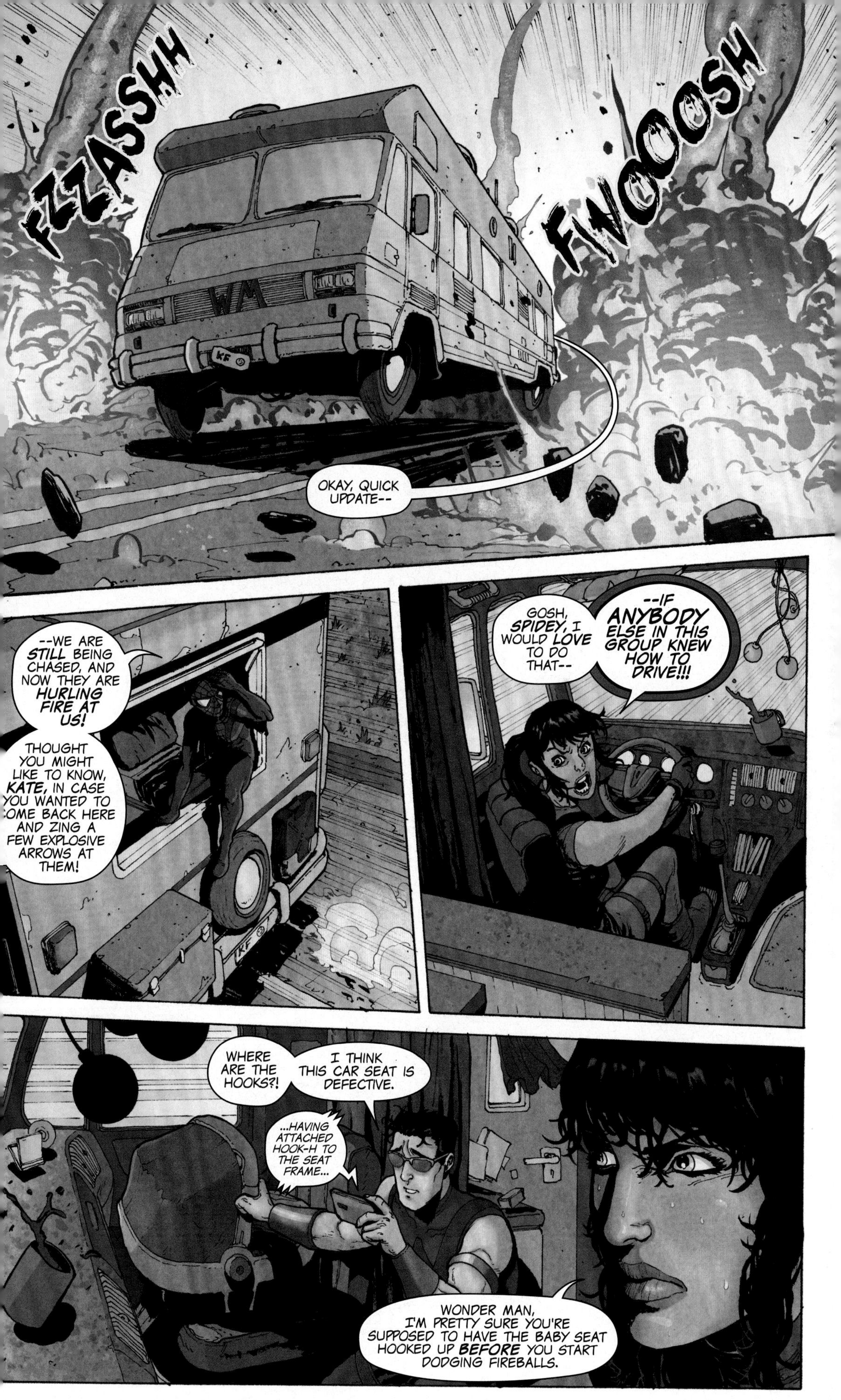
FZZASSHH
FWOOOSH
OKAY, QUICK UPDATE--
--WE ARE STILL BEING CHASED, AND NOW THEY ARE HURLING FIRE AT US!
THOUGHT YOU MIGHT LIKE TO KNOW, KATE, IN CASE YOU WANTED TO COME BACK HERE AND ZING A FEW EXPLOSIVE ARROWS AT THEM!
GOSH, SPIDEY, I WOULD LOVE TO DO THAT--
--IF ANYBODY ELSE IN THIS GROUP KNEW HOW TO DRIVE!!!
WHERE ARE THE HOOKS?!
I THINK THIS CAR SEAT IS DEFECTIVE.
...HAVING ATTACHED HOOK-H TO THE SEAT FRAME...
WONDER MAN, I'M PRETTY SURE YOU'RE SUPPOSED TO HAVE THE BABY SEAT HOOKED UP BEFORE YOU START DODGING FIREBALLS.

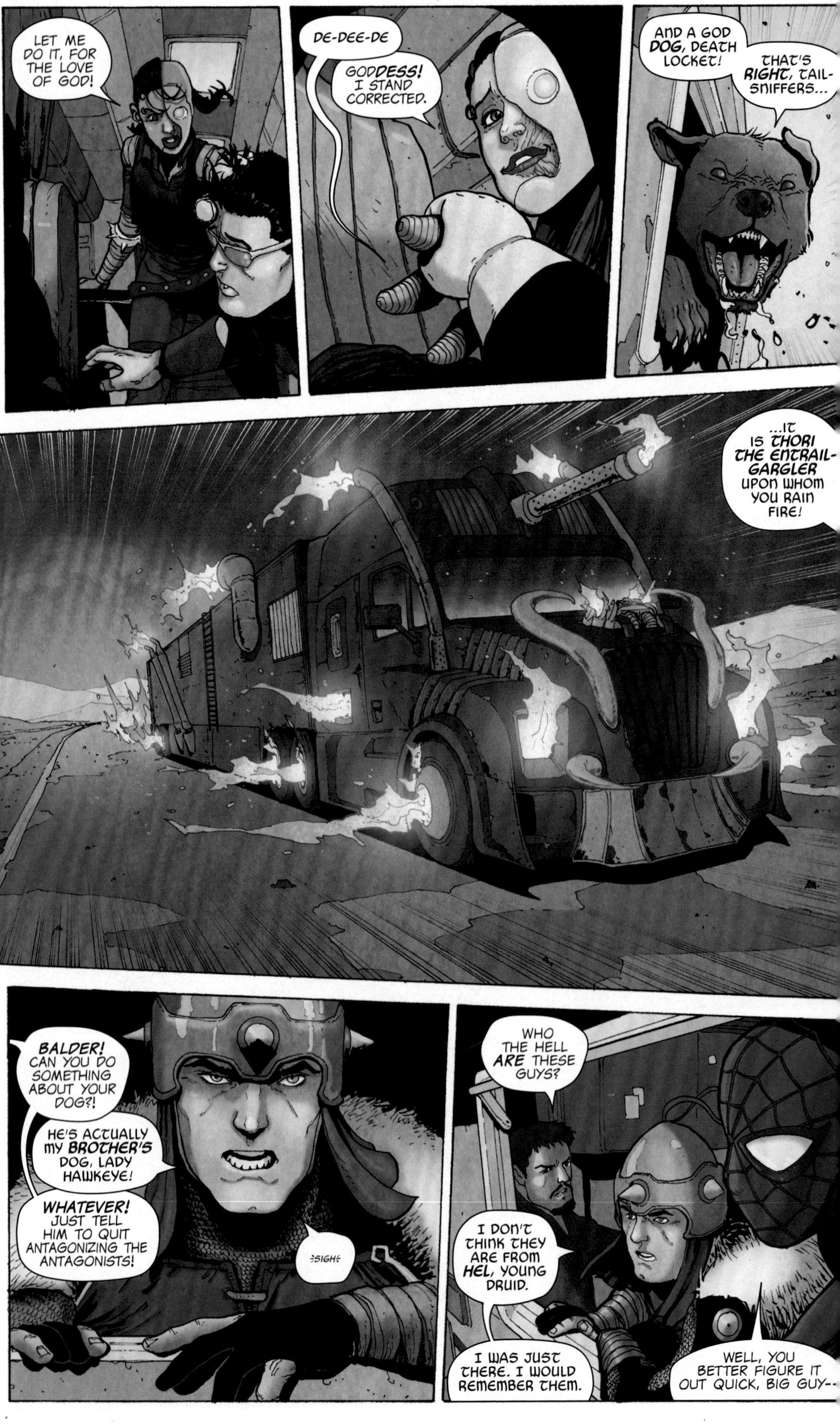
LET ME DO IT, FOR THE LOVE OF GOD!
DE-DEE-DE
GODDESS! I STAND CORRECTED.
AND A GOD DOG, DEATH LOCKET!
THAT'S RIGHT, TAIL-SNIFFERS...
...IT IS THORI THE ENTRAIL-GARGLER UPON WHOM YOU RAIN FIRE!
BALDER! CAN YOU DO SOMETHING ABOUT YOUR DOG?!
HE'S ACTUALLY MY BROTHER'S DOG, LADY HAWKEYE!
WHATEVER! JUST TELL HIM TO QUIT ANTAGONIZING THE ANTAGONISTS!
SIGH
WHO THE HELL ARE THESE GUYS?
I DON'T THINK THEY ARE FROM HEL, YOUNG DRUID.
I WAS JUST THERE. I WOULD REMEMBER THEM.
WELL, YOU BETTER FIGURE IT OUT QUICK, BIG GUY--

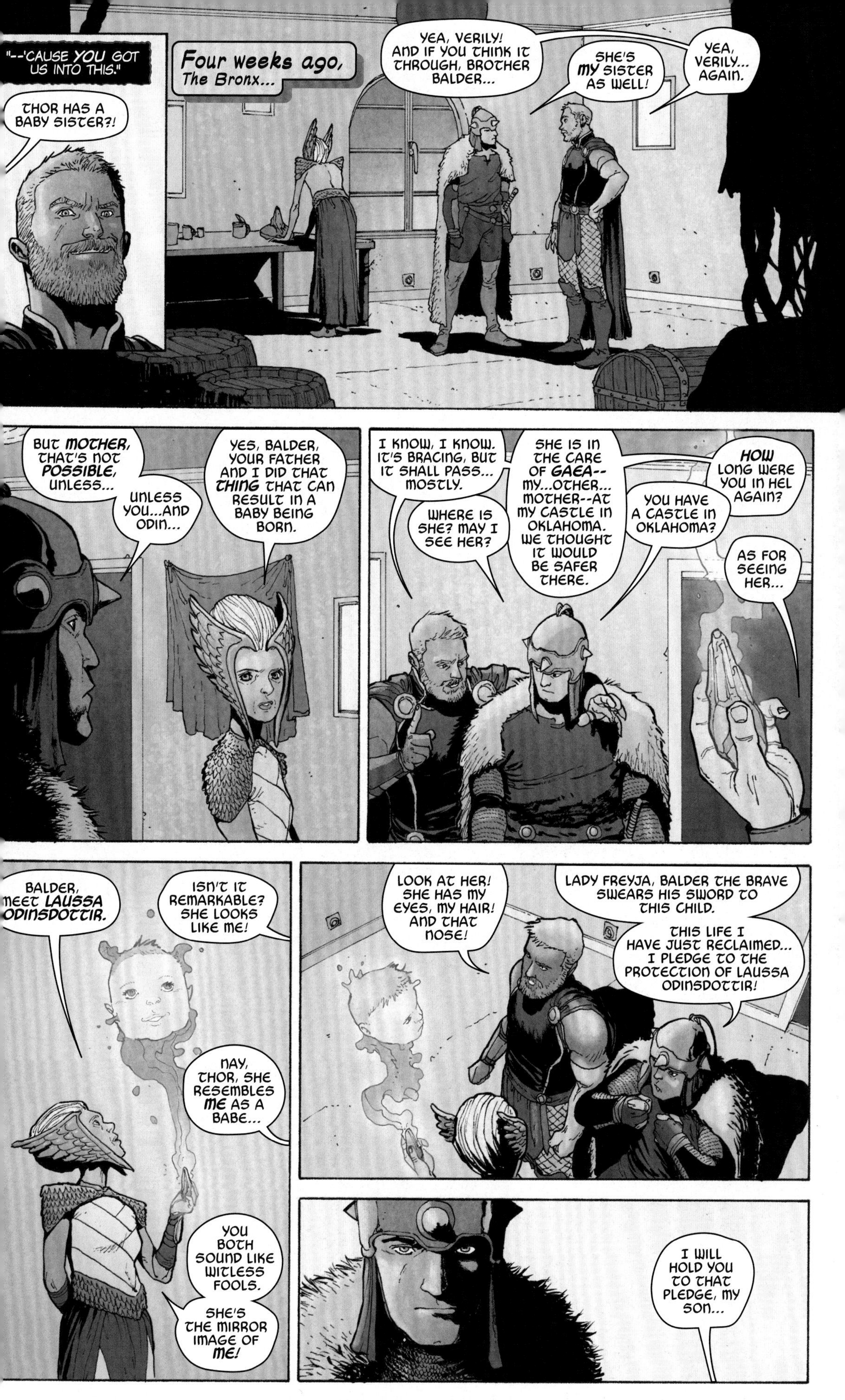
"--'CAUSE YOU GOT US INTO THIS."
THOR HAS A BABY SISTER?!
Four weeks ago, The Bronx...
YEA, VERILY! AND IF YOU THINK IT THROUGH, BROTHER BALDER...
SHE'S MY SISTER AS WELL!
YEA, VERILY... AGAIN.
BUT MOTHER, THAT'S NOT POSSIBLE, UNLESS...
UNLESS YOU...AND ODIN...
YES, BALDER, YOUR FATHER AND I DID THAT THING THAT CAN RESULT IN A BABY BEING BORN.
I KNOW, I KNOW. IT'S BRACING, BUT IT SHALL PASS... MOSTLY.
WHERE IS SHE? MAY I SEE HER?
SHE IS IN THE CARE OF GAEA-- MY...OTHER... MOTHER--AT MY CASTLE IN OKLAHOMA. WE THOUGHT IT WOULD BE SAFER THERE.
YOU HAVE A CASTLE IN OKLAHOMA?
HOW LONG WERE YOU IN HEL AGAIN?
AS FOR SEEING HER...
BALDER, MEET LAUSSA ODINSDOTTIR.
ISN'T IT REMARKABLE? SHE LOOKS LIKE ME!
NAY, THOR, SHE RESEMBLES ME AS A BABE...
YOU BOTH SOUND LIKE WITLESS FOOLS.
SHE'S THE MIRROR IMAGE OF ME!
LOOK AT HER! SHE HAS MY EYES, MY HAIR! AND THAT NOSE!
LADY FREYJA, BALDER THE BRAVE SWEARS HIS SWORD TO THIS CHILD.
THIS LIFE I HAVE JUST RECLAIMED... I PLEDGE TO THE PROTECTION OF LAUSSA ODINSDOTTIR!
I WILL HOLD YOU TO THAT PLEDGE, MY SON...

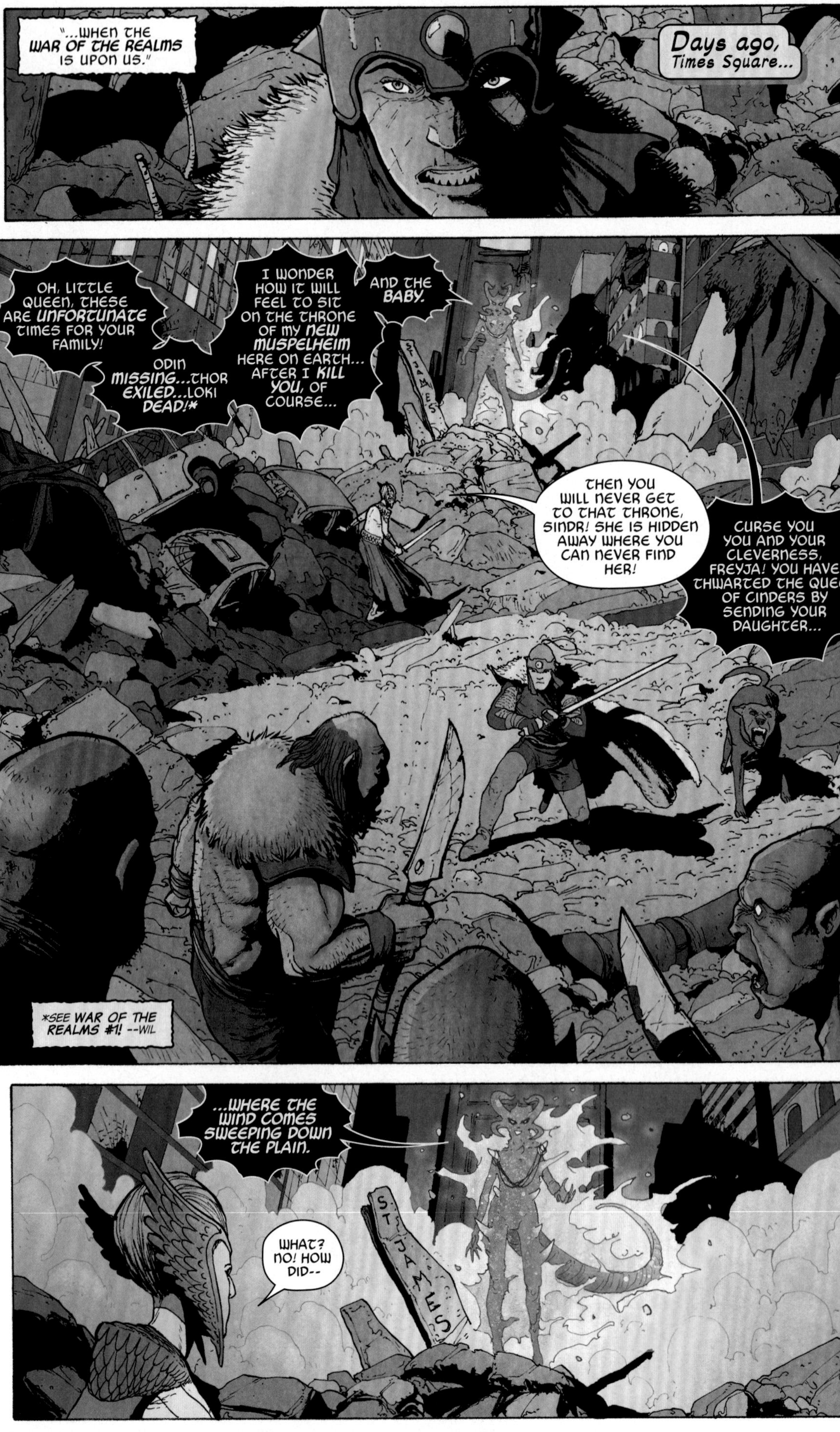
"...WHEN THE WAR OF THE REALMS IS UPON US."
Days ago, Times Square...
OH, LITTLE QUEEN, THESE ARE UNFORTUNATE TIMES FOR YOUR FAMILY!
ODIN MISSING...THOR EXILED...LOKI DEAD!*
I WONDER HOW IT WILL FEEL TO SIT ON THE THRONE OF MY NEW MUSPELHEIM HERE ON EARTH... AFTER I KILL YOU, OF COURSE...
AND THE BABY.
THEN YOU WILL NEVER GET TO THAT THRONE, SINDR! SHE IS HIDDEN AWAY WHERE YOU CAN NEVER FIND HER!
CURSE YOU YOU AND YOUR CLEVERNESS, FREYJA! YOU HAVE THWARTED THE QUEEN OF CINDERS BY SENDING YOUR DAUGHTER...
*SEE WAR OF THE REALMS #1! --WIL
...WHERE THE WIND COMES SWEEPING DOWN THE PLAIN.
WHAT? NO! HOW DID--

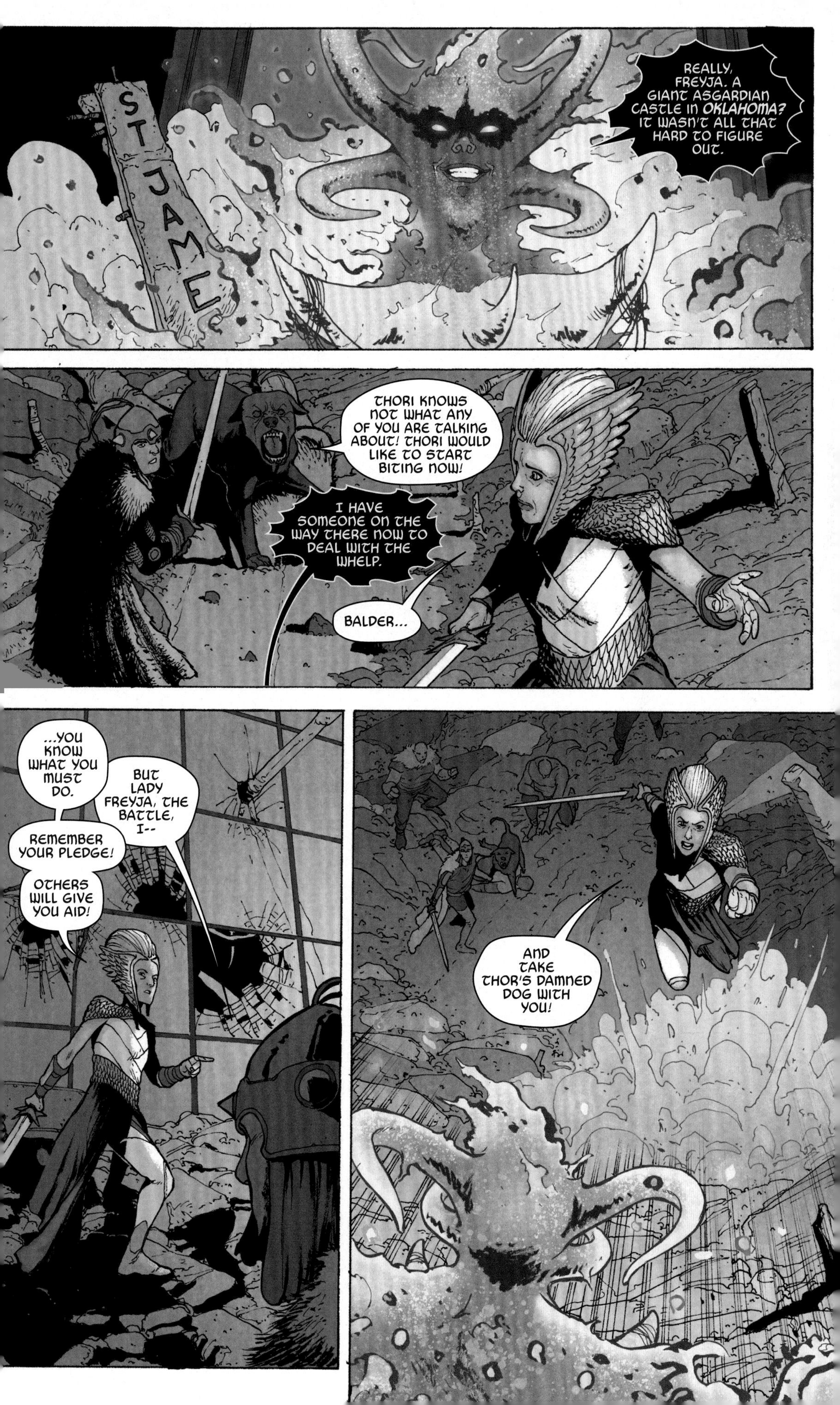

ST JAME
REALLY, FREYJA. A GIANT ASGARDIAN CASTLE IN OKLAHOMA? IT WASN'T ALL THAT HARD TO FIGURE OUT.
THORI KNOWS NOT WHAT ANY OF YOU ARE TALKING ABOUT! THORI WOULD LIKE TO START BITING NOW!
I HAVE SOMEONE ON THE WAY THERE NOW TO DEAL WITH THE WHELP.
BALDER...
...YOU KNOW WHAT YOU MUST DO.
BUT LADY FREYJA, THE BATTLE, I--
REMEMBER YOUR PLEDGE!
OTHERS WILL GIVE YOU AID!
AND TAKE THOR'S DAMNED DOG WITH YOU!

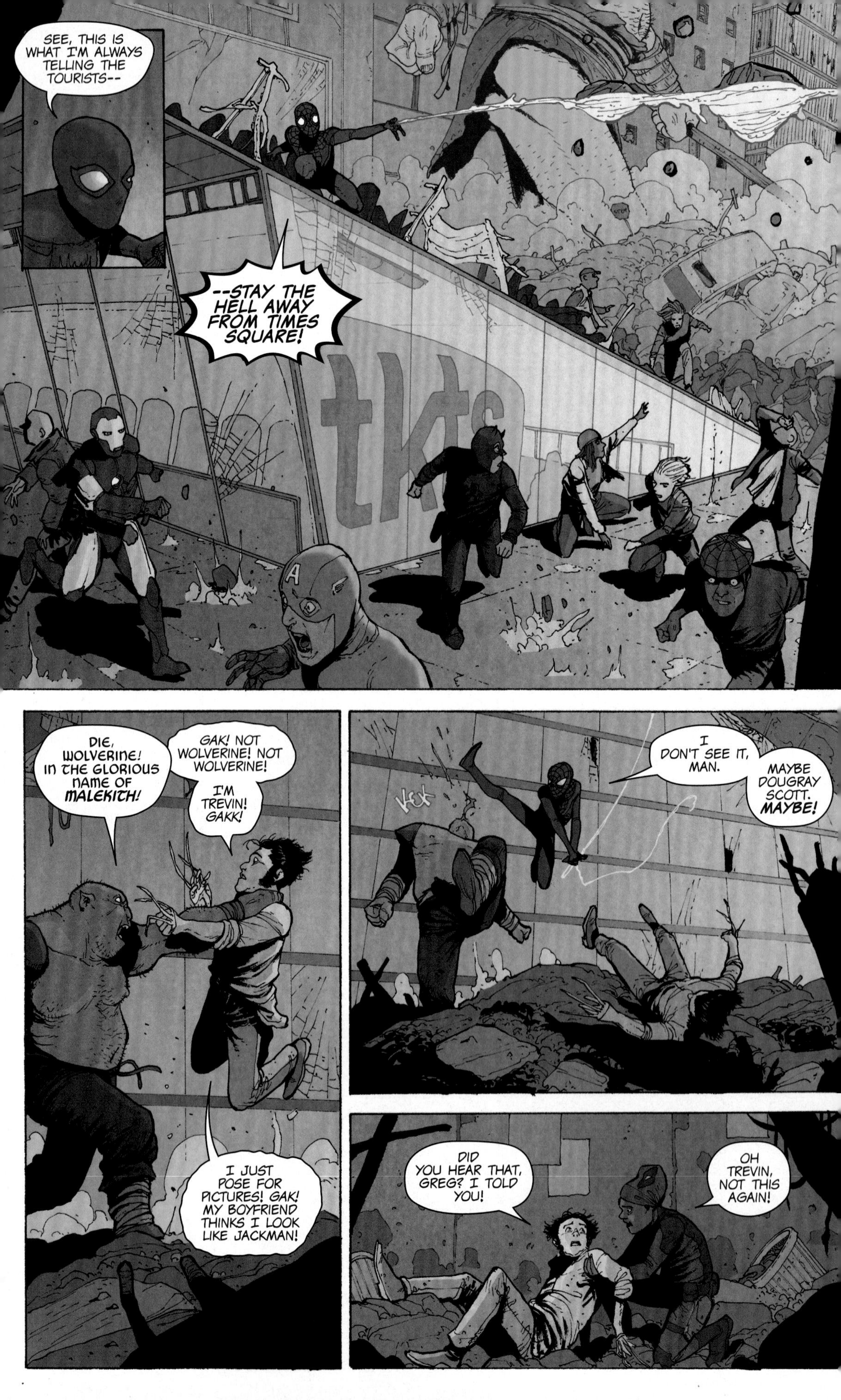
SEE, THIS IS WHAT I'M ALWAYS TELLING THE TOURISTS--
--STAY THE HELL AWAY FROM TIMES SQUARE!
tkts
DIE, WOLVERINE! IN THE GLORIOUS NAME OF MALEKITH!
GAK! NOT WOLVERINE! NOT WOLVERINE!
I'M TREVIN! GAKK!
I JUST POSE FOR PICTURES! GAK! MY BOYFRIEND THINKS I LOOK LIKE JACKMAN!
I DON'T SEE IT, MAN.
MAYBE DOUGRAY SCOTT. MAYBE!
DID YOU HEAR THAT, GREG? I TOLD YOU!
OH TREVIN, NOT THIS AGAIN!

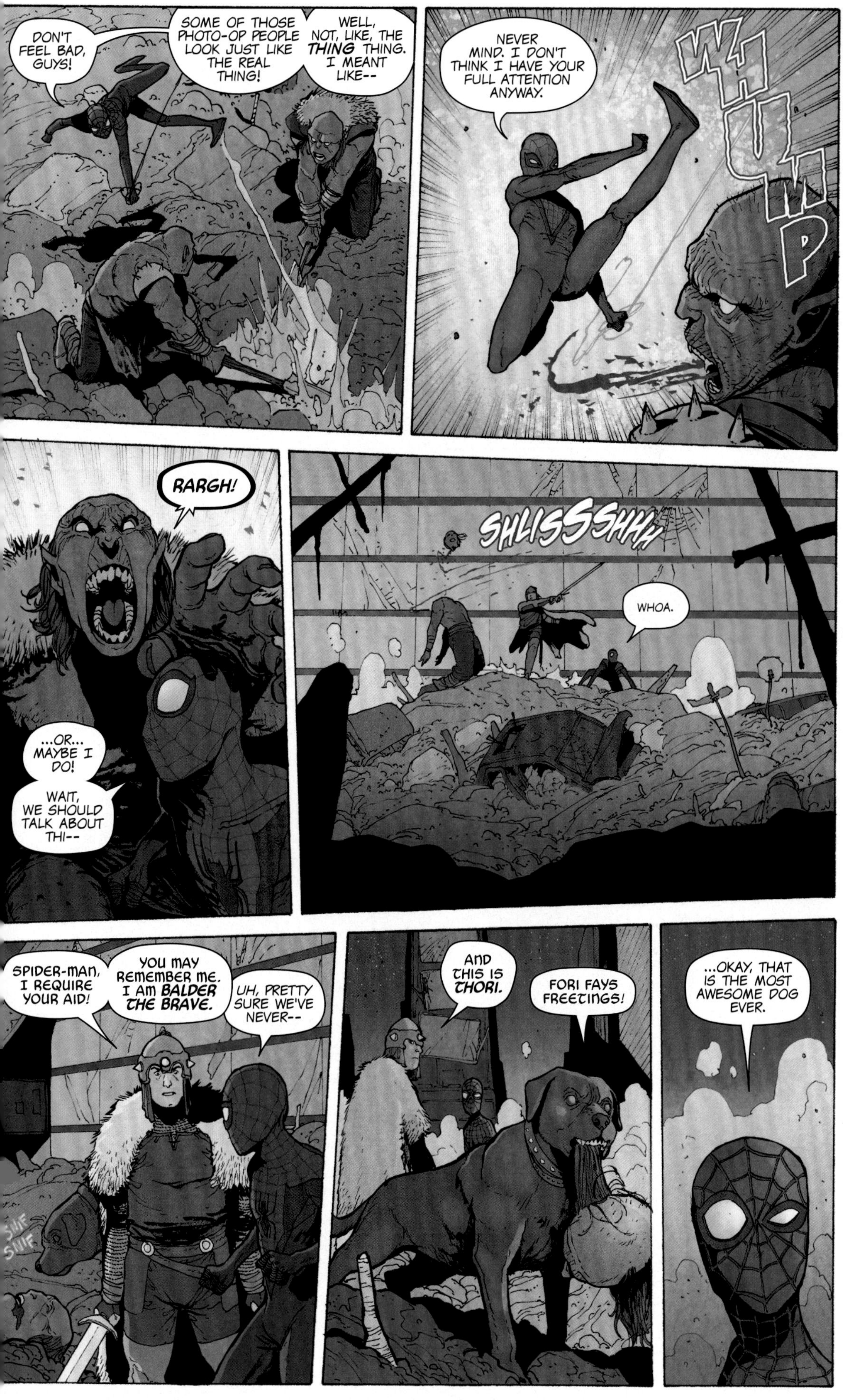
DON'T FEEL BAD, GUYS!
SOME OF THOSE PHOTO-OP PEOPLE LOOK JUST LIKE THE REAL THING!
WELL, NOT, LIKE, THE THING THING. I MEANT LIKE--
NEVER MIND. I DON'T THINK I HAVE YOUR FULL ATTENTION ANYWAY.
WHUMP
RARGH!
...OR... MAYBE I DO!
WAIT, WE SHOULD TALK ABOUT THI--
SHLISSSHHH
WHOA.
SPIDER-MAN, I REQUIRE YOUR AID!
YOU MAY REMEMBER ME. I AM BALDER THE BRAVE.
UH, PRETTY SURE WE'VE NEVER--
AND THIS IS THORI.
FORI FAYS FREETINGS!
...OKAY, THAT IS THE MOST AWESOME DOG EVER.

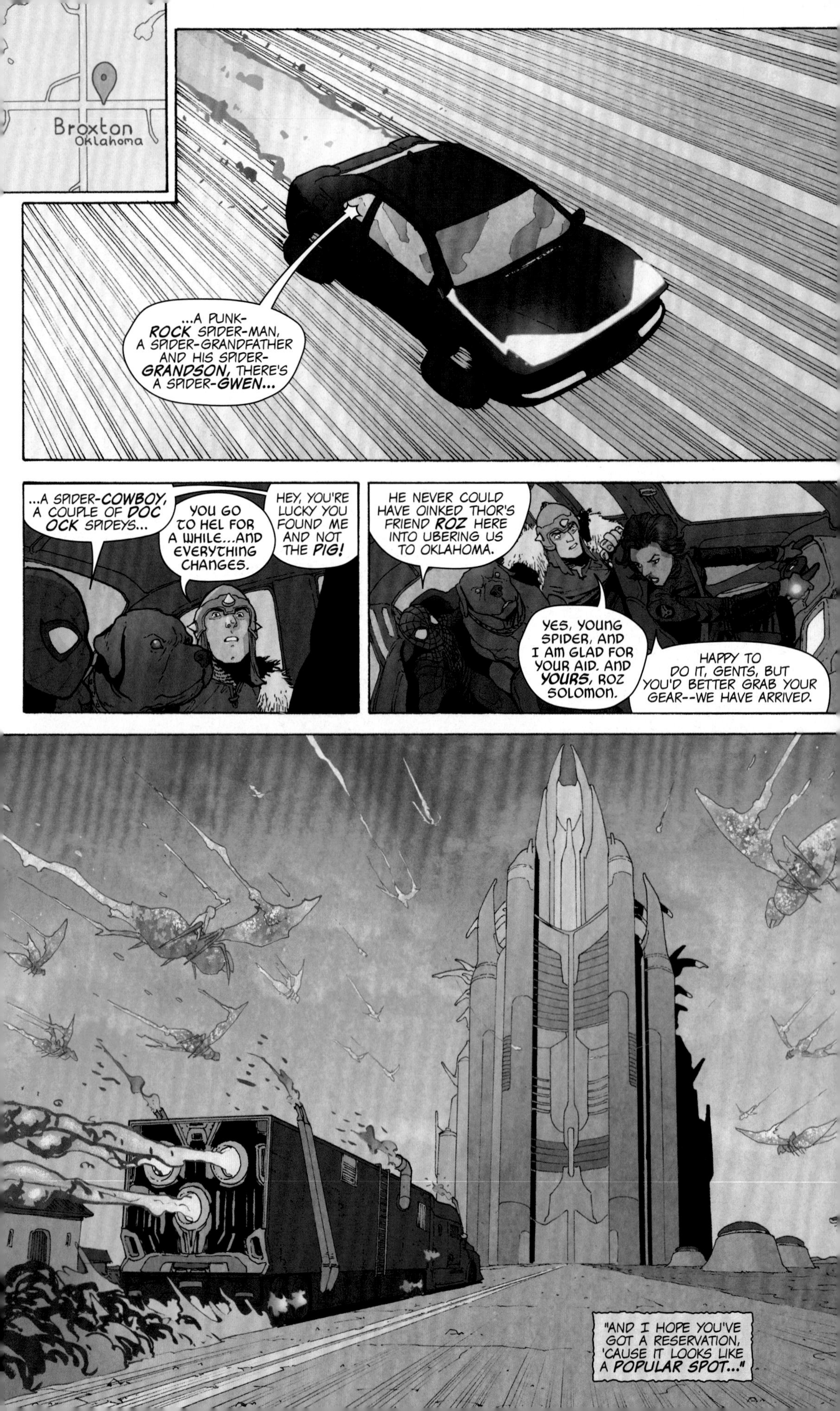
Broxton
Oklahoma
...A PUNK-ROCK SPIDER-MAN, A SPIDER-GRANDFATHER AND HIS SPIDER-GRANDSON, THERE'S A SPIDER-GWEN...
...A SPIDER-COWBOY, A COUPLE OF DOC OCK SPIDEYS...
YOU GO TO HEL FOR A WHILE...AND EVERYTHING CHANGES.
HEY, YOU'RE LUCKY YOU FOUND ME AND NOT THE PIG!
HE NEVER COULD HAVE OINKED THOR'S FRIEND ROZ HERE INTO UBERING US TO OKLAHOMA.
YES, YOUNG SPIDER, AND I AM GLAD FOR YOUR AID. AND YOURS, ROZ SOLOMON.
HAPPY TO DO IT, GENTS, BUT YOU'D BETTER GRAB YOUR GEAR--WE HAVE ARRIVED.
"AND I HOPE YOU'VE GOT A RESERVATION, 'CAUSE IT LOOKS LIKE A POPULAR SPOT..."

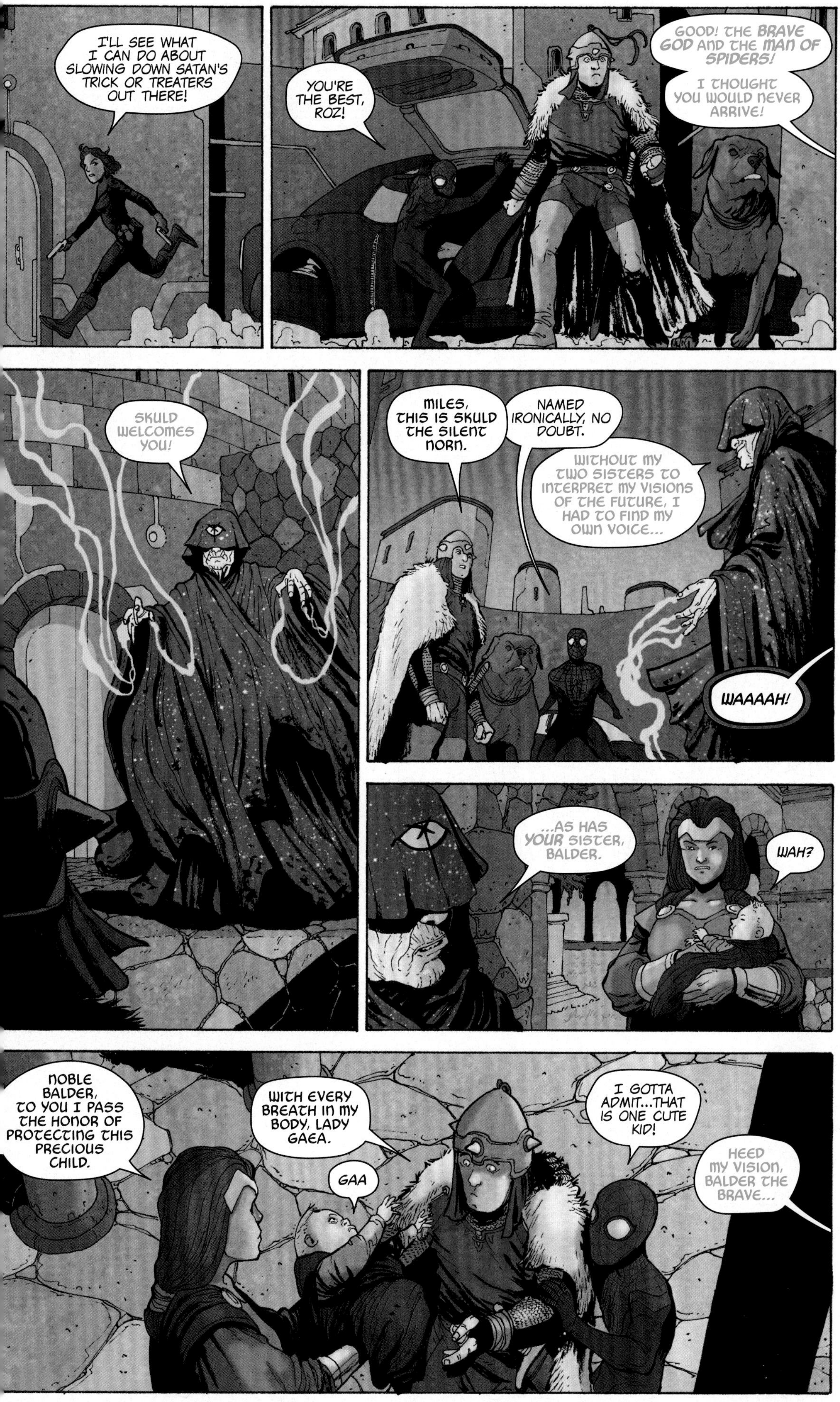
I'LL SEE WHAT I CAN DO ABOUT SLOWING DOWN SATAN'S TRICK OR TREATERS OUT THERE!
YOU'RE THE BEST, ROZ!
GOOD! THE BRAVE GOD AND THE MAN OF SPIDERS!
I THOUGHT YOU WOULD NEVER ARRIVE!
SKULD WELCOMES YOU!
MILES, THIS IS SKULD THE SILENT NORN.
NAMED IRONICALLY, NO DOUBT.
WITHOUT MY TWO SISTERS TO INTERPRET MY VISIONS OF THE FUTURE, I HAD TO FIND MY OWN VOICE...
WAAAAH!
...AS HAS YOUR SISTER, BALDER.
WAH?
NOBLE BALDER, TO YOU I PASS THE HONOR OF PROTECTING THIS PRECIOUS CHILD.
WITH EVERY BREATH IN MY BODY, LADY GAEA.
GAA
I GOTTA ADMIT...THAT IS ONE CUTE KID!
HEED MY VISION, BALDER THE BRAVE...

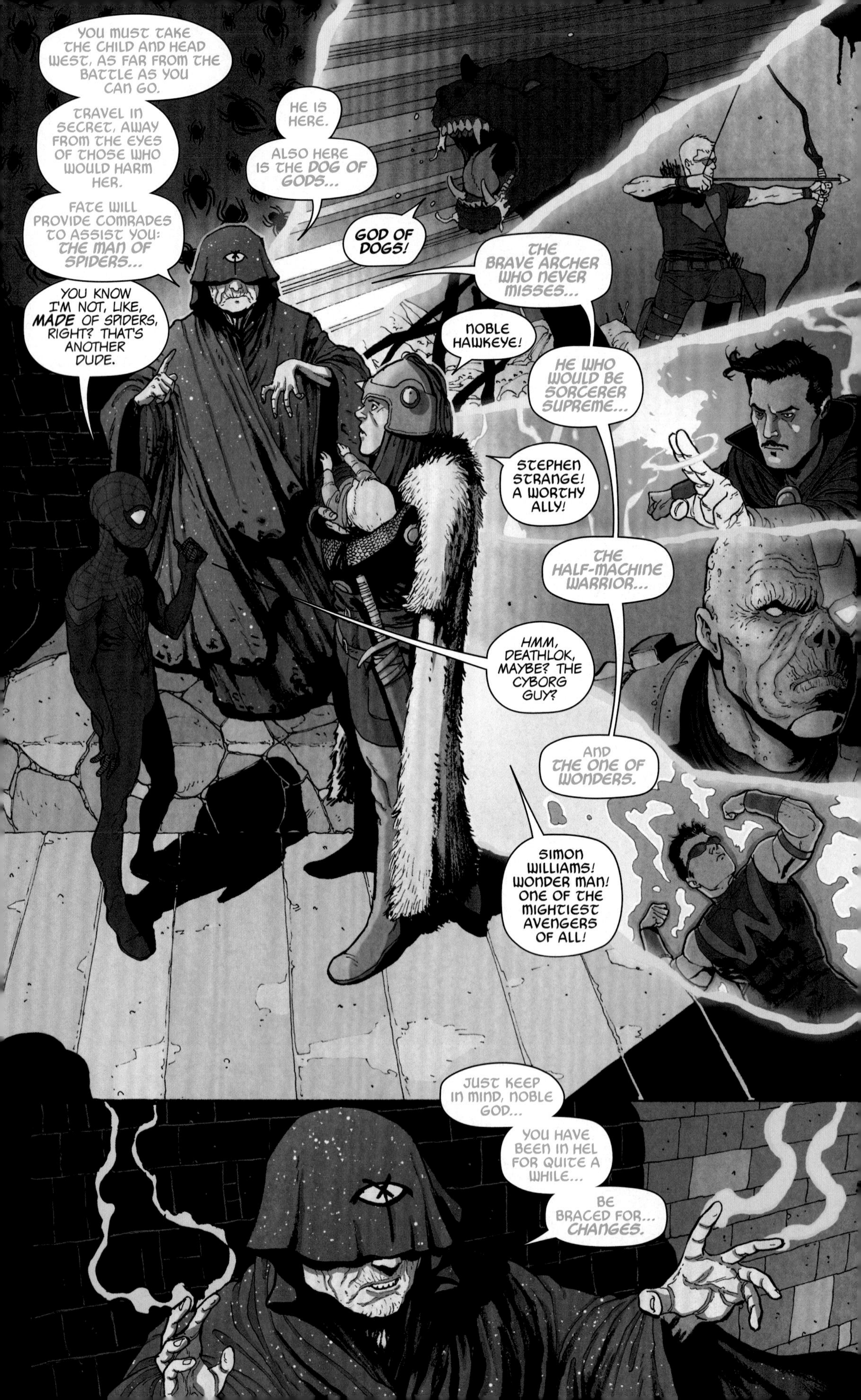
YOU MUST TAKE THE CHILD AND HEAD WEST, AS FAR FROM THE BATTLE AS YOU CAN GO.
TRAVEL IN SECRET, AWAY FROM THE EYES OF THOSE WHO WOULD HARM HER.
FATE WILL PROVIDE COMRADES TO ASSIST YOU: THE MAN OF SPIDERS...
YOU KNOW I'M NOT, LIKE, MADE OF SPIDERS, RIGHT? THAT'S ANOTHER DUDE.
HE IS HERE.
ALSO HERE IS THE DOG OF GODS...
GOD OF DOGS!
THE BRAVE ARCHER WHO NEVER MISSES...
NOBLE HAWKEYE!
HE WHO WOULD BE SORCERER SUPREME...
STEPHEN STRANGE! A WORTHY ALLY!
THE HALF-MACHINE WARRIOR...
HMM, DEATHLOK, MAYBE? THE CYBORG GUY?
AND THE ONE OF WONDERS.
SIMON WILLIAMS! WONDER MAN! ONE OF THE MIGHTIEST AVENGERS OF ALL!
JUST KEEP IN MIND, NOBLE GOD...
YOU HAVE BEEN IN HEL FOR QUITE A WHILE...
BE BRACED FOR... CHANGES.

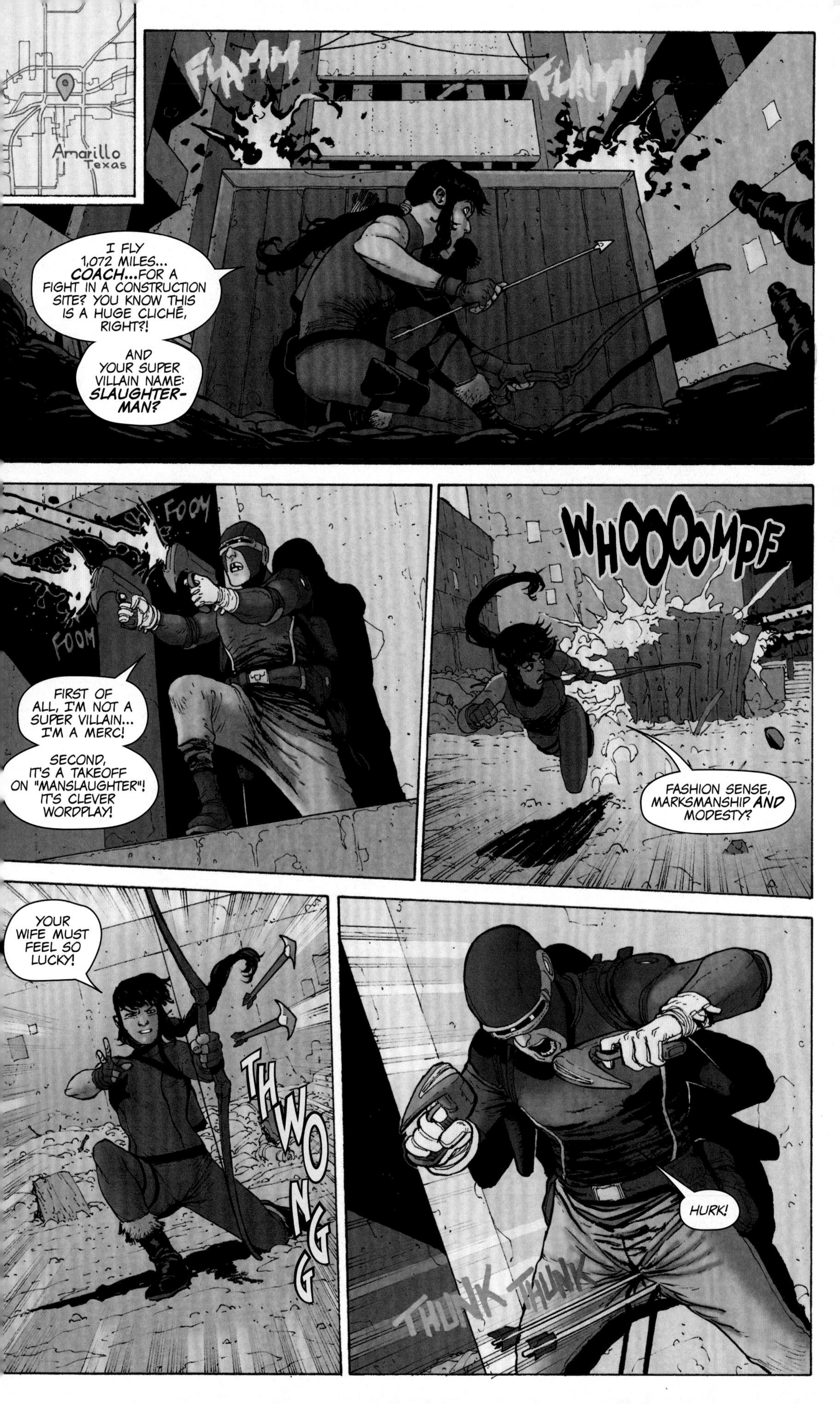
Amarillo
Texas
FLAMM
FLAMM
I FLY 1,072 MILES... COACH...FOR A FIGHT IN A CONSTRUCTION SITE? YOU KNOW THIS IS A HUGE CLICHÉ, RIGHT?!
AND YOUR SUPER VILLAIN NAME: SLAUGHTER-MAN?
FOOM
FOOM
FIRST OF ALL, I'M NOT A SUPER VILLAIN... I'M A MERC!
SECOND, IT'S A TAKEOFF ON "MANSLAUGHTER"! IT'S CLEVER WORDPLAY!
WHOOOOOMPF
FASHION SENSE, MARKSMANSHIP AND MODESTY?
YOUR WIFE MUST FEEL SO LUCKY!
THWONG
HURK!
THUNK THUNK

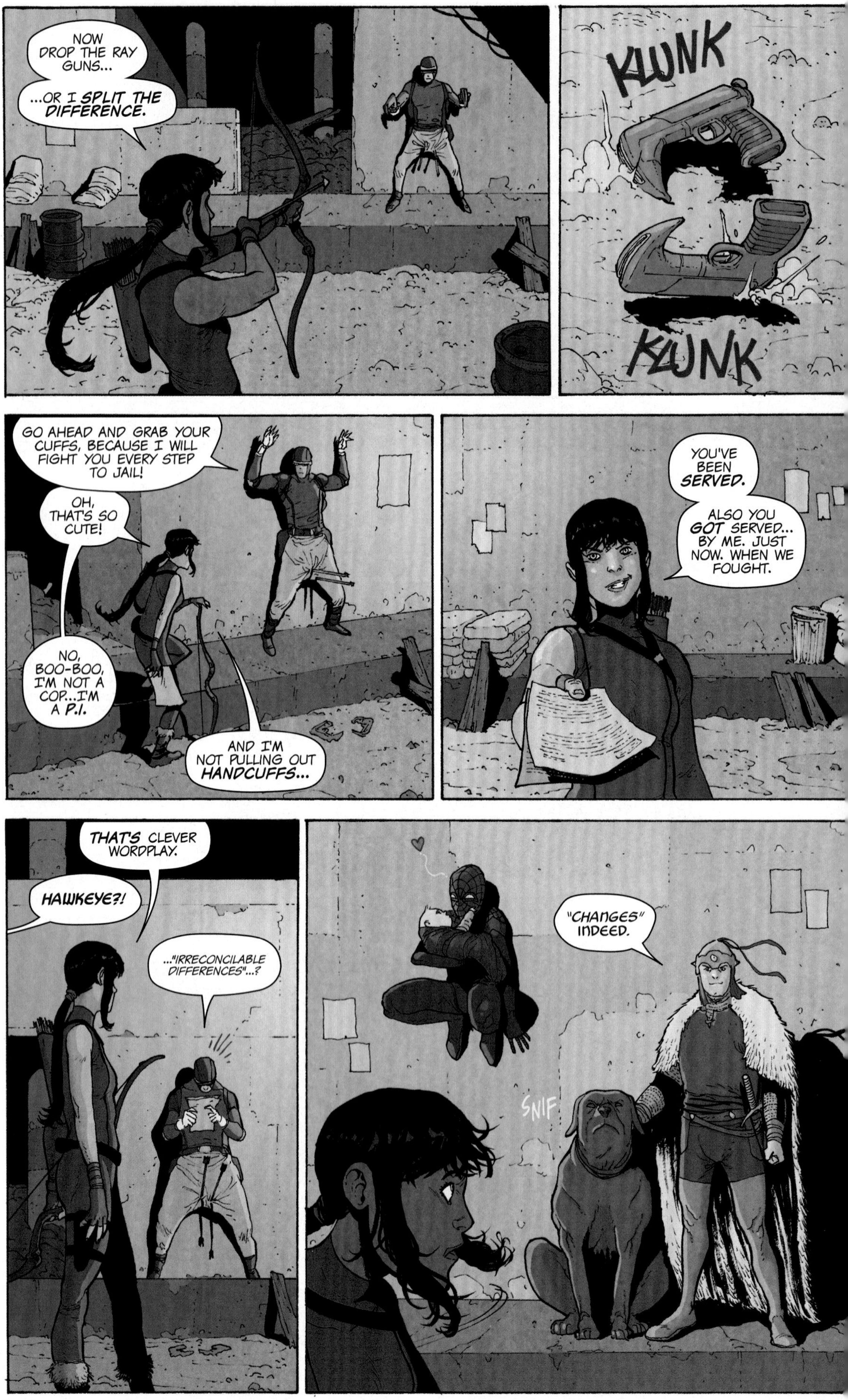
NOW DROP THE RAY GUNS...
...OR I SPLIT THE DIFFERENCE.
KLUNK
KLUNK
GO AHEAD AND GRAB YOUR CUFFS, BECAUSE I WILL FIGHT YOU EVERY STEP TO JAIL!
OH, THAT'S SO CUTE!
NO, BOO-BOO, I'M NOT A COP...I'M A P.I.
AND I'M NOT PULLING OUT HANDCUFFS...
YOU'VE BEEN SERVED.
ALSO YOU GOT SERVED... BY ME. JUST NOW. WHEN WE FOUGHT.
THAT'S CLEVER WORDPLAY.
HAWKEYE?!
..."IRRECONCILABLE DIFFERENCES"...?
"CHANGES" INDEED.
SNIF

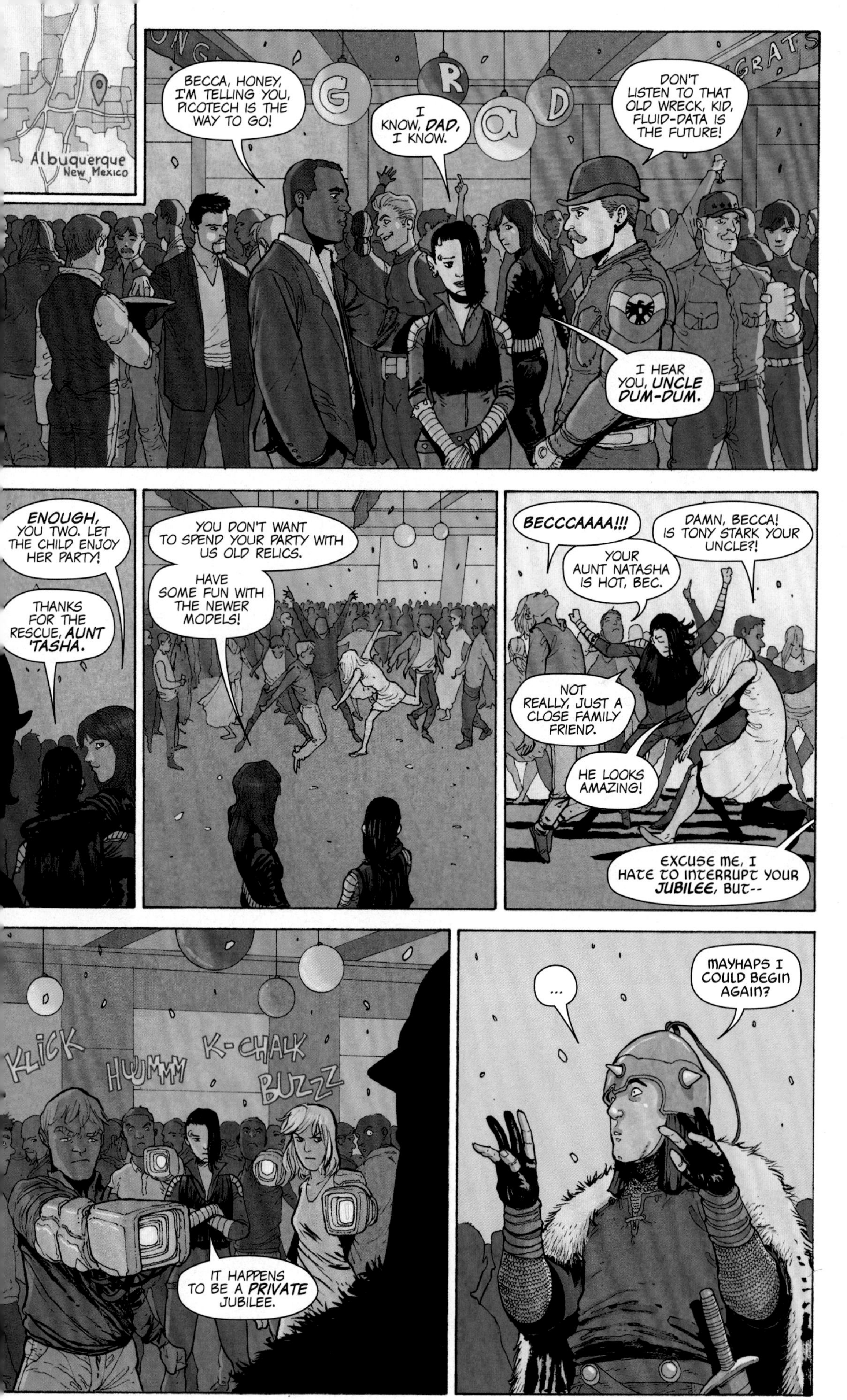
Albuquerque
New Mexico
CONGRATS
BECCA, HONEY, I'M TELLING YOU, PICOTECH IS THE WAY TO GO!
G R a D
I KNOW, DAD, I KNOW.
CONGRATS
DON'T LISTEN TO THAT OLD WRECK, KID, FLUID-DATA IS THE FUTURE!
I HEAR YOU, UNCLE DUM-DUM.
ENOUGH, YOU TWO. LET THE CHILD ENJOY HER PARTY!
THANKS FOR THE RESCUE, AUNT 'TASHA.
YOU DON'T WANT TO SPEND YOUR PARTY WITH US OLD RELICS.
HAVE SOME FUN WITH THE NEWER MODELS!
BECCCAAAA!!!
YOUR AUNT NATASHA IS HOT, BEC.
DAMN, BECCA! IS TONY STARK YOUR UNCLE?!
NOT REALLY, JUST A CLOSE FAMILY FRIEND.
HE LOOKS AMAZING!
EXCUSE ME, I HATE TO INTERRUPT YOUR JUBILEE, BUT--
KLICK
HUUMMM
K-CHALK
BUZZZ
IT HAPPENS TO BE A PRIVATE JUBILEE.
...
MAYHAPS I COULD BEGIN AGAIN?

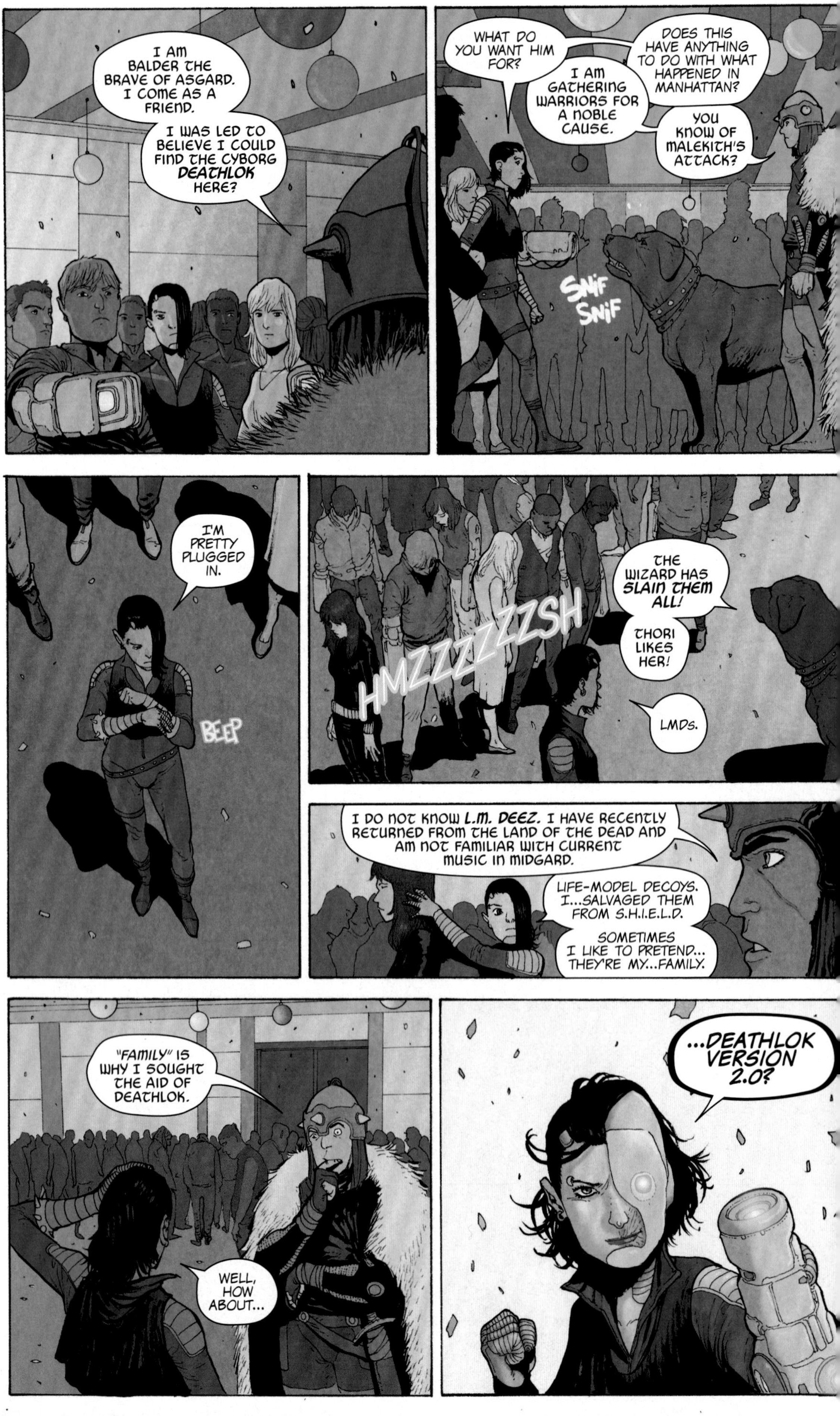
I AM BALDER THE BRAVE OF ASGARD. I COME AS A FRIEND.
I WAS LED TO BELIEVE I COULD FIND THE CYBORG DEATHLOK HERE?
WHAT DO YOU WANT HIM FOR?
I AM GATHERING WARRIORS FOR A NOBLE CAUSE.
DOES THIS HAVE ANYTHING TO DO WITH WHAT HAPPENED IN MANHATTAN?
YOU KNOW OF MALEKITH'S ATTACK?
SNIF SNIF
I'M PRETTY PLUGGED IN.
BEEP
HMZZZZZZZSH
THE WIZARD HAS SLAIN THEM ALL!
THORI LIKES HER!
LMDs.
I DO NOT KNOW L.M. DEEZ. I HAVE RECENTLY RETURNED FROM THE LAND OF THE DEAD AND AM NOT FAMILIAR WITH CURRENT MUSIC IN MIDGARD.
LIFE-MODEL DECOYS. I...SALVAGED THEM FROM S.H.I.E.L.D.
SOMETIMES I LIKE TO PRETEND... THEY'RE MY...FAMILY.
"FAMILY" IS WHY I SOUGHT THE AID OF DEATHLOK.
WELL, HOW ABOUT...
...DEATHLOK VERSION 2.0?

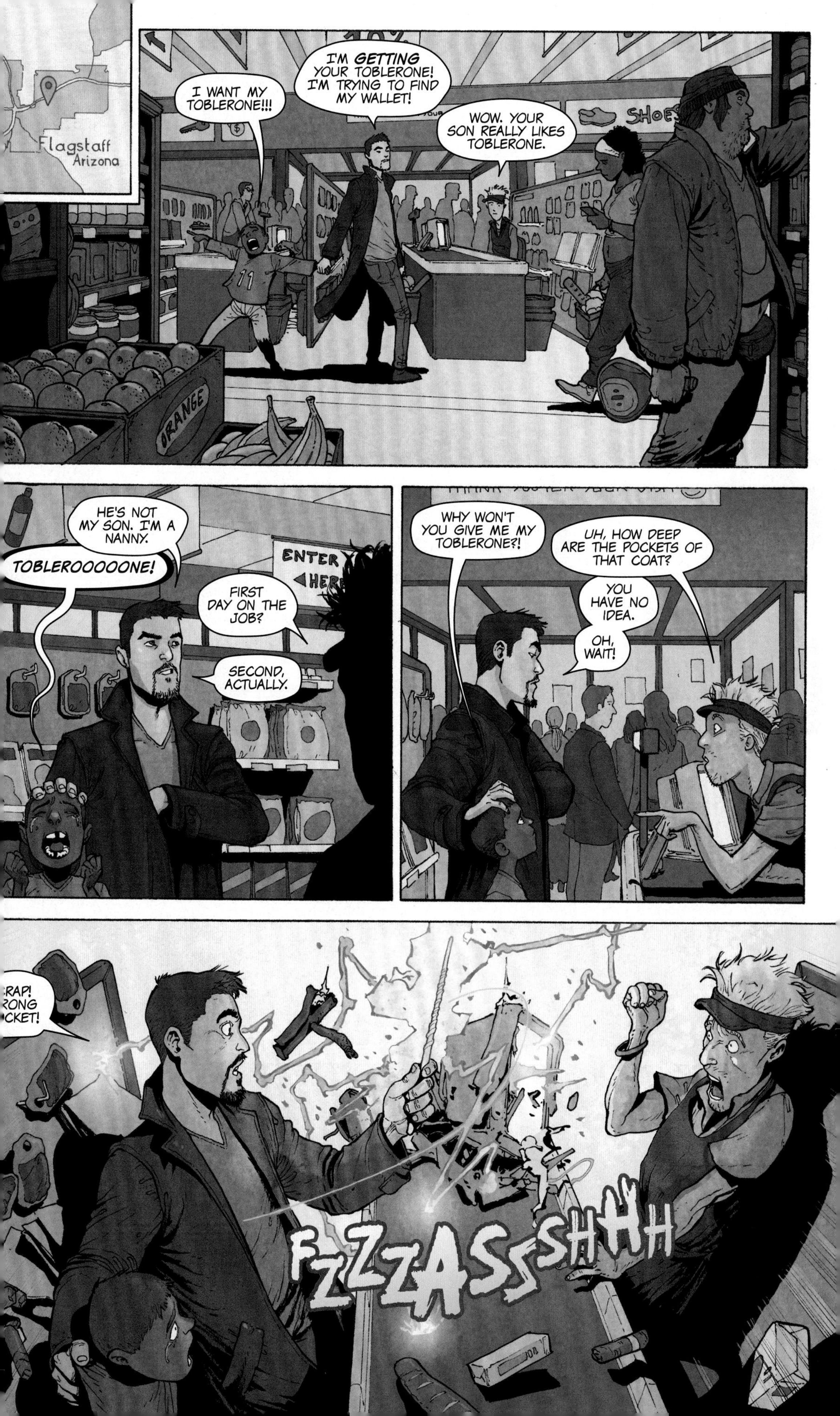

Flagstaff
Arizona
I WANT MY TOBLERONE!!!
I'M **GETTING** YOUR TOBLERONE! I'M TRYING TO FIND MY WALLET!
WOW. YOUR SON REALLY LIKES TOBLERONE.
SHOES
ORANGE
HE'S NOT MY SON. I'M A NANNY.
TOBLEROOOOONE!
ENTER HERE
FIRST DAY ON THE JOB?
SECOND, ACTUALLY.
WHY WON'T YOU GIVE ME MY TOBLERONE?!
UH, HOW DEEP ARE THE POCKETS OF THAT COAT?
YOU HAVE NO IDEA.
OH, WAIT!
RAP!
RONG
CKET!
FZZZASSSHHH

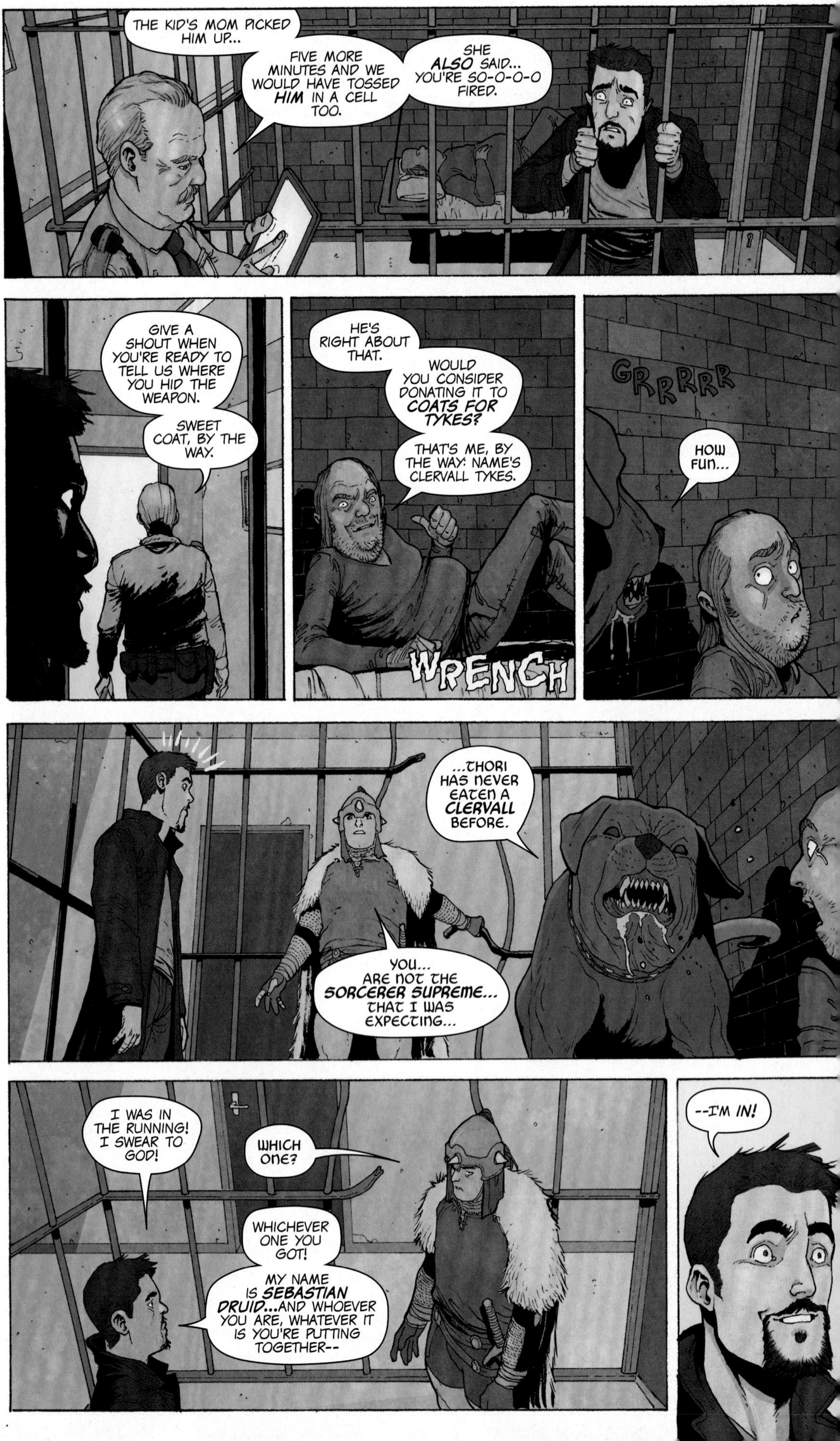
THE KID'S MOM PICKED HIM UP...
FIVE MORE MINUTES AND WE WOULD HAVE TOSSED HIM IN A CELL TOO.
SHE ALSO SAID... YOU'RE SO-O-O-O FIRED.
GIVE A SHOUT WHEN YOU'RE READY TO TELL US WHERE YOU HID THE WEAPON.
SWEET COAT, BY THE WAY.
HE'S RIGHT ABOUT THAT.
WOULD YOU CONSIDER DONATING IT TO COATS FOR TYKES?
THAT'S ME, BY THE WAY: NAME'S CLERVALL TYKES.
WRENCH
GRRRRR
HOW FUN...
...THORI HAS NEVER EATEN A CLERVALL BEFORE.
YOU... ARE NOT THE SORCERER SUPREME... THAT I WAS EXPECTING...
I WAS IN THE RUNNING! I SWEAR TO GOD!
WHICH ONE?
WHICHEVER ONE YOU GOT!
MY NAME IS SEBASTIAN DRUID...AND WHOEVER YOU ARE, WHATEVER IT IS YOU'RE PUTTING TOGETHER--
--I'M IN!

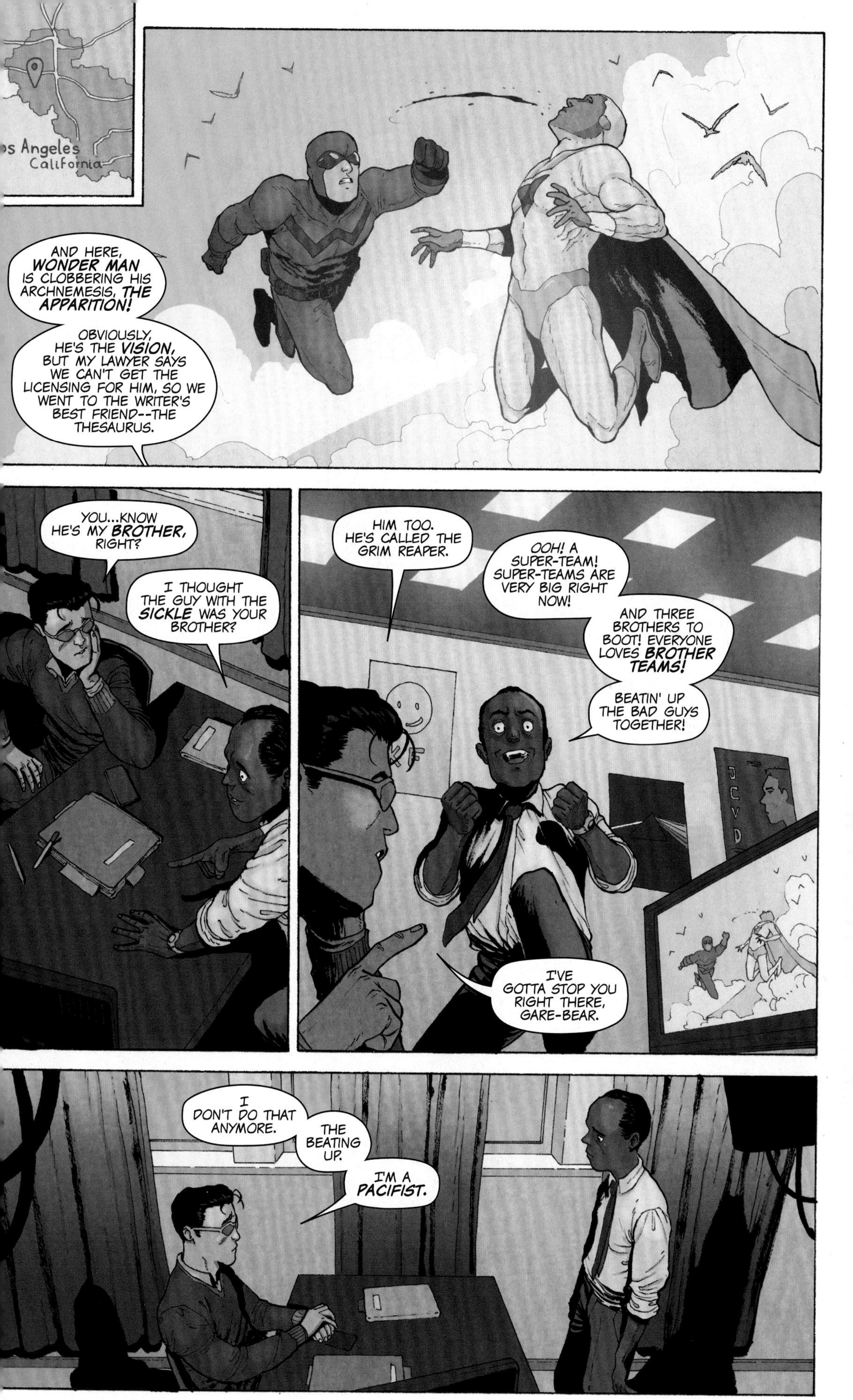
os Angeles
California
AND HERE, WONDER MAN IS CLOBBERING HIS ARCHNEMESIS, THE APPARITION!
OBVIOUSLY, HE'S THE VISION, BUT MY LAWYER SAYS WE CAN'T GET THE LICENSING FOR HIM, SO WE WENT TO THE WRITER'S BEST FRIEND--THE THESAURUS.
YOU...KNOW HE'S MY BROTHER, RIGHT?
I THOUGHT THE GUY WITH THE SICKLE WAS YOUR BROTHER?
HIM TOO. HE'S CALLED THE GRIM REAPER.
OOH! A SUPER-TEAM! SUPER-TEAMS ARE VERY BIG RIGHT NOW!
AND THREE BROTHERS TO BOOT! EVERYONE LOVES BROTHER TEAMS!
BEATIN' UP THE BAD GUYS TOGETHER!
JCVD
I'VE GOTTA STOP YOU RIGHT THERE, GARE-BEAR.
I DON'T DO THAT ANYMORE.
THE BEATING UP.
I'M A PACIFIST.

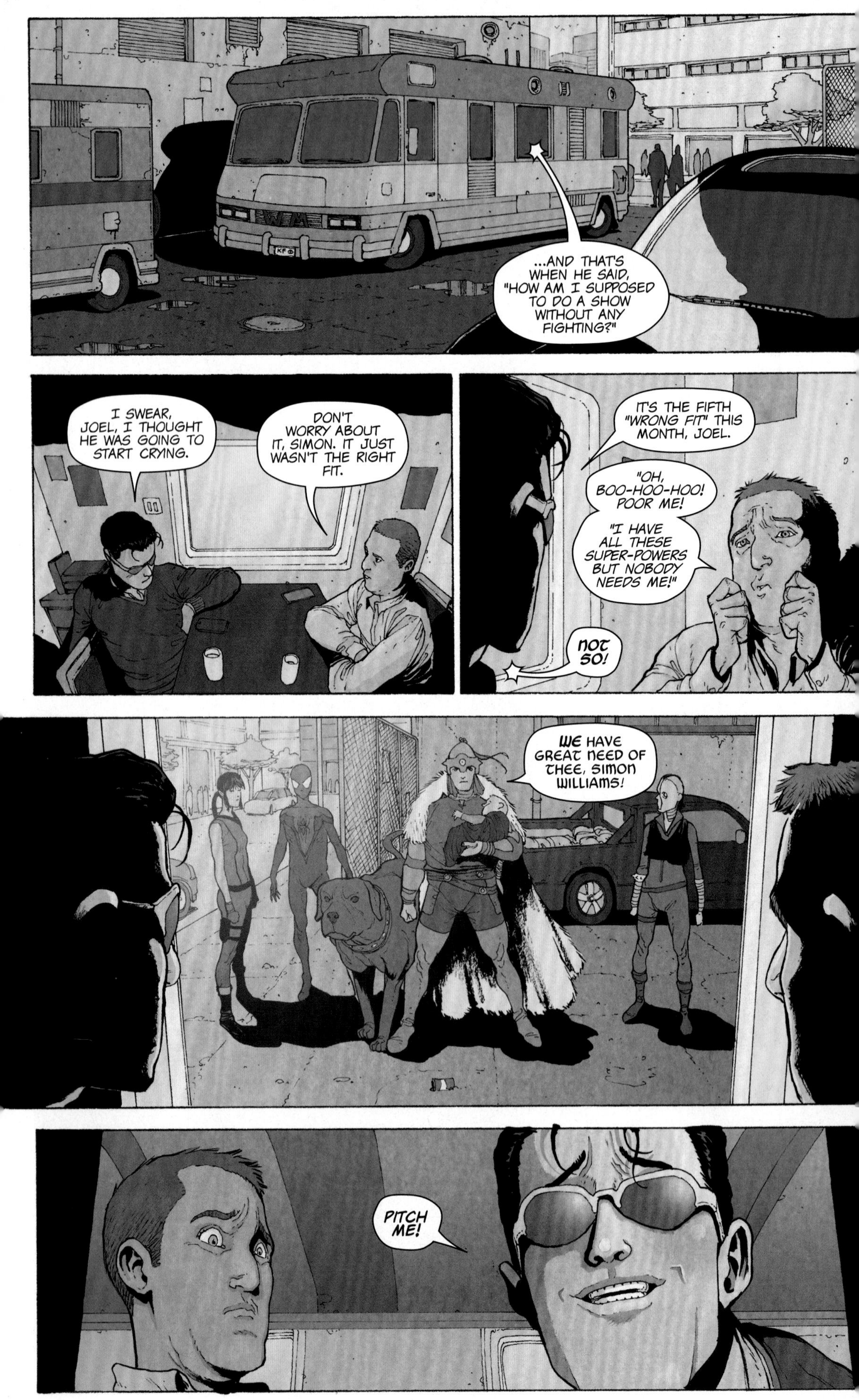
...AND THAT'S WHEN HE SAID, "HOW AM I SUPPOSED TO DO A SHOW WITHOUT ANY FIGHTING?"
I SWEAR, JOEL, I THOUGHT HE WAS GOING TO START CRYING.
DON'T WORRY ABOUT IT, SIMON. IT JUST WASN'T THE RIGHT FIT.
IT'S THE FIFTH "WRONG FIT" THIS MONTH, JOEL.
"OH, BOO-HOO-HOO! POOR ME!
"I HAVE ALL THESE SUPER-POWERS BUT NOBODY NEEDS ME!"
NOT SO!
WE HAVE GREAT NEED OF THEE, SIMON WILLIAMS!
PITCH ME!

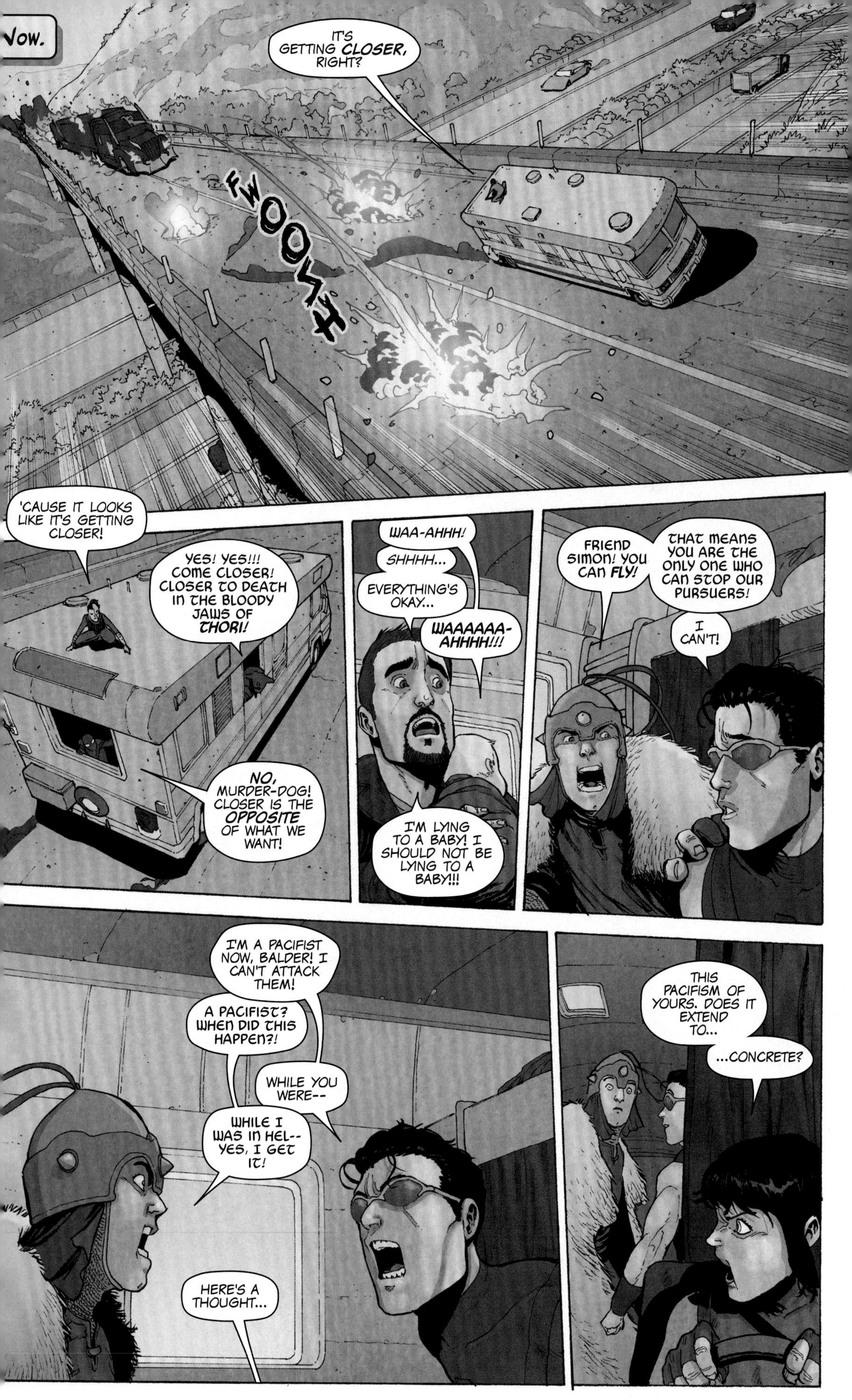

VOW.
IT'S GETTING CLOSER, RIGHT?
FWOOSH
'CAUSE IT LOOKS LIKE IT'S GETTING CLOSER!
YES! YES!!! COME CLOSER! CLOSER TO DEATH IN THE BLOODY JAWS OF THORI!
NO, MURDER-DOG! CLOSER IS THE OPPOSITE OF WHAT WE WANT!
WAA-AHHH!
SHHHH...
EVERYTHING'S OKAY...
WAAAAAA-AHHHH!!!
I'M LYING TO A BABY! I SHOULD NOT BE LYING TO A BABY!!!
FRIEND SIMON! YOU CAN FLY!
THAT MEANS YOU ARE THE ONLY ONE WHO CAN STOP OUR PURSUERS!
I CAN'T!
I'M A PACIFIST NOW, BALDER! I CAN'T ATTACK THEM!
A PACIFIST? WHEN DID THIS HAPPEN?!
WHILE YOU WERE--
WHILE I WAS IN HEL-- YES, I GET IT!
HERE'S A THOUGHT...
THIS PACIFISM OF YOURS. DOES IT EXTEND TO...
...CONCRETE?

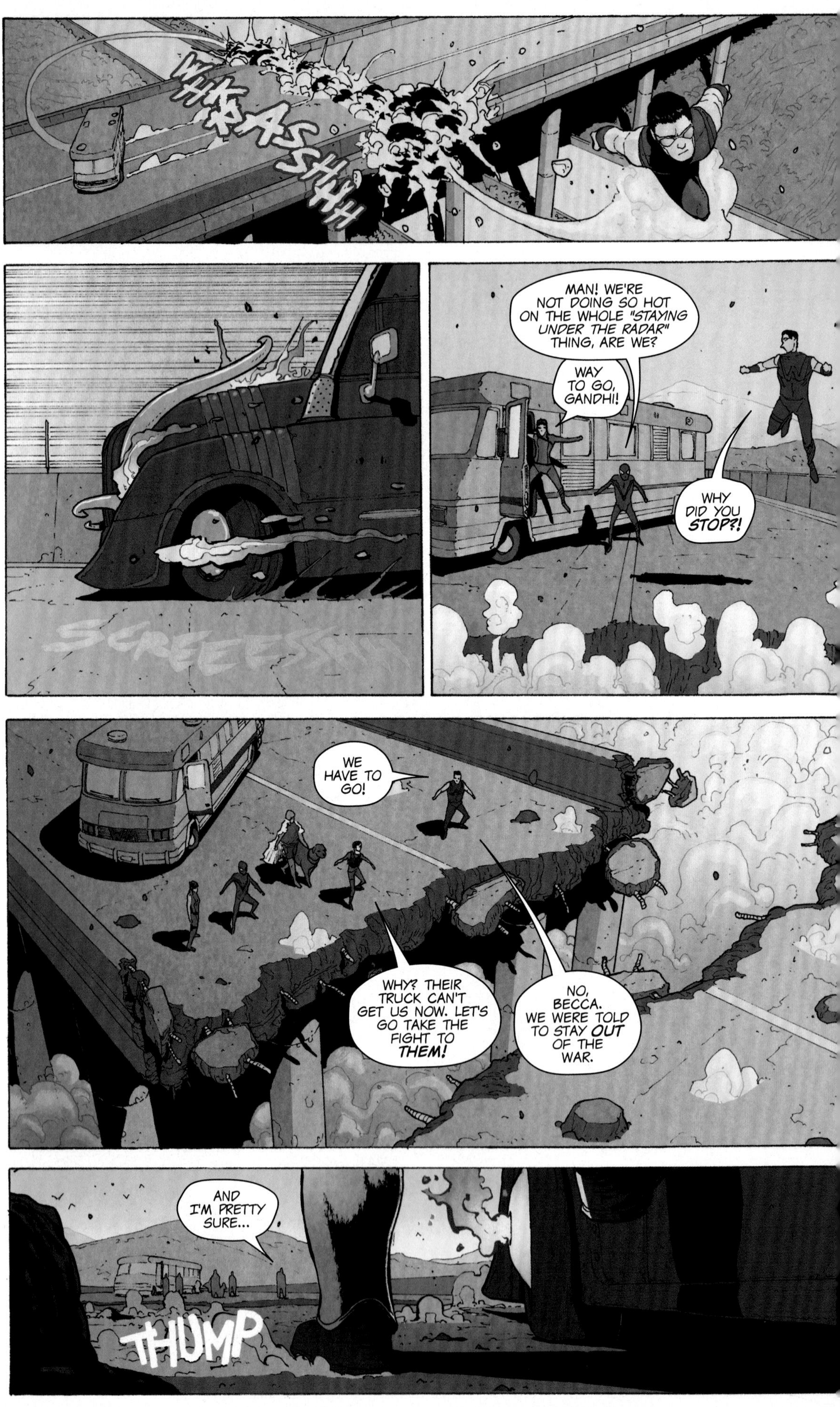
WHRASHHH
SCREEESHH
MAN! WE'RE NOT DOING SO HOT ON THE WHOLE "STAYING UNDER THE RADAR" THING, ARE WE?
WAY TO GO, GANDHI!
WHY DID YOU STOP?!
WE HAVE TO GO!
WHY? THEIR TRUCK CAN'T GET US NOW. LET'S GO TAKE THE FIGHT TO THEM!
NO, BECCA. WE WERE TOLD TO STAY OUT OF THE WAR.
AND I'M PRETTY SURE...
THUMP

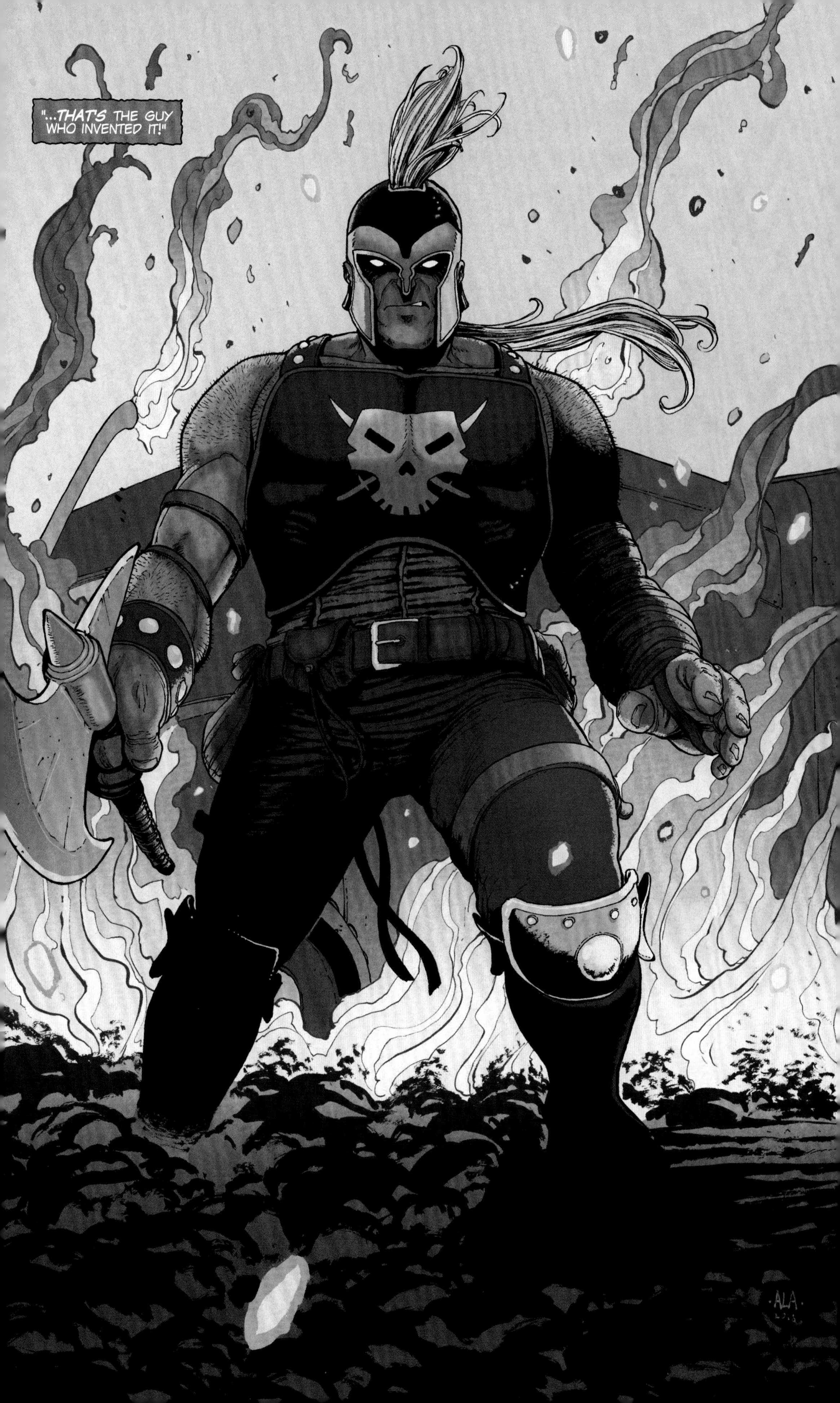
"...THAT'S THE GUY WHO INVENTED IT!"
ALA

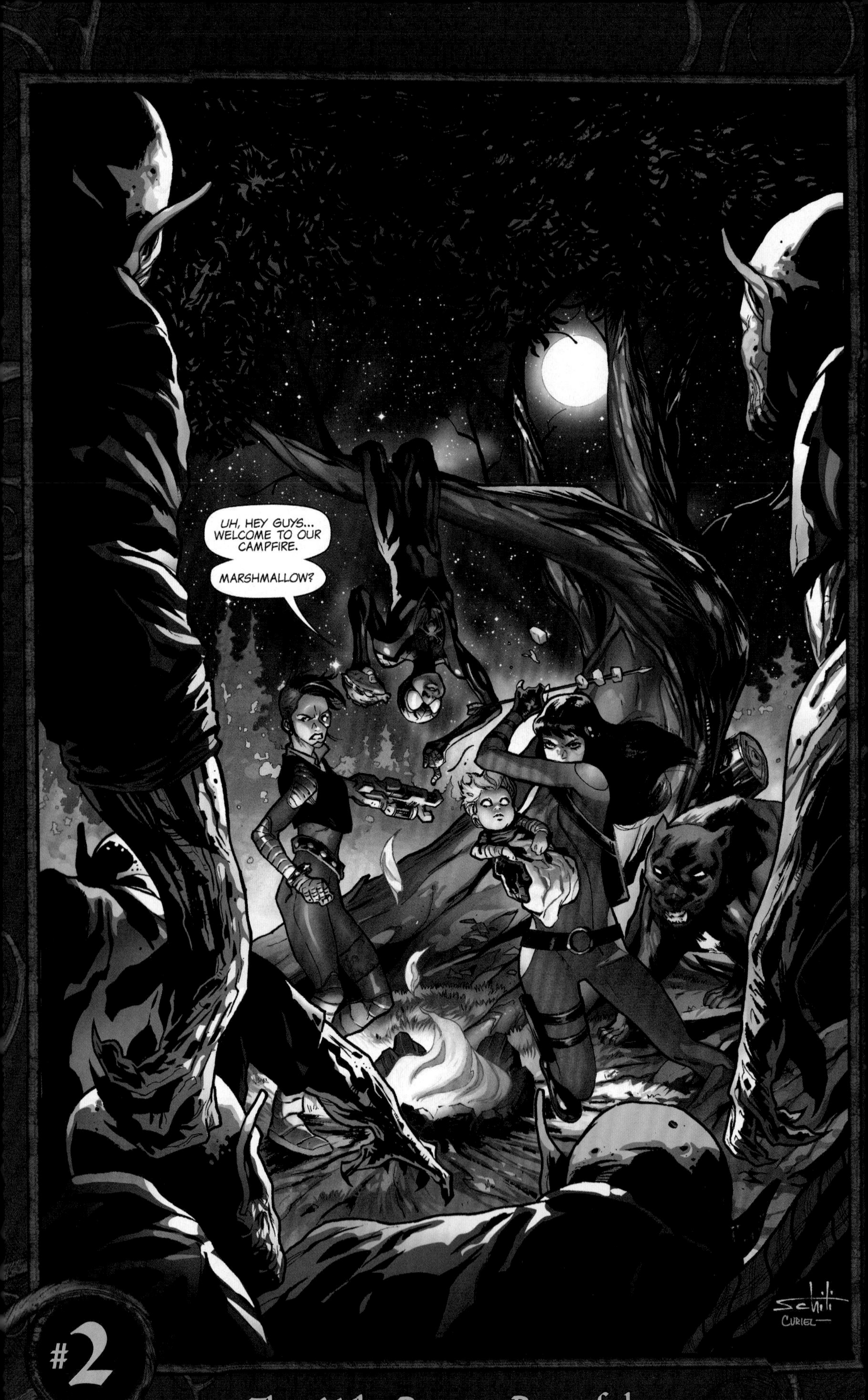
UH, HEY GUYS... WELCOME TO OUR CAMPFIRE.
MARSHMALLOW?
#2

They Who Became Powerful

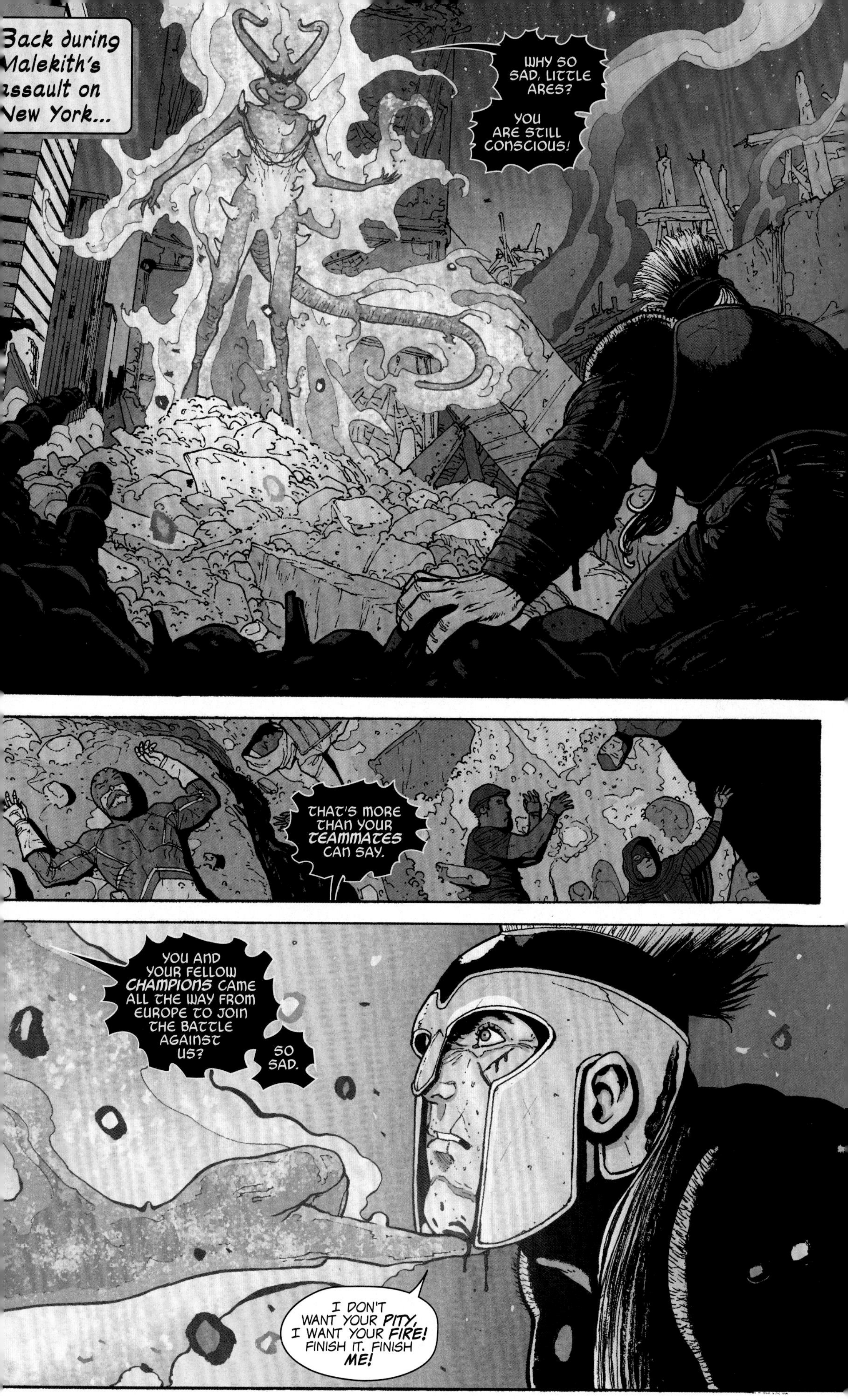
Back during Malekith's assault on New York...
WHY SO SAD, LITTLE ARES?
YOU ARE STILL CONSCIOUS!
THAT'S MORE THAN YOUR TEAMMATES CAN SAY.
YOU AND YOUR FELLOW CHAMPIONS CAME ALL THE WAY FROM EUROPE TO JOIN THE BATTLE AGAINST US?
SO SAD.
I DON'T WANT YOUR PITY, I WANT YOUR FIRE! FINISH IT. FINISH ME!

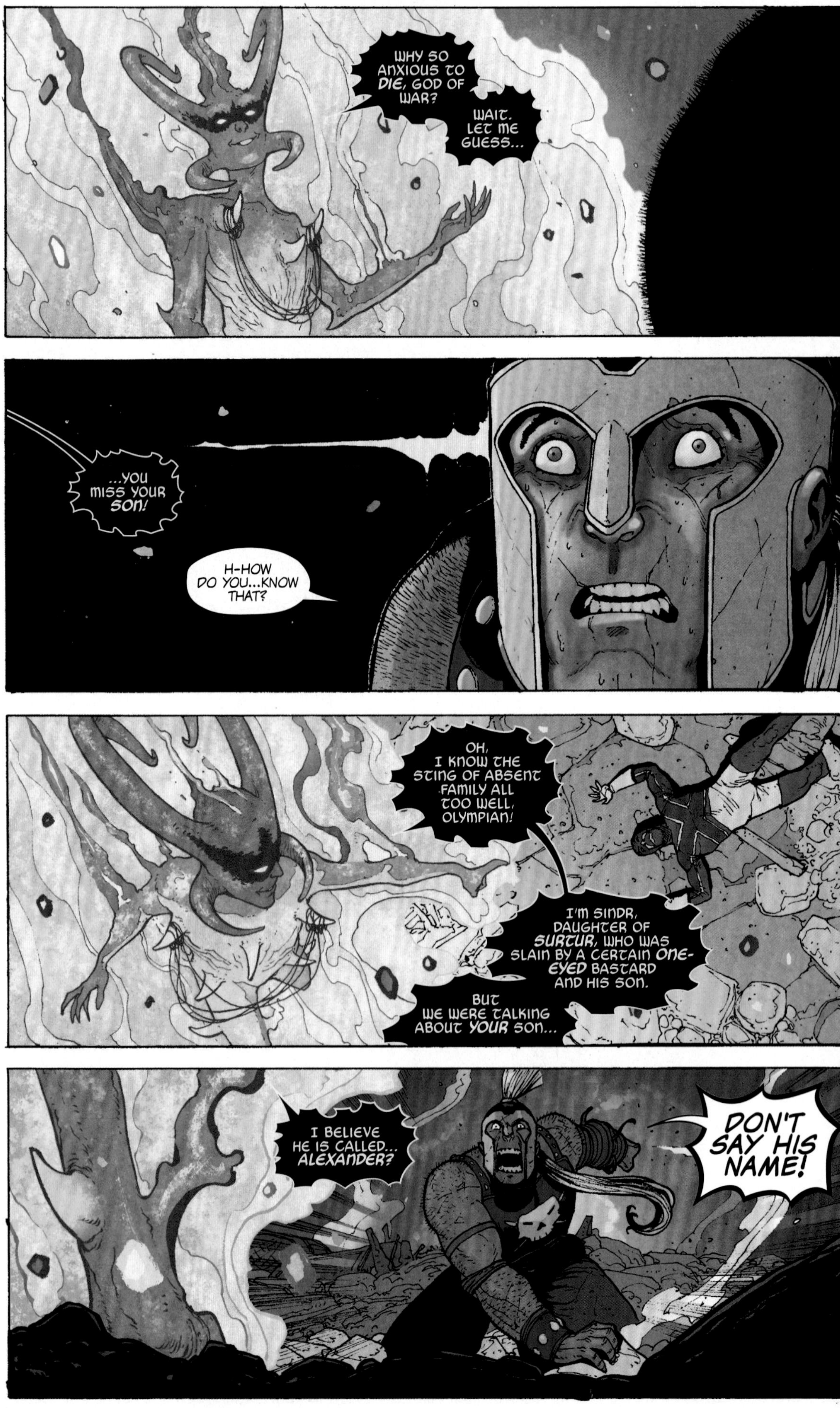
WHY SO ANXIOUS TO DIE, GOD OF WAR?
WAIT. LET ME GUESS...
...YOU MISS YOUR SON!
H-HOW DO YOU...KNOW THAT?
OH, I KNOW THE STING OF ABSENT FAMILY ALL TOO WELL, OLYMPIAN!
I'M SINDR, DAUGHTER OF SURTUR, WHO WAS SLAIN BY A CERTAIN ONE-EYED BASTARD AND HIS SON.
BUT WE WERE TALKING ABOUT YOUR SON...
I BELIEVE HE IS CALLED... ALEXANDER?
DON'T SAY HIS NAME!

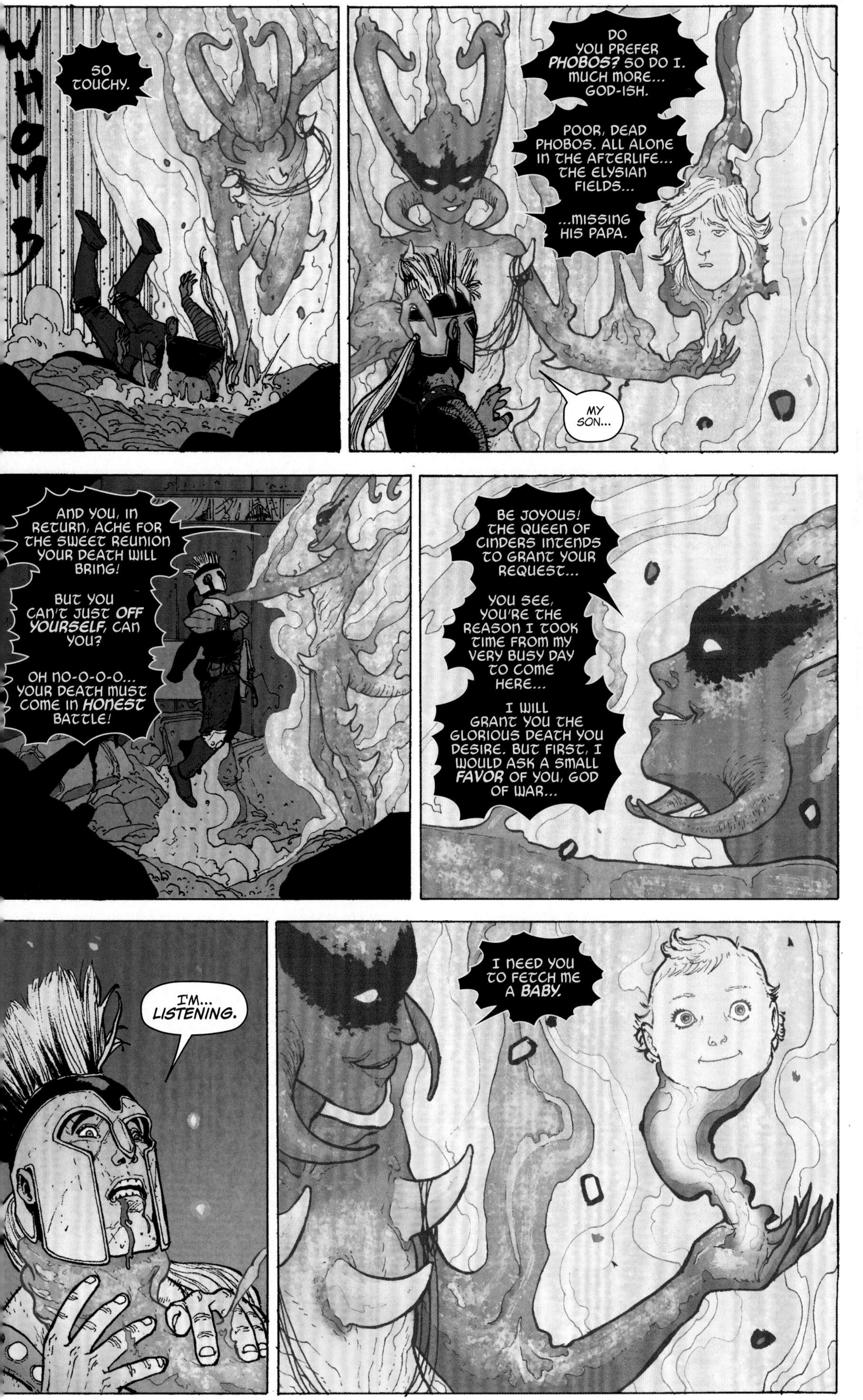
WHOMB
SO TOUCHY.
DO YOU PREFER PHOBOS? SO DO I. MUCH MORE... GOD-ISH.
POOR, DEAD PHOBOS. ALL ALONE IN THE AFTERLIFE... THE ELYSIAN FIELDS...
...MISSING HIS PAPA.
MY SON...
AND YOU, IN RETURN, ACHE FOR THE SWEET REUNION YOUR DEATH WILL BRING!
BUT YOU CAN'T JUST OFF YOURSELF, CAN YOU?
OH NO-O-O-O... YOUR DEATH MUST COME IN HONEST BATTLE!
BE JOYOUS! THE QUEEN OF CINDERS INTENDS TO GRANT YOUR REQUEST...
YOU SEE, YOU'RE THE REASON I TOOK TIME FROM MY VERY BUSY DAY TO COME HERE...
I WILL GRANT YOU THE GLORIOUS DEATH YOU DESIRE. BUT FIRST, I WOULD ASK A SMALL FAVOR OF YOU, GOD OF WAR...
I'M... LISTENING.
I NEED YOU TO FETCH ME A BABY.

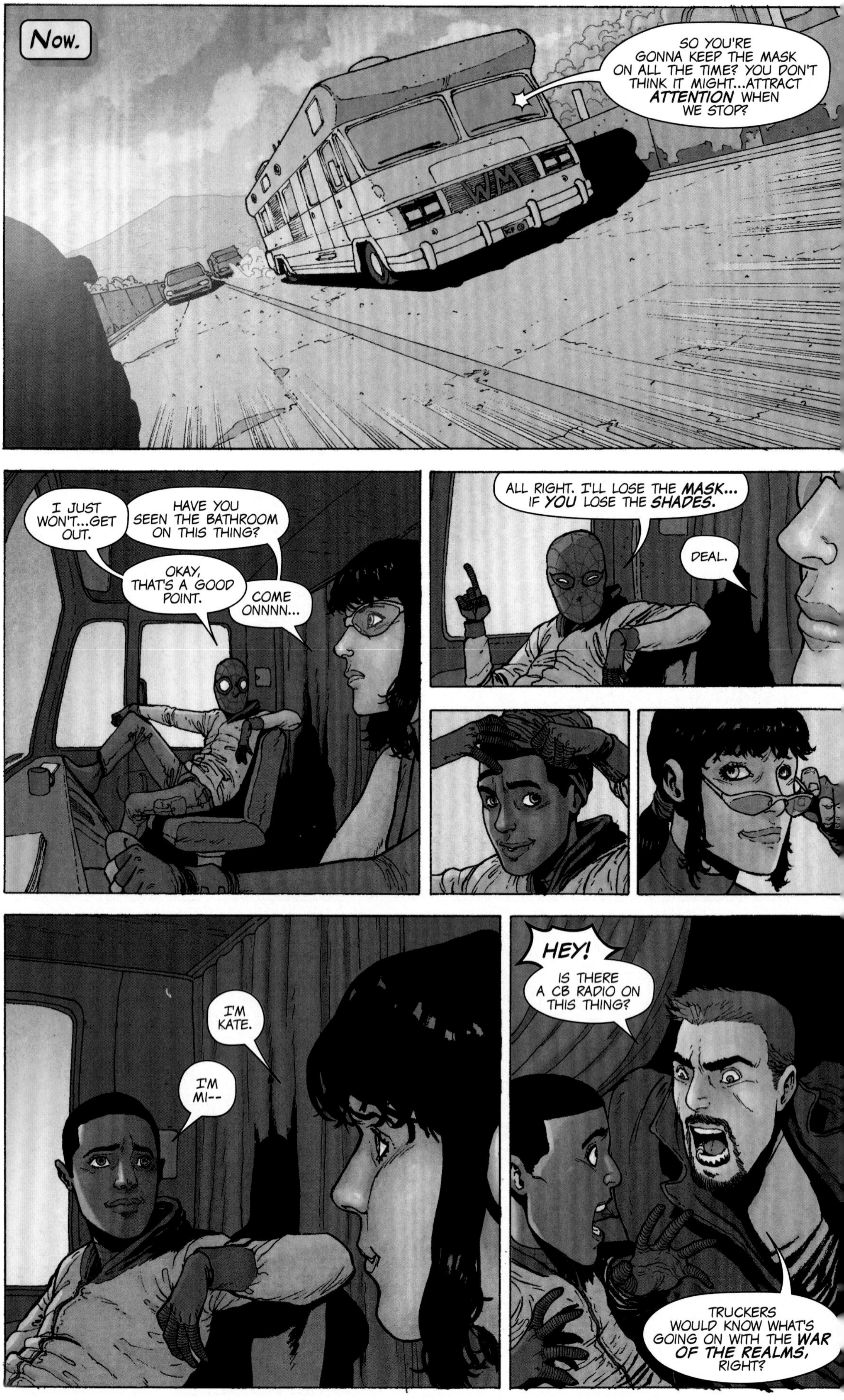

Now.
SO YOU'RE GONNA KEEP THE MASK ON ALL THE TIME? YOU DON'T THINK IT MIGHT...ATTRACT ATTENTION WHEN WE STOP?
I JUST WON'T...GET OUT.
HAVE YOU SEEN THE BATHROOM ON THIS THING?
OKAY, THAT'S A GOOD POINT.
COME ONNNN...
ALL RIGHT. I'LL LOSE THE MASK... IF YOU LOSE THE SHADES.
DEAL.
I'M KATE.
I'M MI--
HEY!
IS THERE A CB RADIO ON THIS THING?
TRUCKERS WOULD KNOW WHAT'S GOING ON WITH THE WAR OF THE REALMS, RIGHT?

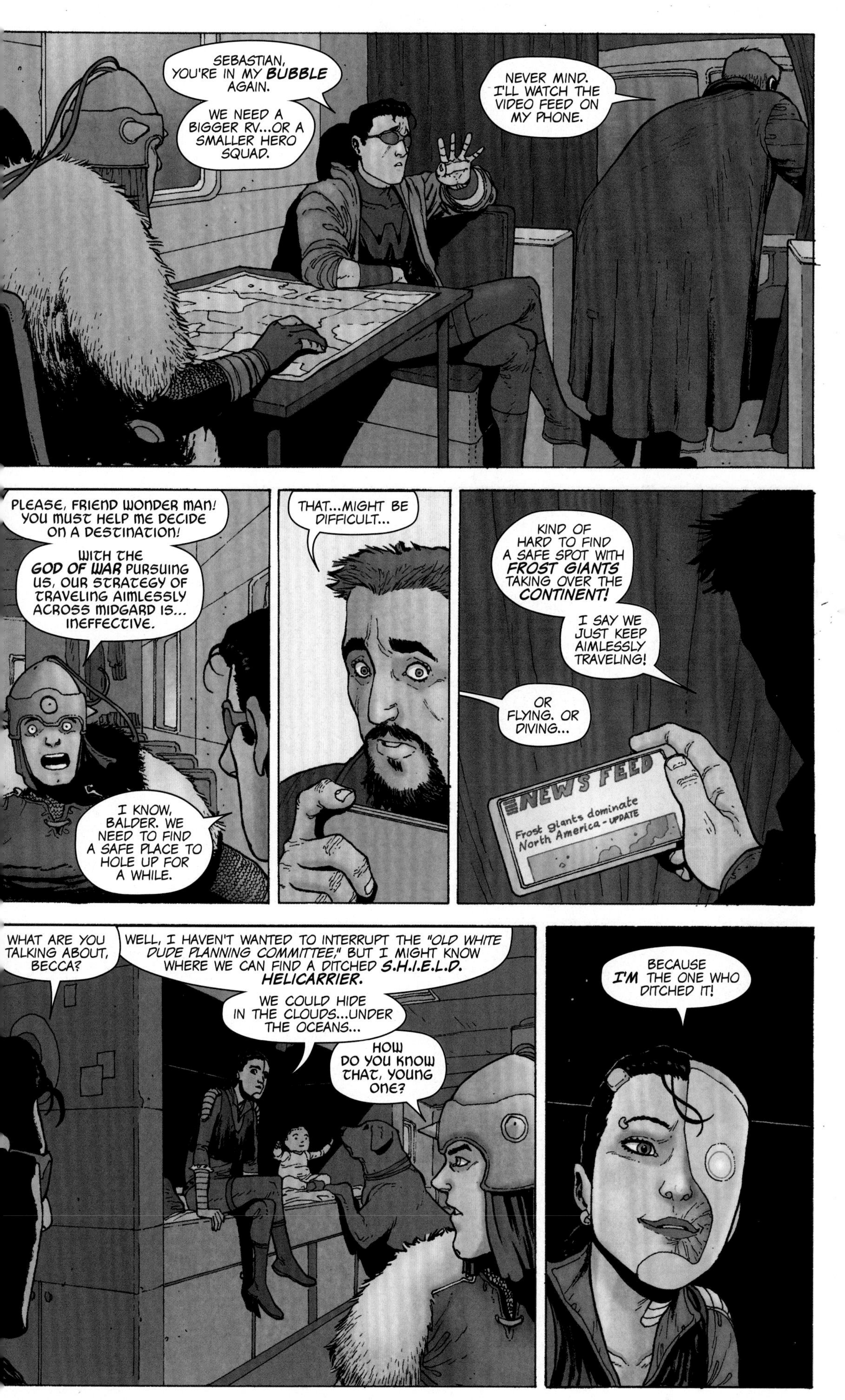

SEBASTIAN, YOU'RE IN MY **BUBBLE** AGAIN.
WE NEED A BIGGER RV...OR A SMALLER HERO SQUAD.
NEVER MIND. I'LL WATCH THE VIDEO FEED ON MY PHONE.
PLEASE, FRIEND WONDER MAN! YOU MUST HELP ME DECIDE ON A DESTINATION!
WITH THE **GOD OF WAR** PURSUING US, OUR STRATEGY OF TRAVELING AIMLESSLY ACROSS MIDGARD IS... INEFFECTIVE.
I KNOW, BALDER. WE NEED TO FIND A SAFE PLACE TO HOLE UP FOR A WHILE.
THAT...MIGHT BE DIFFICULT...
KIND OF HARD TO FIND A SAFE SPOT WITH **FROST GIANTS** TAKING OVER THE **CONTINENT!**
I SAY WE JUST KEEP AIMLESSLY TRAVELING!
OR FLYING. OR DIVING...
NEWS FEED
Frost giants dominate North America - UPDATE
WHAT ARE YOU TALKING ABOUT, BECCA?
WELL, I HAVEN'T WANTED TO INTERRUPT THE *"OLD WHITE DUDE PLANNING COMMITTEE,"* BUT I MIGHT KNOW WHERE WE CAN FIND A DITCHED **S.H.I.E.L.D. HELICARRIER.**
WE COULD HIDE IN THE CLOUDS...UNDER THE OCEANS...
HOW DO YOU KNOW THAT, YOUNG ONE?
BECAUSE **I'M** THE ONE WHO DITCHED IT!

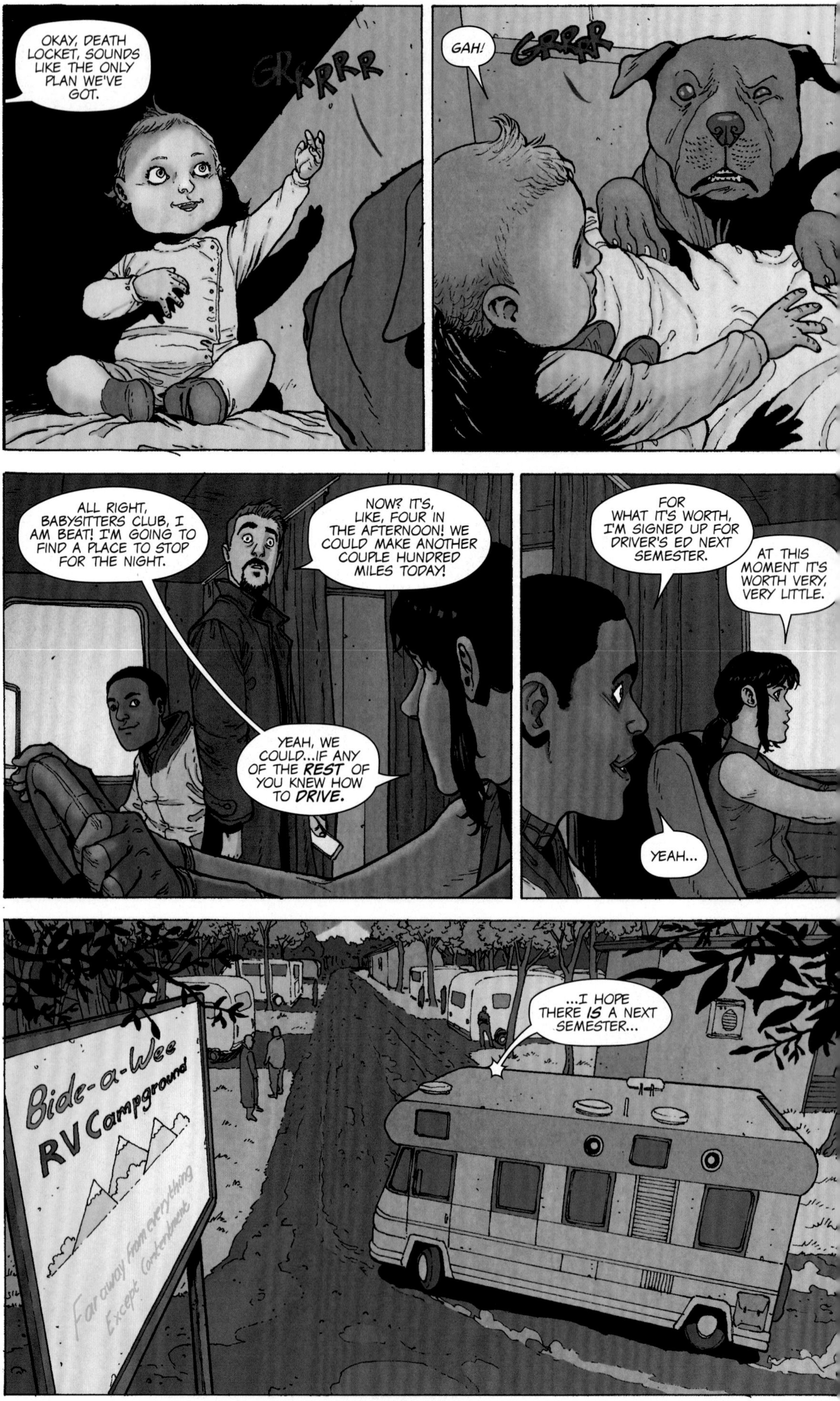
OKAY, DEATH LOCKET, SOUNDS LIKE THE ONLY PLAN WE'VE GOT.
GRRRRR
GAH!
GRRRR
ALL RIGHT, BABYSITTERS CLUB, I AM BEAT! I'M GOING TO FIND A PLACE TO STOP FOR THE NIGHT.
NOW? IT'S, LIKE, FOUR IN THE AFTERNOON! WE COULD MAKE ANOTHER COUPLE HUNDRED MILES TODAY!
YEAH, WE COULD...IF ANY OF THE REST OF YOU KNEW HOW TO DRIVE.
FOR WHAT IT'S WORTH, I'M SIGNED UP FOR DRIVER'S ED NEXT SEMESTER.
AT THIS MOMENT IT'S WORTH VERY, VERY LITTLE.
YEAH...
Bide-a-Wee
RV Campground
Faraway from everything
Except Contentment
...I HOPE THERE IS A NEXT SEMESTER...

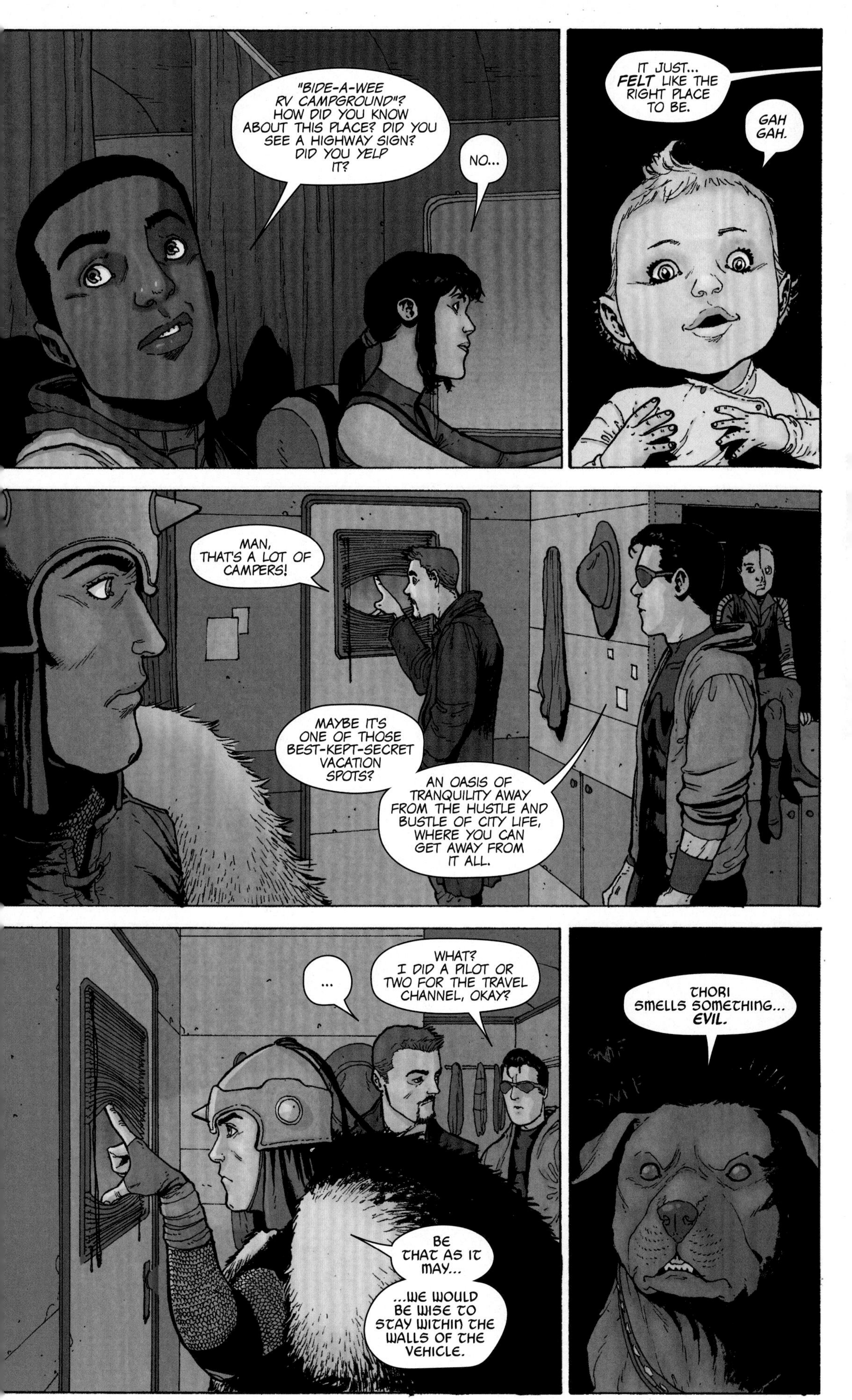
"BIDE-A-WEE RV CAMPGROUND"? HOW DID YOU KNOW ABOUT THIS PLACE? DID YOU SEE A HIGHWAY SIGN? DID YOU YELP IT?
NO...
IT JUST... **FELT** LIKE THE RIGHT PLACE TO BE.
GAH GAH.
MAN, THAT'S A LOT OF CAMPERS!
MAYBE IT'S ONE OF THOSE BEST-KEPT-SECRET VACATION SPOTS?
AN OASIS OF TRANQUILITY AWAY FROM THE HUSTLE AND BUSTLE OF CITY LIFE, WHERE YOU CAN GET AWAY FROM IT ALL.
...
WHAT? I DID A PILOT OR TWO FOR THE TRAVEL CHANNEL, OKAY?
BE THAT AS IT MAY...
...WE WOULD BE WISE TO STAY WITHIN THE WALLS OF THE VEHICLE.
THORI SMELLS SOMETHING... **EVIL.**

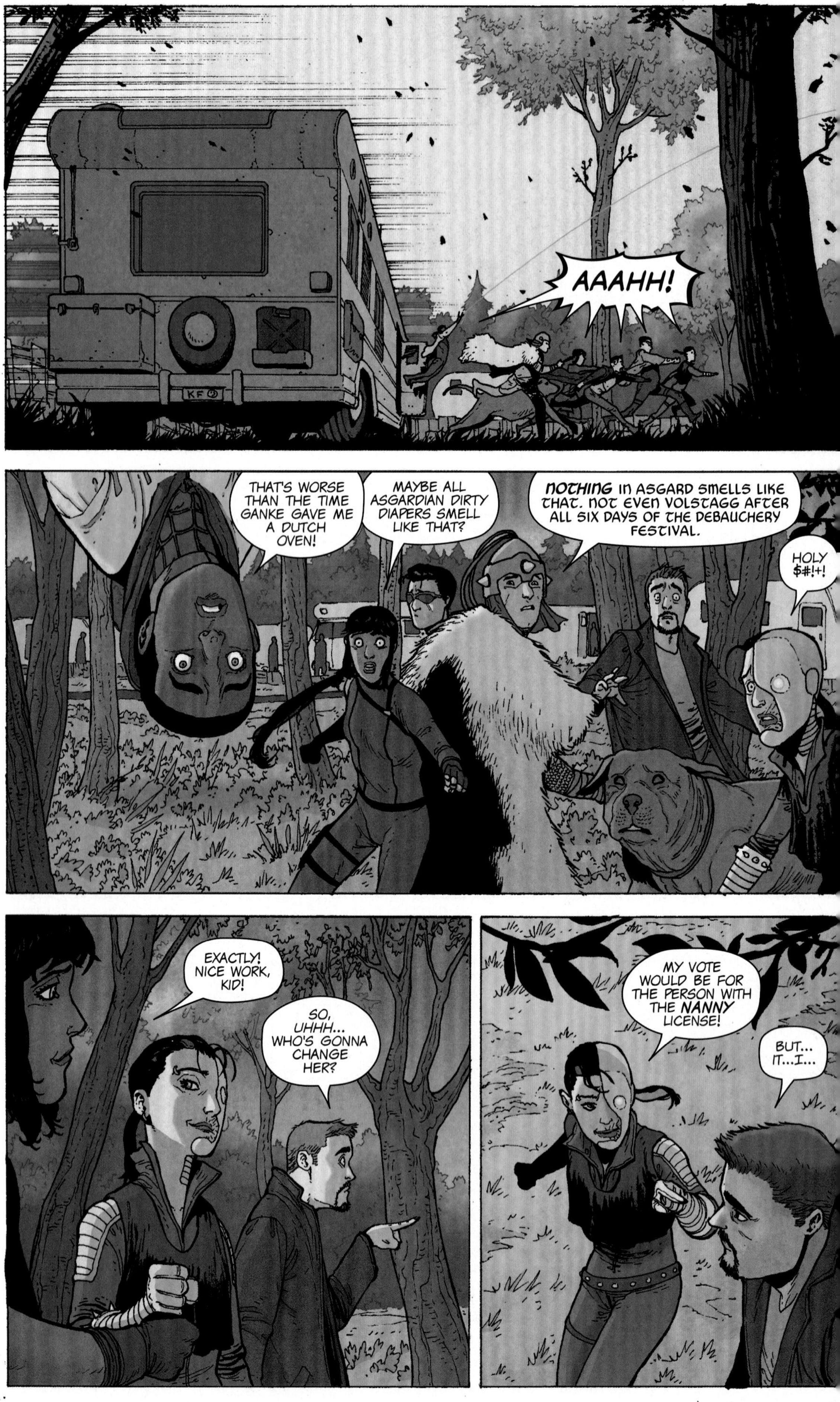

AAAHH!
THAT'S WORSE THAN THE TIME GANKE GAVE ME A DUTCH OVEN!
MAYBE ALL ASGARDIAN DIRTY DIAPERS SMELL LIKE THAT?
NOTHING IN ASGARD SMELLS LIKE THAT. NOT EVEN VOLSTAGG AFTER ALL SIX DAYS OF THE DEBAUCHERY FESTIVAL.
HOLY $#!+!
EXACTLY! NICE WORK, KID!
SO, UHHH... WHO'S GONNA CHANGE HER?
MY VOTE WOULD BE FOR THE PERSON WITH THE NANNY LICENSE!
BUT... IT...I...

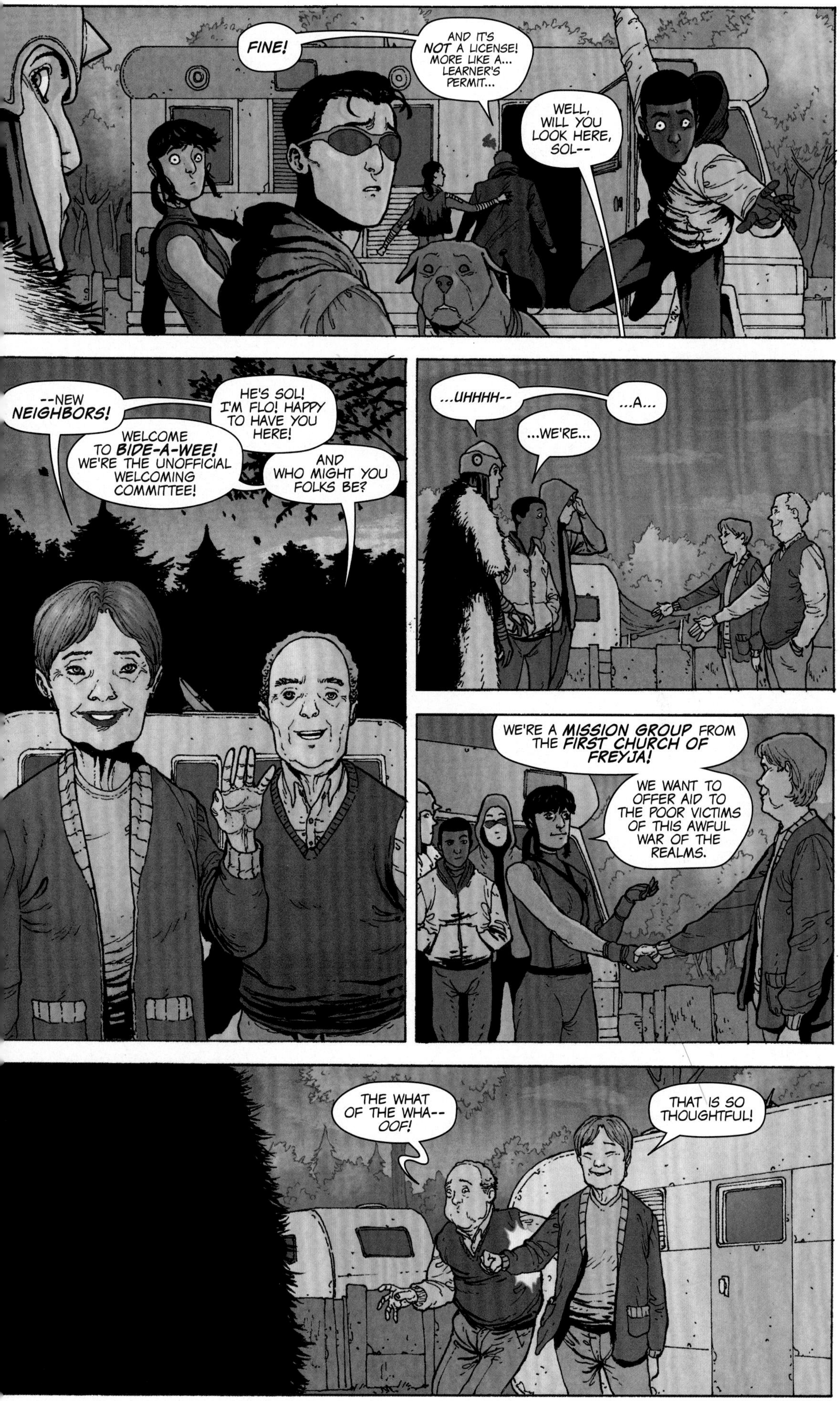
FINE!
AND IT'S NOT A LICENSE! MORE LIKE A... LEARNER'S PERMIT...
WELL, WILL YOU LOOK HERE, SOL--
--NEW NEIGHBORS!
HE'S SOL! I'M FLO! HAPPY TO HAVE YOU HERE!
WELCOME TO BIDE-A-WEE! WE'RE THE UNOFFICIAL WELCOMING COMMITTEE!
AND WHO MIGHT YOU FOLKS BE?
...UHHHH--
...A...
...WE'RE...
WE'RE A MISSION GROUP FROM THE FIRST CHURCH OF FREYJA!
WE WANT TO OFFER AID TO THE POOR VICTIMS OF THIS AWFUL WAR OF THE REALMS.
THE WHAT OF THE WHA-- OOF!
THAT IS SO THOUGHTFUL!

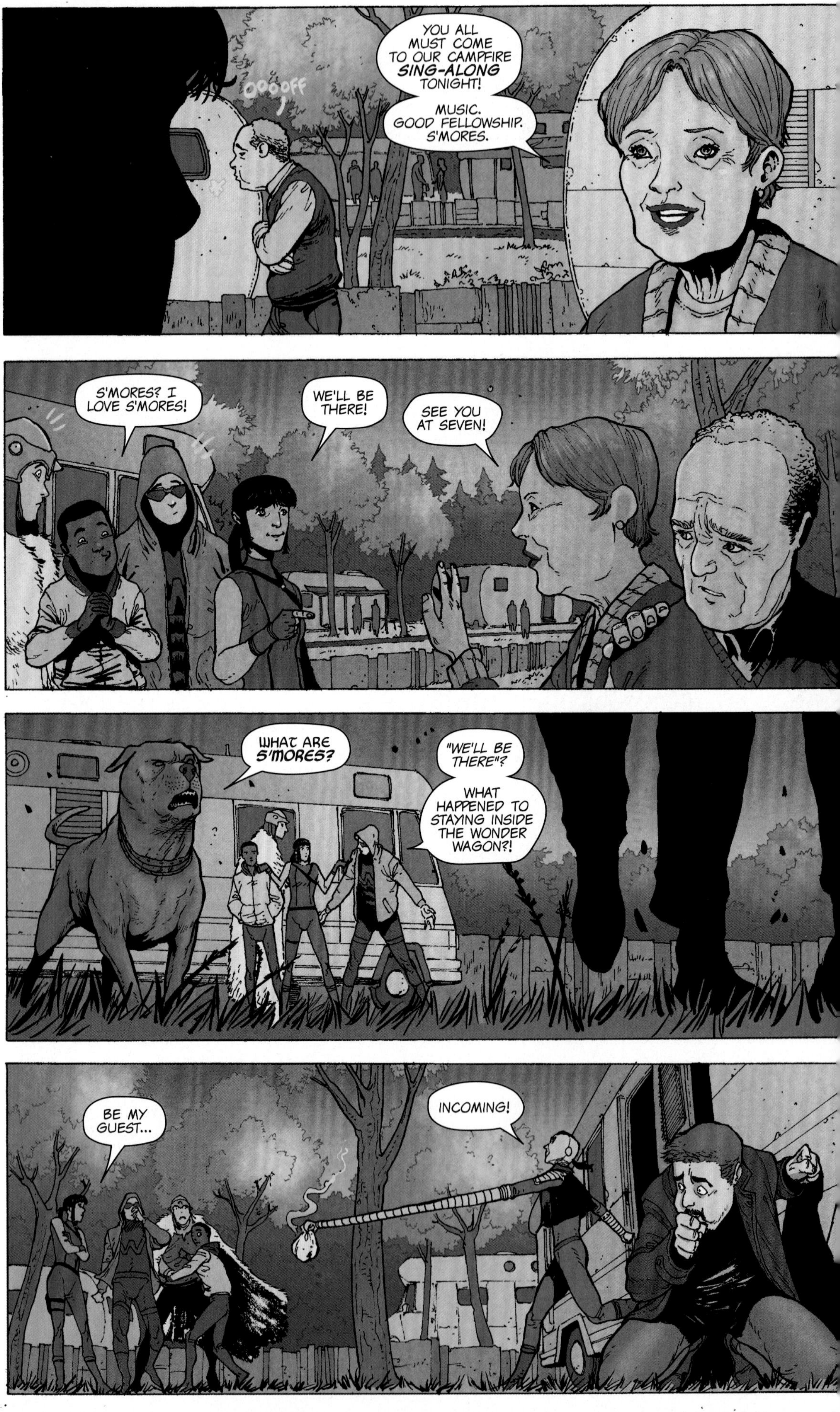

OOOOFF
YOU ALL MUST COME TO OUR CAMPFIRE SING-ALONG TONIGHT!
MUSIC. GOOD FELLOWSHIP. S'MORES.
S'MORES? I LOVE S'MORES!
WE'LL BE THERE!
SEE YOU AT SEVEN!
WHAT ARE S'MORES?
"WE'LL BE THERE"?
WHAT HAPPENED TO STAYING INSIDE THE WONDER WAGON?!
BE MY GUEST...
INCOMING!

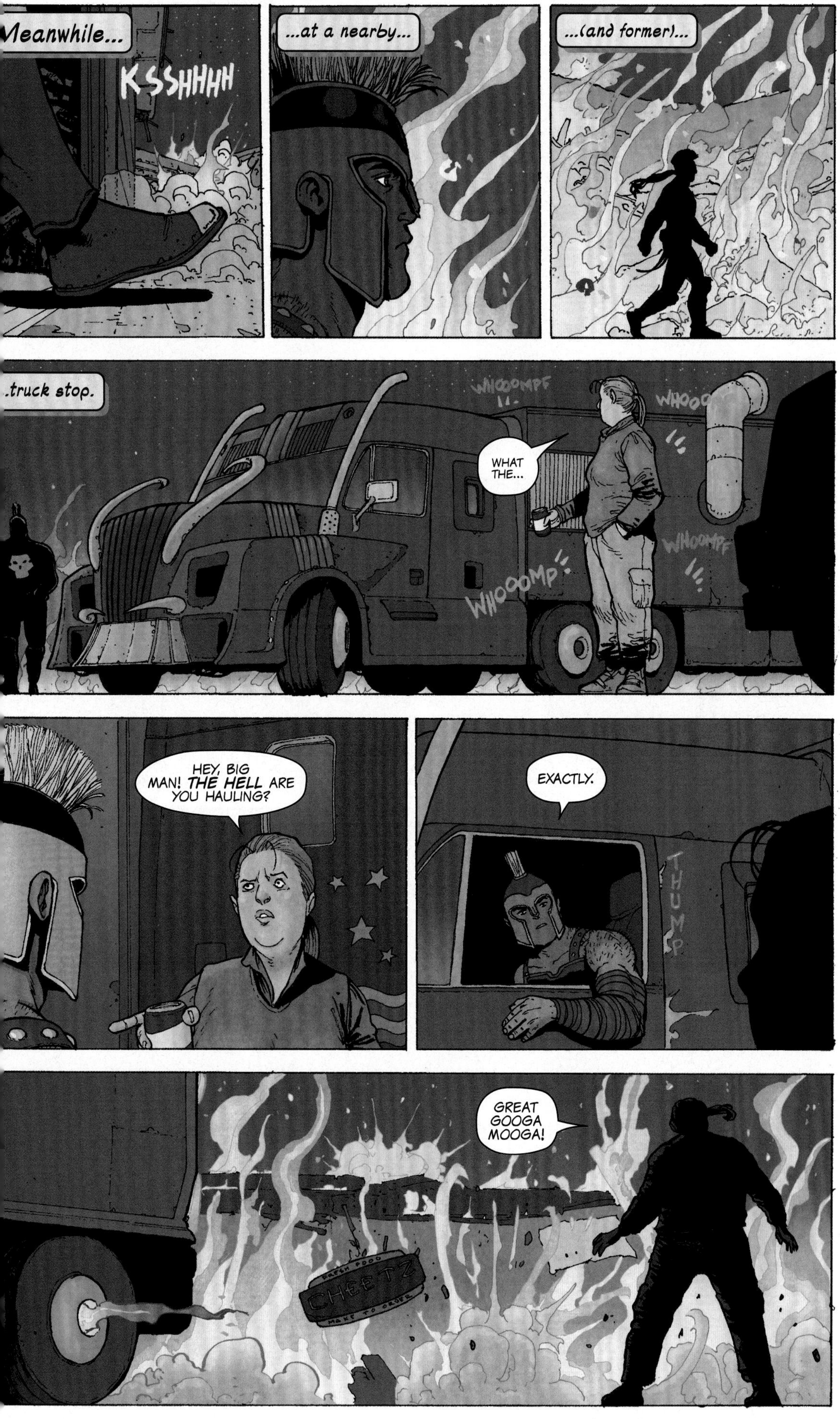
Meanwhile...
KSSHHHH
...at a nearby...
...(and former)...
...truck stop.
WHOOOMPF
WHOOOMPF
WHAT THE...
WHOOOMPF
WHOOOMP
HEY, BIG MAN! THE HELL ARE YOU HAULING?
EXACTLY.
THUMP
GREAT GOOGA MOOGA!
CHEETZ

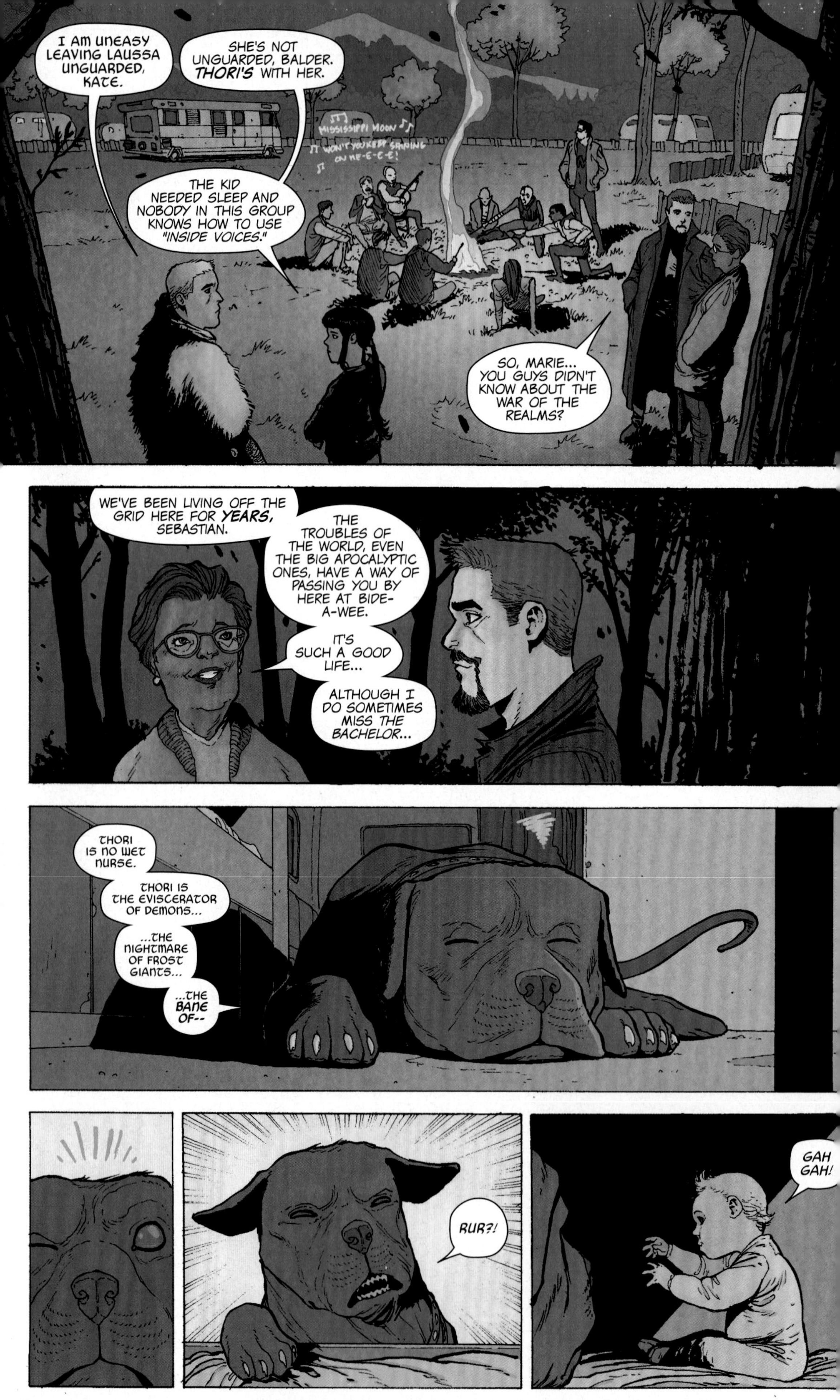
I AM UNEASY LEAVING LAUSSA UNGUARDED, KATE.
SHE'S NOT UNGUARDED, BALDER. THORI'S WITH HER.
♫ MISSISSIPPI MOON ♫
♫ WON'T YOU KEEP SHINING ON ME-E-E-E!
THE KID NEEDED SLEEP AND NOBODY IN THIS GROUP KNOWS HOW TO USE "INSIDE VOICES."
SO, MARIE... YOU GUYS DIDN'T KNOW ABOUT THE WAR OF THE REALMS?
WE'VE BEEN LIVING OFF THE GRID HERE FOR YEARS, SEBASTIAN.
THE TROUBLES OF THE WORLD, EVEN THE BIG APOCALYPTIC ONES, HAVE A WAY OF PASSING YOU BY HERE AT BIDE-A-WEE.
IT'S SUCH A GOOD LIFE...
ALTHOUGH I DO SOMETIMES MISS THE BACHELOR...
THORI IS NO WET NURSE.
THORI IS THE EVISCERATOR OF DEMONS...
...THE NIGHTMARE OF FROST GIANTS...
...THE BANE OF--
RUR?!
GAH GAH!

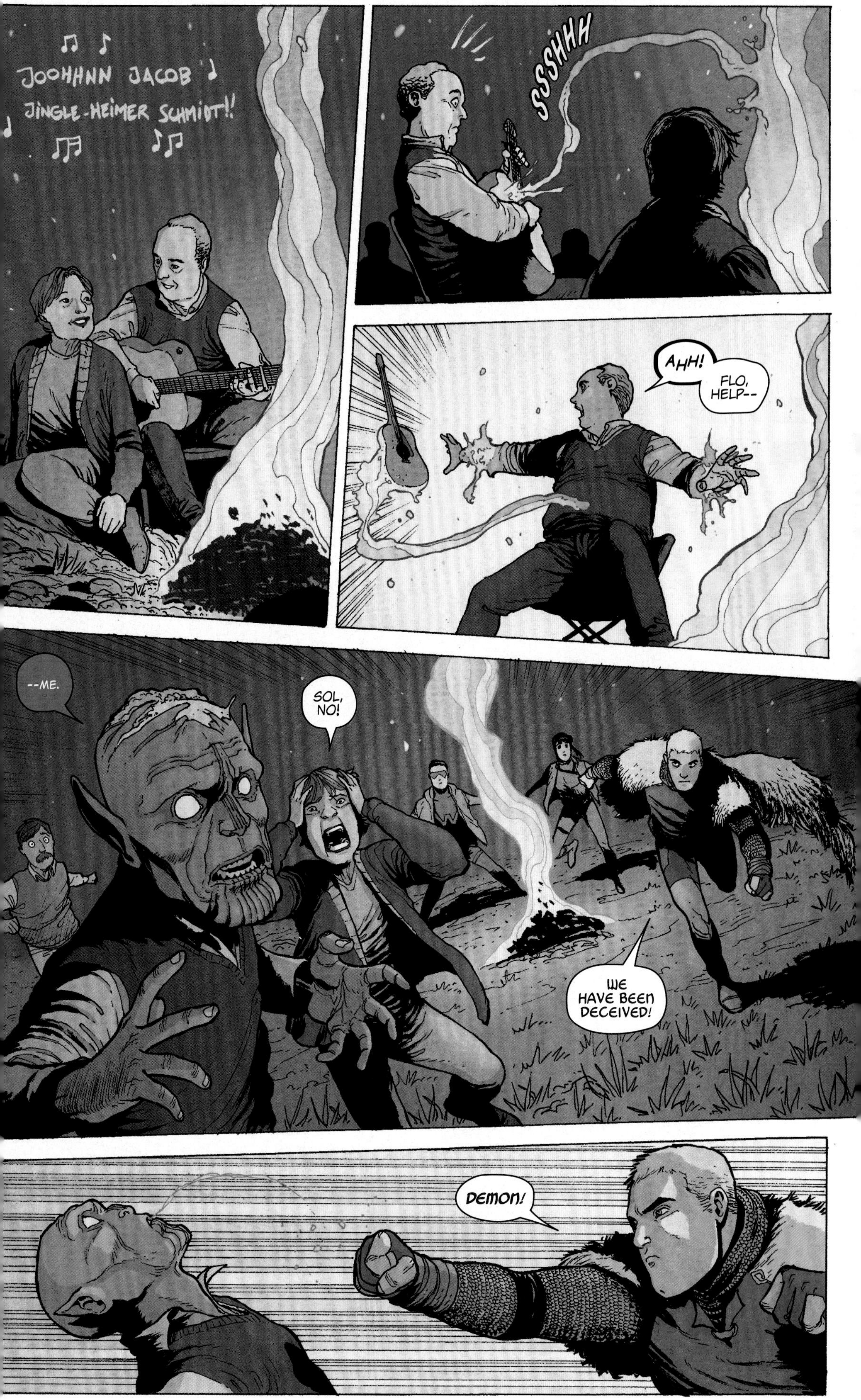
JOOHHNN JACOB
JINGLE-HEIMER SCHMIDT!!
SSSHHH
AHH!
FLO, HELP--
--ME.
SOL, NO!
WE HAVE BEEN DECEIVED!
DEMON!

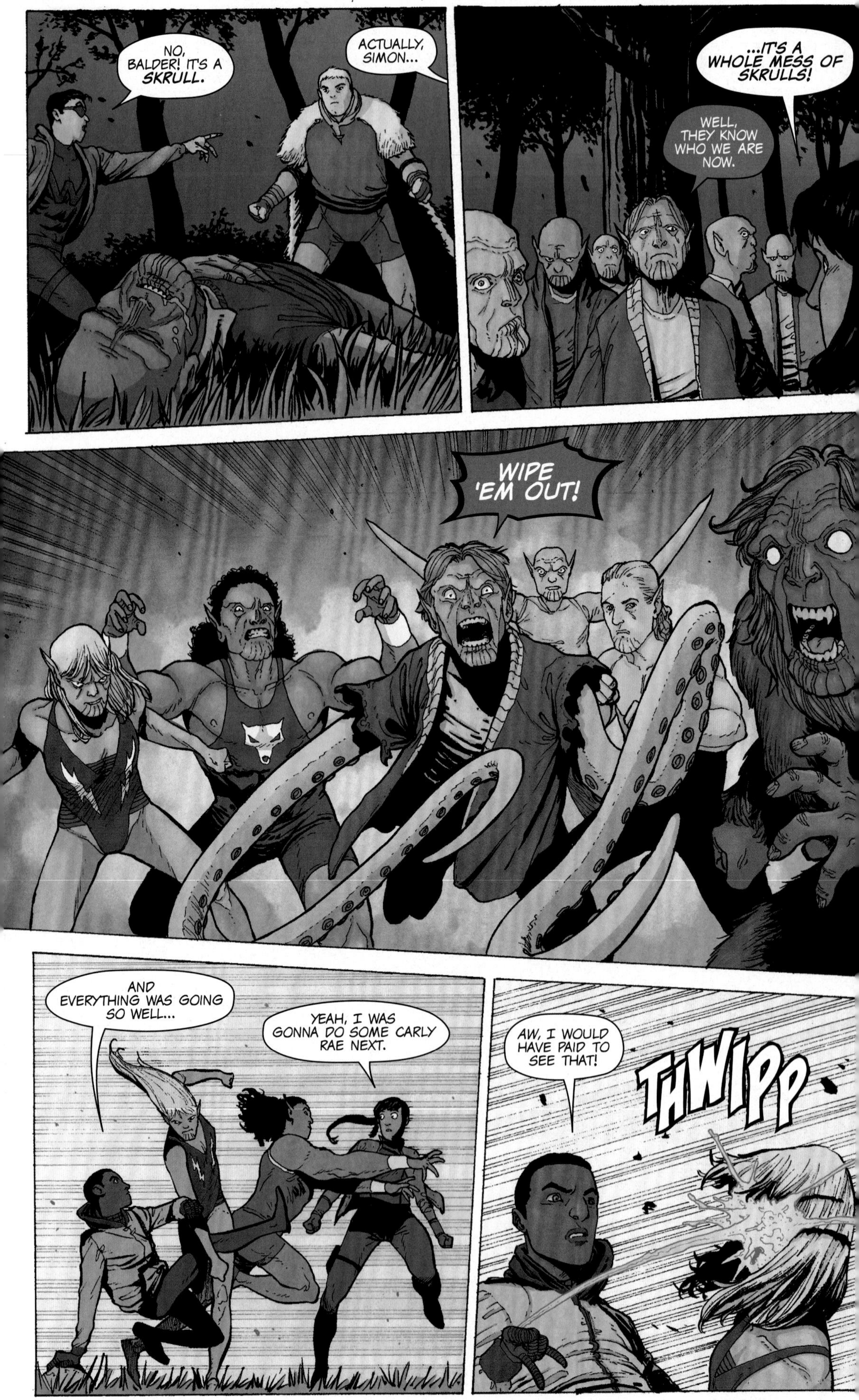
NO, BALDER! IT'S A SKRULL.
ACTUALLY, SIMON...
...IT'S A WHOLE MESS OF SKRULLS!
WELL, THEY KNOW WHO WE ARE NOW.
WIPE 'EM OUT!
AND EVERYTHING WAS GOING SO WELL...
YEAH, I WAS GONNA DO SOME CARLY RAE NEXT.
AW, I WOULD HAVE PAID TO SEE THAT!
THWIPP

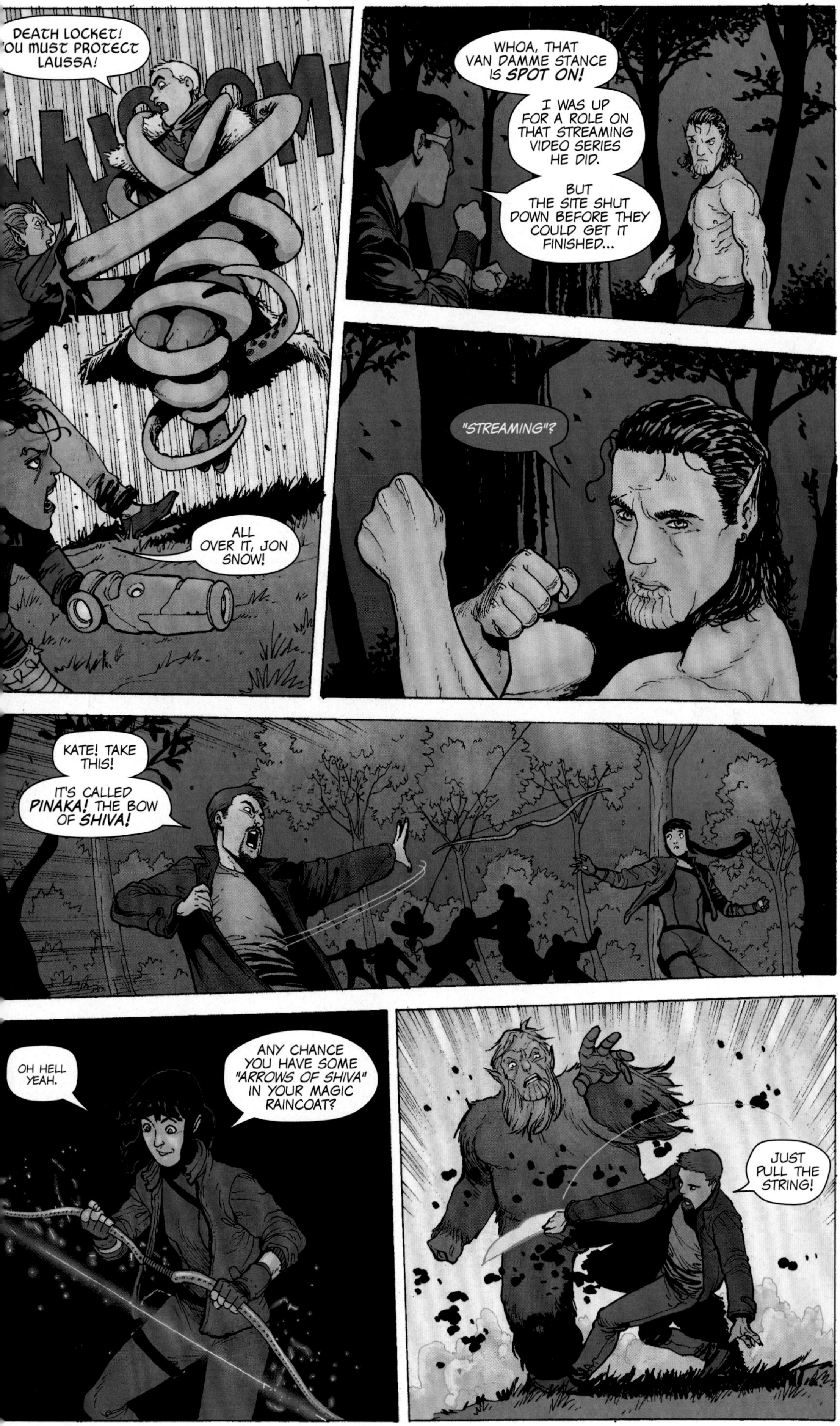
DEATH LOCKET! YOU MUST PROTECT LAUSSA!
WHOA, THAT VAN DAMME STANCE IS SPOT ON!
I WAS UP FOR A ROLE ON THAT STREAMING VIDEO SERIES HE DID.
BUT THE SITE SHUT DOWN BEFORE THEY COULD GET IT FINISHED...
ALL OVER IT, JON SNOW!
"STREAMING"?
KATE! TAKE THIS!
IT'S CALLED PINAKA! THE BOW OF SHIVA!
OH HELL YEAH.
ANY CHANCE YOU HAVE SOME "ARROWS OF SHIVA" IN YOUR MAGIC RAINCOAT?
JUST PULL THE STRING!

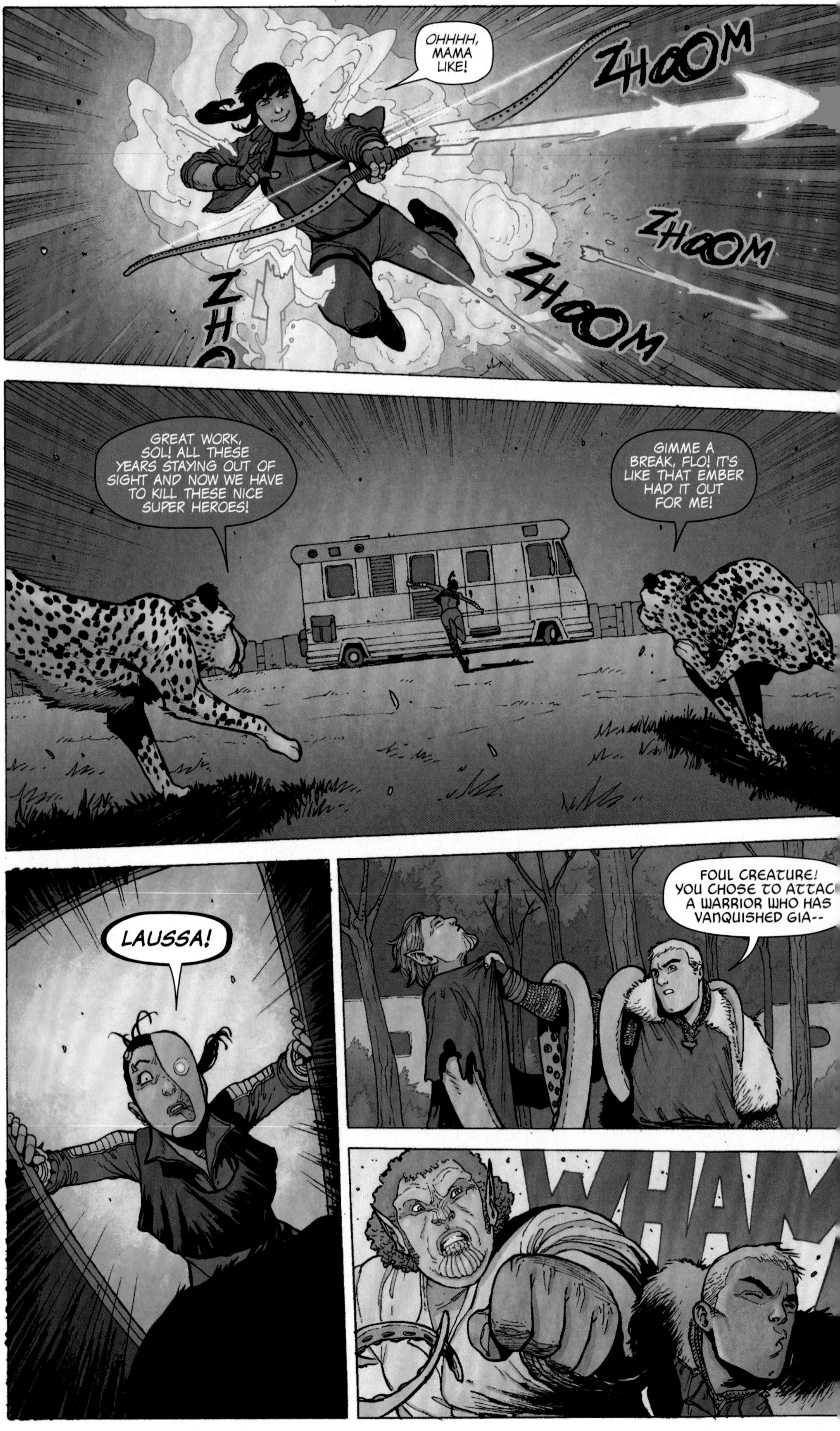
OHHHH, MAMA LIKE!
ZHOOM
ZHOOM
ZHOOM
GREAT WORK, SOL! ALL THESE YEARS STAYING OUT OF SIGHT AND NOW WE HAVE TO KILL THESE NICE SUPER HEROES!
GIMME A BREAK, FLO! IT'S LIKE THAT EMBER HAD IT OUT FOR ME!
LAUSSA!
FOUL CREATURE! YOU CHOSE TO ATTAC A WARRIOR WHO HAS VANQUISHED GIA--

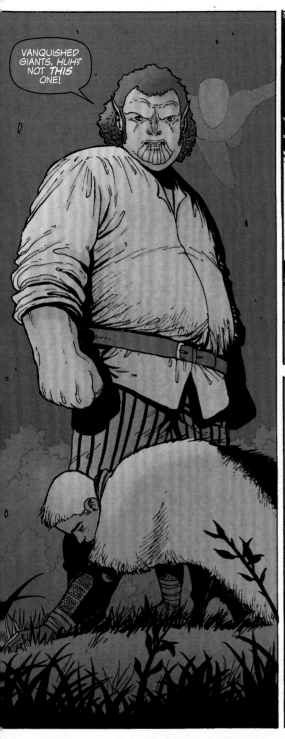

VANQUISHED GIANTS, HUH? NOT *THIS* ONE!

WHAT'S WITH ALL THE '90S JUNK? YOU PEOPLE REALLY *HAVE* BEEN OFF THE GRID!

FZZSHAM

AGH!

FIRST OFF, THE PRINCESS BRIDE CAME OUT IN 19*87.*

AND *SECOND,* IT'S A TIMELESS CLASSIC THAT SHAPED--

NOT *NOW,* DRUID--

--THE SKRULLS HAVE SET UPON LAUSSA!

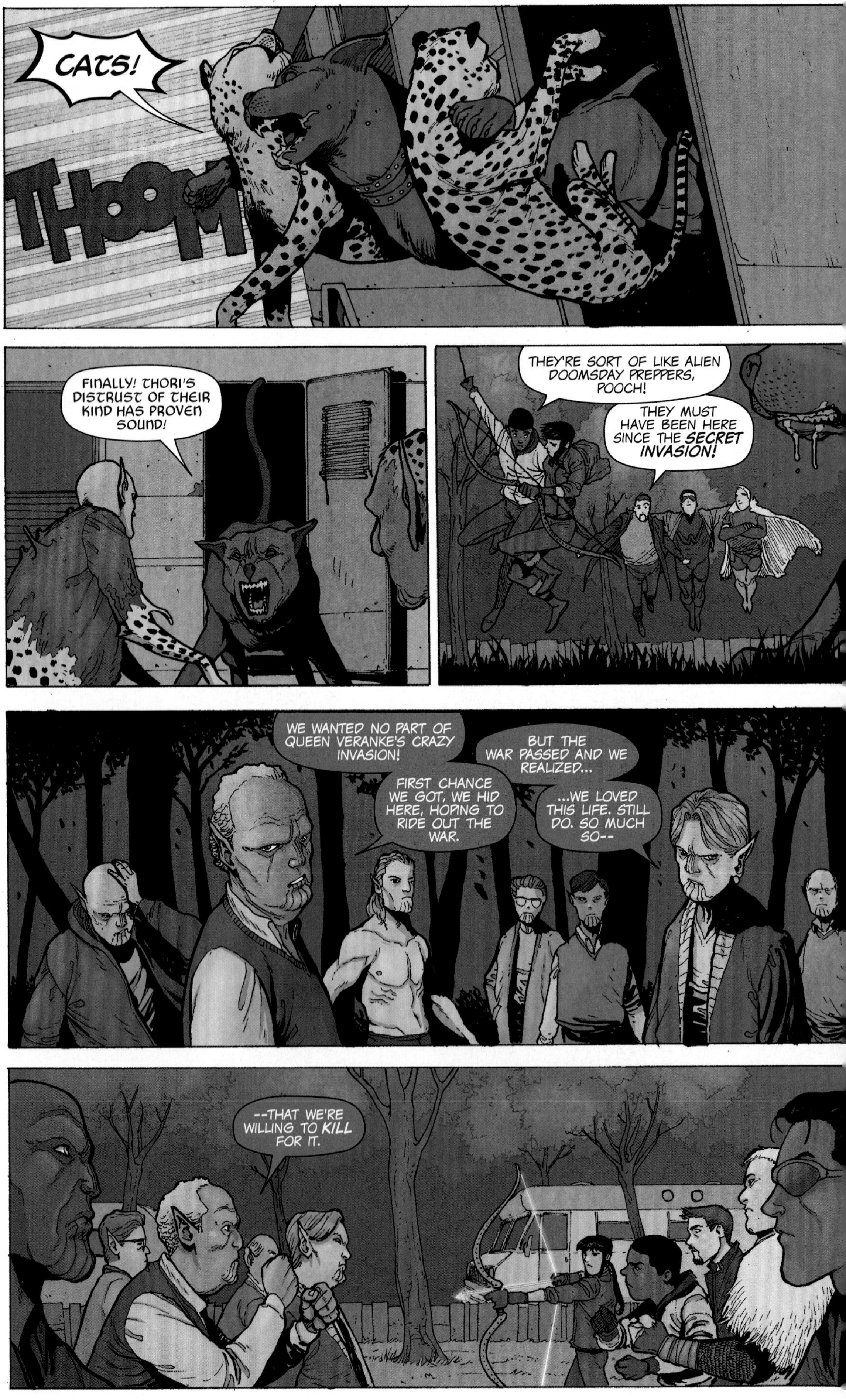
CATS!
THOOM
FINALLY! THORI'S DISTRUST OF THEIR KIND HAS PROVEN SOUND!
THEY'RE SORT OF LIKE ALIEN DOOMSDAY PREPPERS, POOCH!
THEY MUST HAVE BEEN HERE SINCE THE SECRET INVASION!
WE WANTED NO PART OF QUEEN VERANKE'S CRAZY INVASION!
FIRST CHANCE WE GOT, WE HID HERE, HOPING TO RIDE OUT THE WAR.
BUT THE WAR PASSED AND WE REALIZED...
...WE LOVED THIS LIFE. STILL DO. SO MUCH SO--
--THAT WE'RE WILLING TO KILL FOR IT.

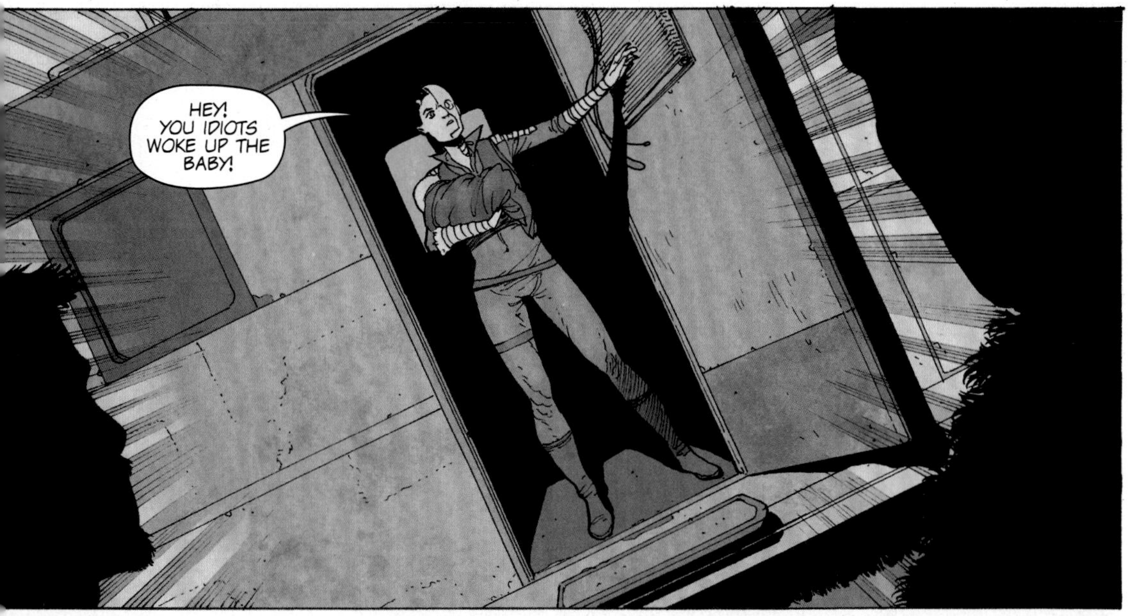
HEY! YOU IDIOTS WOKE UP THE BABY!

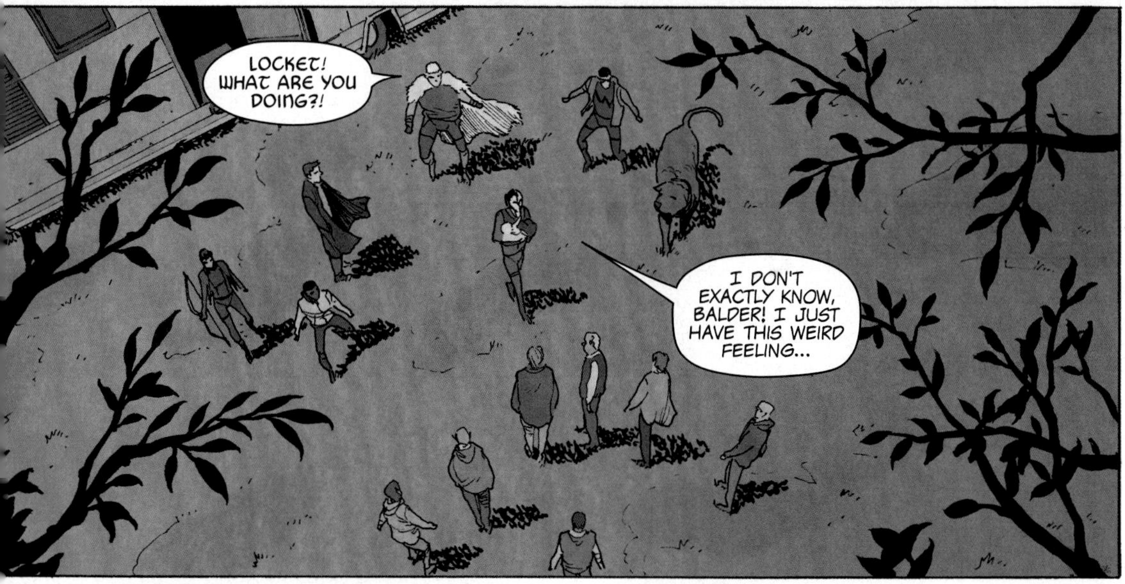
LOCKET! WHAT ARE YOU DOING?!
I DON'T EXACTLY KNOW, BALDER! I JUST HAVE THIS WEIRD FEELING...

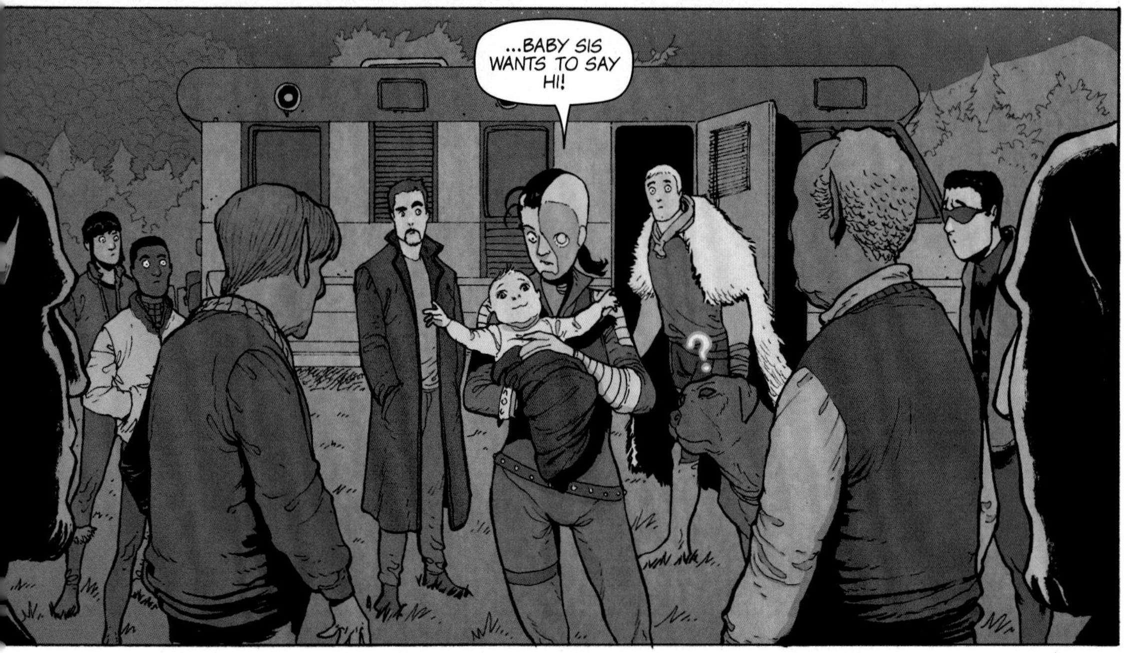
...BABY SIS WANTS TO SAY HI!
?

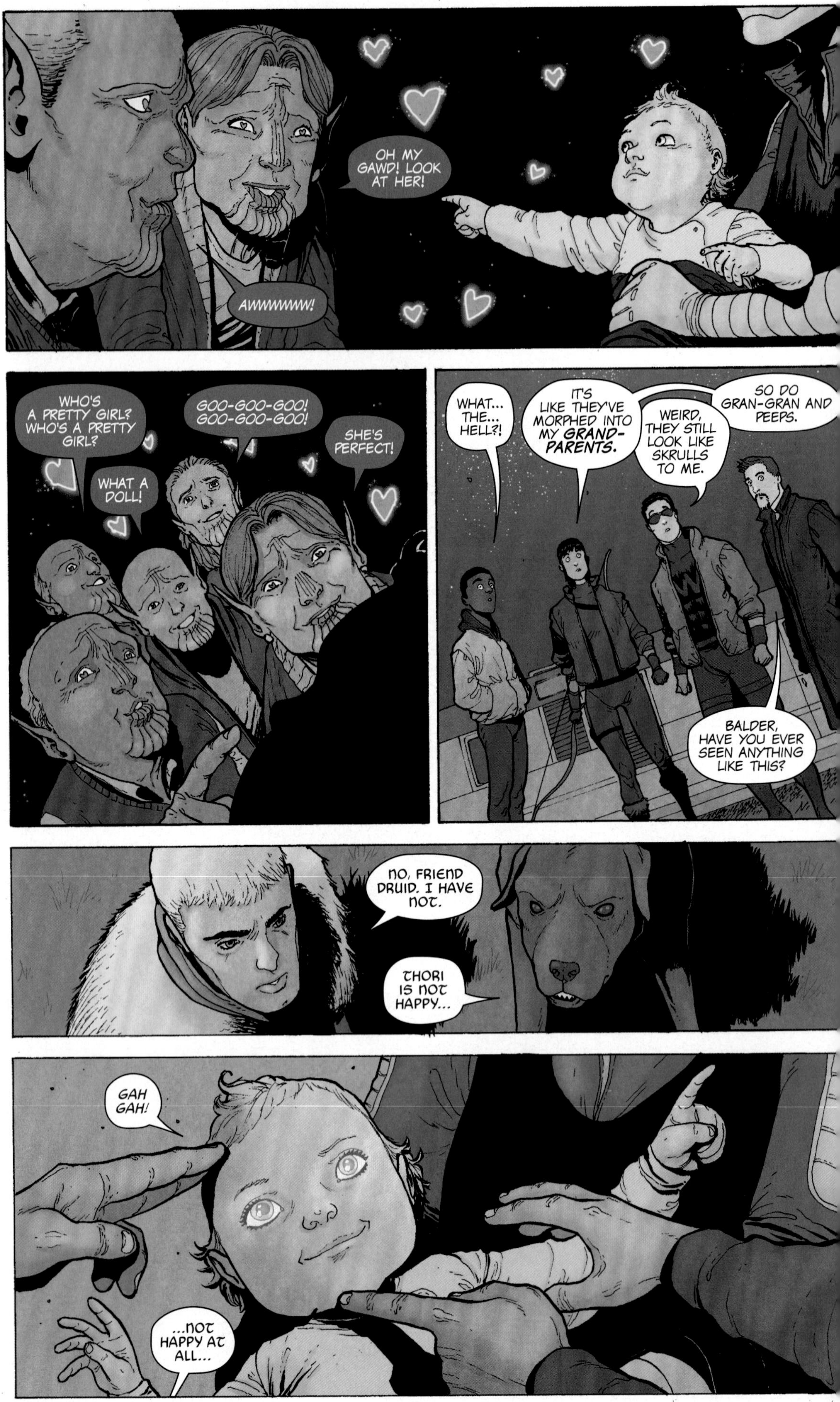

OH MY GAWD! LOOK AT HER!
AWWWWWWW!
WHO'S A PRETTY GIRL? WHO'S A PRETTY GIRL?
WHAT A DOLL!
GOO-GOO-GOO! GOO-GOO-GOO!
SHE'S PERFECT!
WHAT... THE... HELL?!
IT'S LIKE THEY'VE MORPHED INTO MY GRAND-PARENTS.
WEIRD, THEY STILL LOOK LIKE SKRULLS TO ME.
SO DO GRAN-GRAN AND PEEPS.
BALDER, HAVE YOU EVER SEEN ANYTHING LIKE THIS?
NO, FRIEND DRUID. I HAVE NOT.
THORI IS NOT HAPPY...
GAH GAH!
...NOT HAPPY AT ALL...

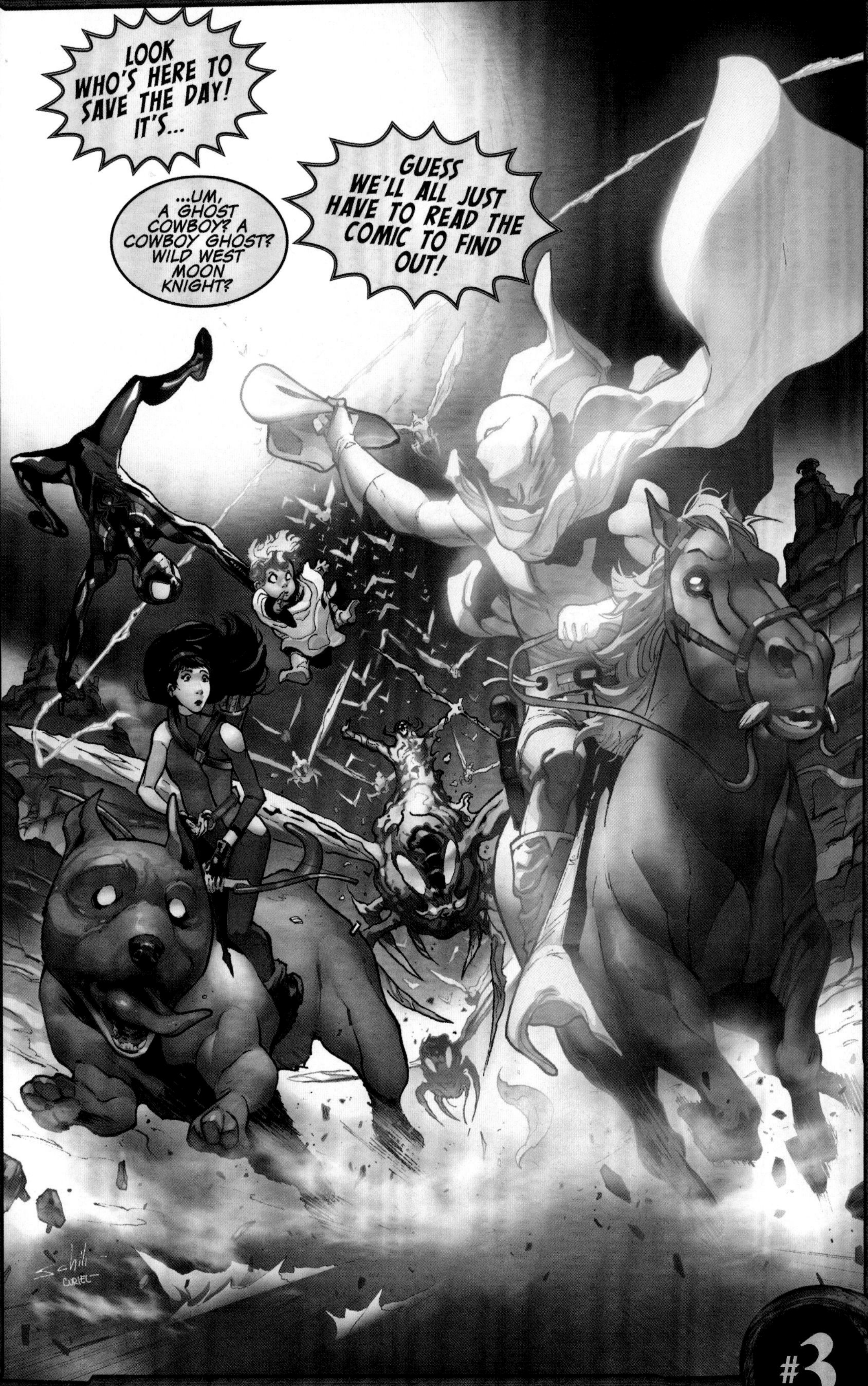
LOOK WHO'S HERE TO SAVE THE DAY! IT'S...
...UM, A GHOST COWBOY? A COWBOY GHOST? WILD WEST MOON KNIGHT?
GUESS WE'LL ALL JUST HAVE TO READ THE COMIC TO FIND OUT!
Schiti
Curiel

#3

Overseers of the Community

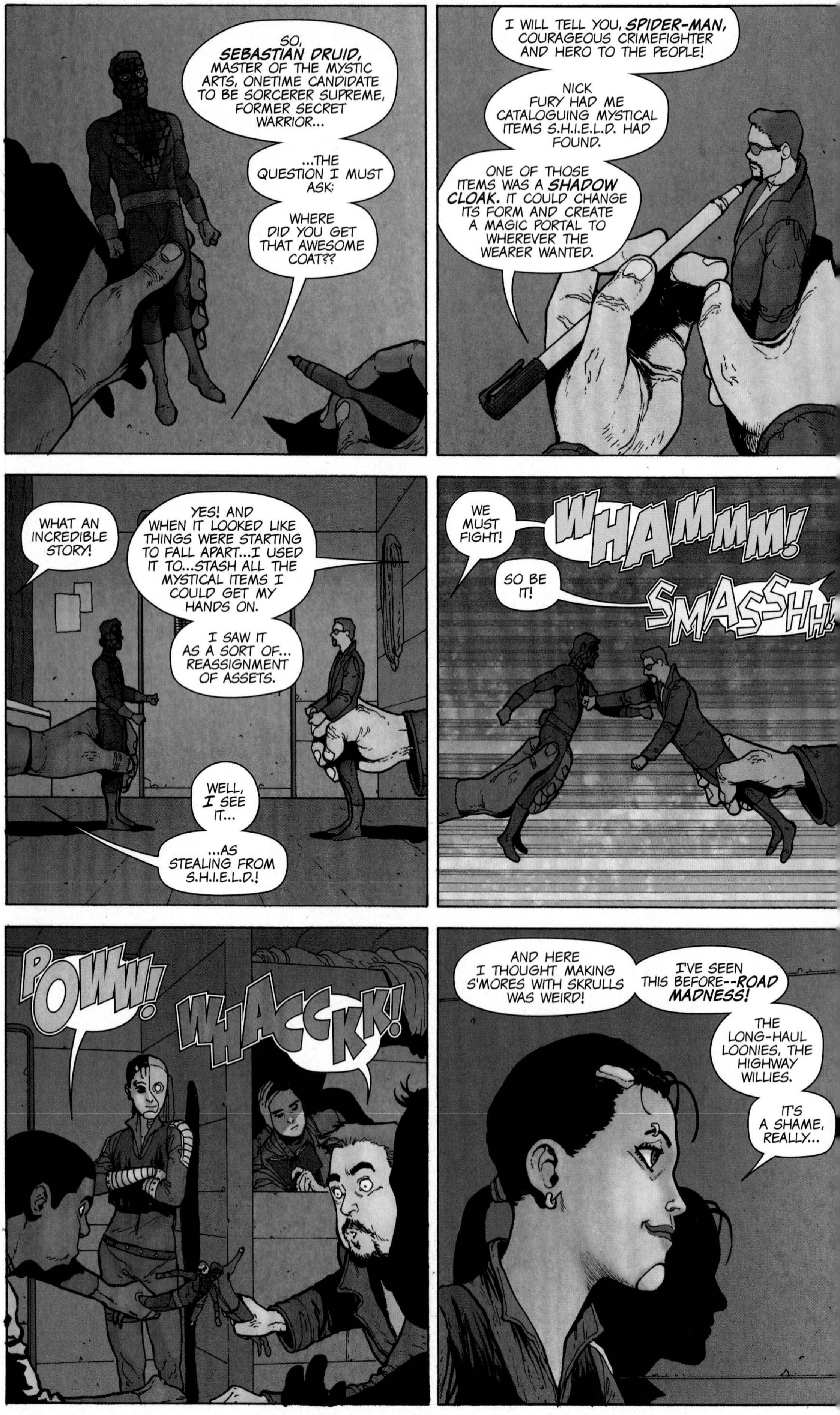
SO, SEBASTIAN DRUID, MASTER OF THE MYSTIC ARTS, ONETIME CANDIDATE TO BE SORCERER SUPREME, FORMER SECRET WARRIOR...
...THE QUESTION I MUST ASK:
WHERE DID YOU GET THAT AWESOME COAT??
I WILL TELL YOU, SPIDER-MAN, COURAGEOUS CRIMEFIGHTER AND HERO TO THE PEOPLE!
NICK FURY HAD ME CATALOGUING MYSTICAL ITEMS S.H.I.E.L.D. HAD FOUND.
ONE OF THOSE ITEMS WAS A SHADOW CLOAK. IT COULD CHANGE ITS FORM AND CREATE A MAGIC PORTAL TO WHEREVER THE WEARER WANTED.
WHAT AN INCREDIBLE STORY!
YES! AND WHEN IT LOOKED LIKE THINGS WERE STARTING TO FALL APART...I USED IT TO...STASH ALL THE MYSTICAL ITEMS I COULD GET MY HANDS ON.
I SAW IT AS A SORT OF... REASSIGNMENT OF ASSETS.
WELL, I SEE IT...
...AS STEALING FROM S.H.I.E.L.D.!
WE MUST FIGHT!
WHAMMM!
SO BE IT!
SMASSHH!
POWW!
WHACCKK!
AND HERE I THOUGHT MAKING S'MORES WITH SKRULLS WAS WEIRD!
I'VE SEEN THIS BEFORE--ROAD MADNESS!
THE LONG-HAUL LOONIES, THE HIGHWAY WILLIES.
IT'S A SHAME, REALLY...

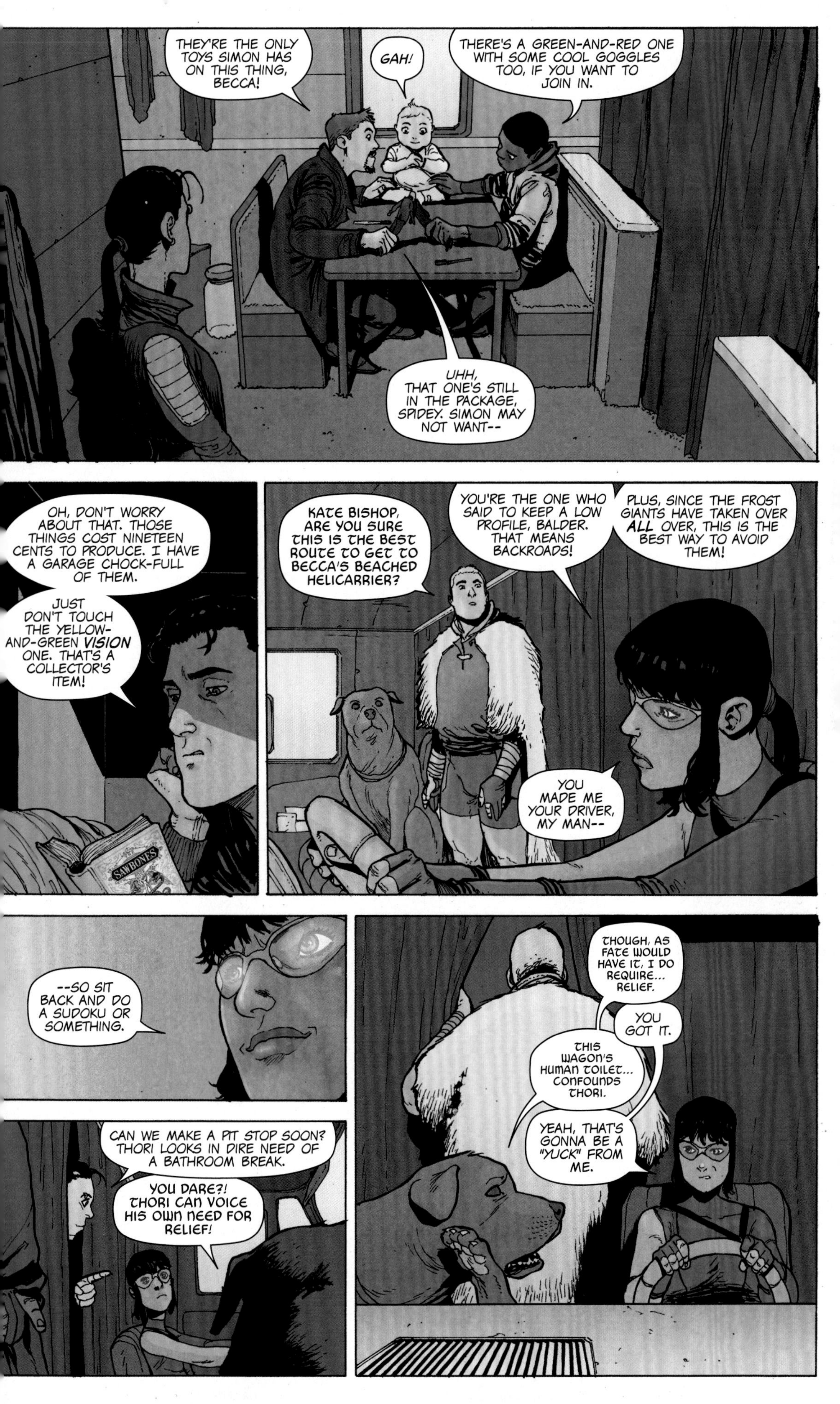

THEY'RE THE ONLY TOYS SIMON HAS ON THIS THING, BECCA!
GAH!
THERE'S A GREEN-AND-RED ONE WITH SOME COOL GOGGLES TOO, IF YOU WANT TO JOIN IN.
UHH, THAT ONE'S STILL IN THE PACKAGE, SPIDEY. SIMON MAY NOT WANT--
OH, DON'T WORRY ABOUT THAT. THOSE THINGS COST NINETEEN CENTS TO PRODUCE. I HAVE A GARAGE CHOCK-FULL OF THEM.
JUST DON'T TOUCH THE YELLOW-AND-GREEN VISION ONE. THAT'S A COLLECTOR'S ITEM!
SAWBONES
KATE BISHOP, ARE YOU SURE THIS IS THE BEST ROUTE TO GET TO BECCA'S BEACHED HELICARRIER?
YOU'RE THE ONE WHO SAID TO KEEP A LOW PROFILE, BALDER. THAT MEANS BACKROADS!
PLUS, SINCE THE FROST GIANTS HAVE TAKEN OVER ALL OVER, THIS IS THE BEST WAY TO AVOID THEM!
YOU MADE ME YOUR DRIVER, MY MAN--
--SO SIT BACK AND DO A SUDOKU OR SOMETHING.
CAN WE MAKE A PIT STOP SOON? THORI LOOKS IN DIRE NEED OF A BATHROOM BREAK.
YOU DARE?! THORI CAN VOICE HIS OWN NEED FOR RELIEF!
THOUGH, AS FATE WOULD HAVE IT, I DO REQUIRE... RELIEF.
YOU GOT IT.
THIS WAGON'S HUMAN TOILET... CONFOUNDS THORI.
YEAH, THAT'S GONNA BE A "YUCK" FROM ME.

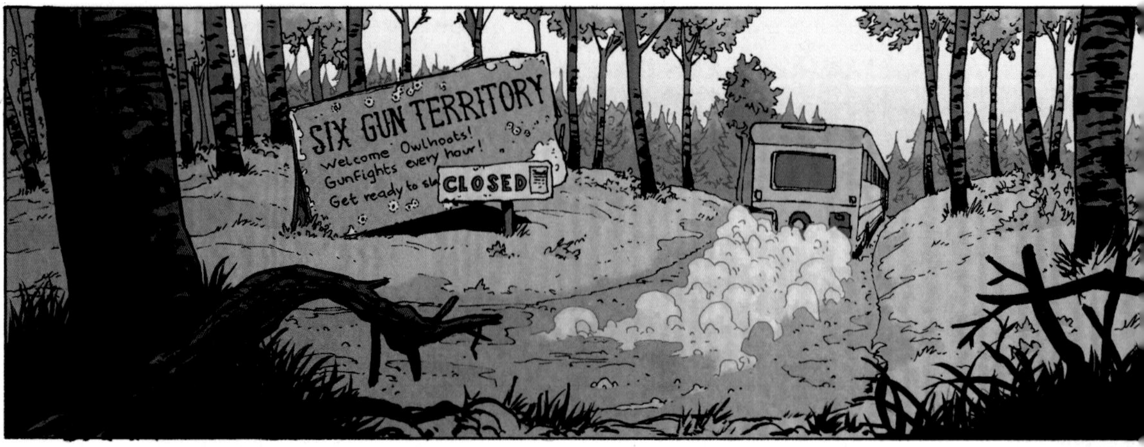
SIX GUN TERRITORY
Welcome Owlhoots!
Gunfights every hour!
CLOSED

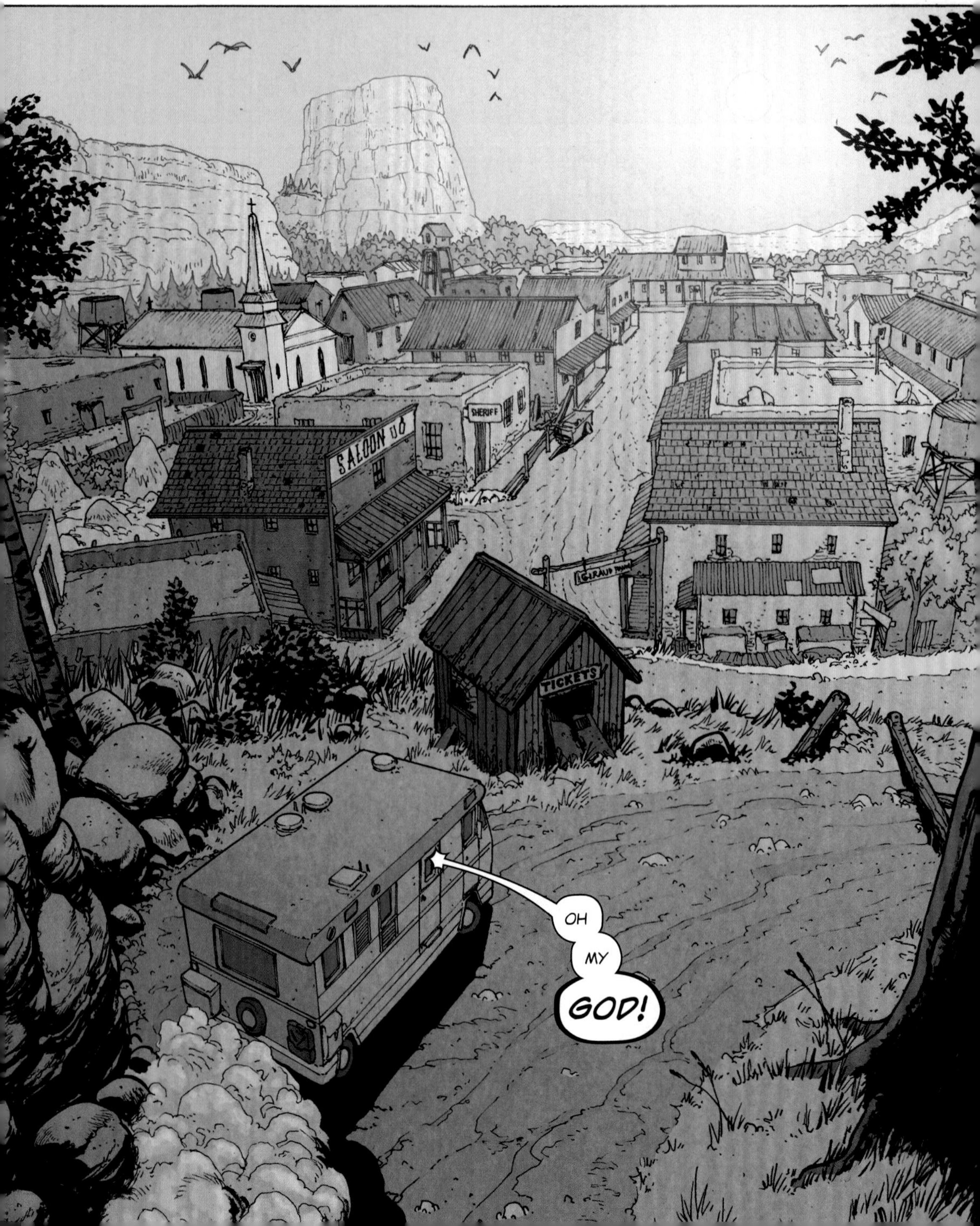
SALOON
SHERIFF
TICKETS
OH MY GOD!

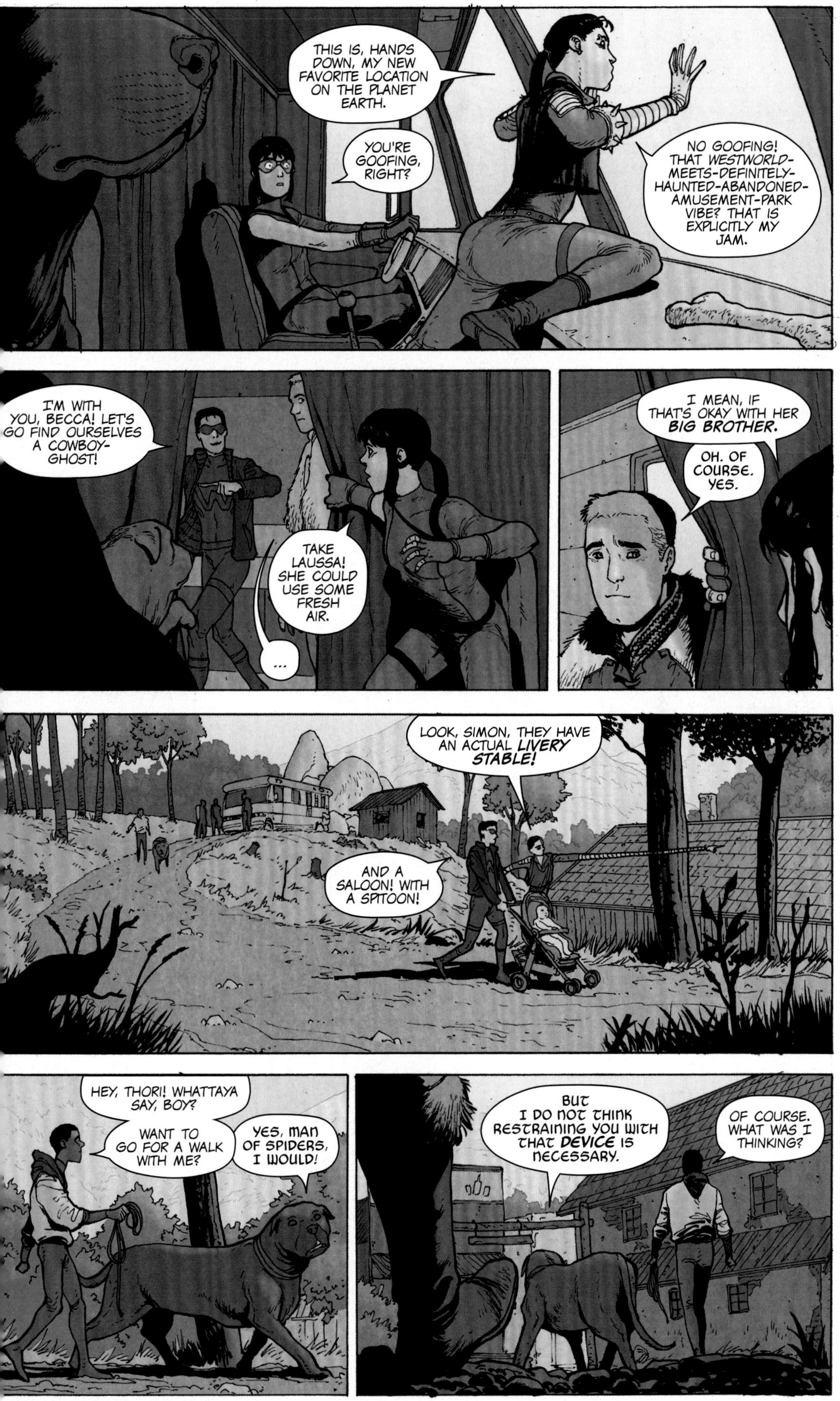
THIS IS, HANDS DOWN, MY NEW FAVORITE LOCATION ON THE PLANET EARTH.
YOU'RE GOOFING, RIGHT?
NO GOOFING! THAT WESTWORLD-MEETS-DEFINITELY-HAUNTED-ABANDONED-AMUSEMENT-PARK VIBE? THAT IS EXPLICITLY MY JAM.
I'M WITH YOU, BECCA! LET'S GO FIND OURSELVES A COWBOY-GHOST!
TAKE LAUSSA! SHE COULD USE SOME FRESH AIR.
...
I MEAN, IF THAT'S OKAY WITH HER BIG BROTHER.
OH. OF COURSE. YES.
LOOK, SIMON, THEY HAVE AN ACTUAL LIVERY STABLE!
AND A SALOON! WITH A SPITOON!
HEY, THORI! WHATTAYA SAY, BOY?
WANT TO GO FOR A WALK WITH ME?
YES, MAN OF SPIDERS, I WOULD!
BUT I DO NOT THINK RESTRAINING YOU WITH THAT DEVICE IS NECESSARY.
OF COURSE. WHAT WAS I THINKING?

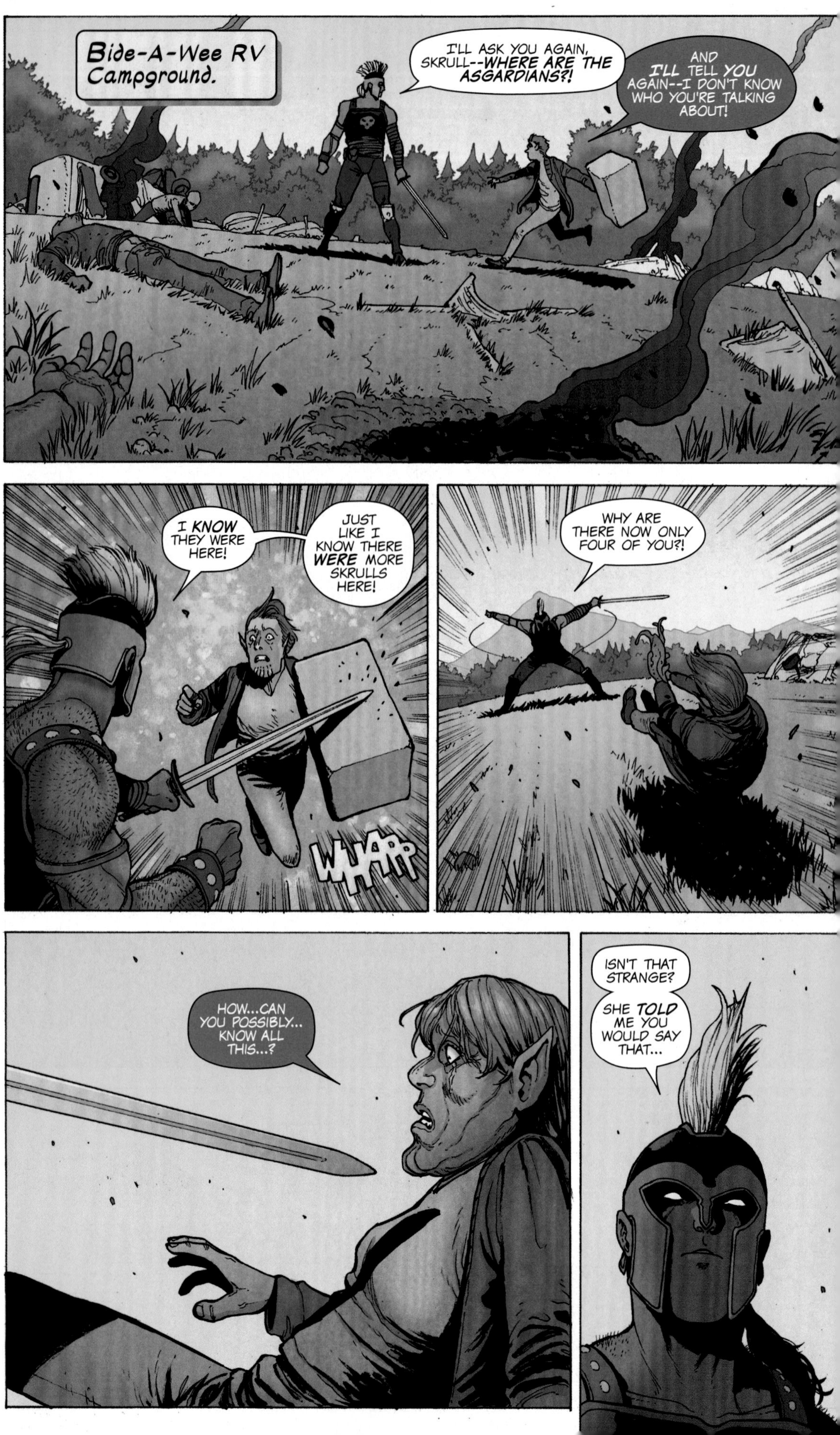
Bide-A-Wee RV Campground.
I'LL ASK YOU AGAIN, SKRULL--WHERE ARE THE ASGARDIANS?!
AND I'LL TELL YOU AGAIN--I DON'T KNOW WHO YOU'RE TALKING ABOUT!
I KNOW THEY WERE HERE!
JUST LIKE I KNOW THERE WERE MORE SKRULLS HERE!
WHARP
WHY ARE THERE NOW ONLY FOUR OF YOU?!
HOW...CAN YOU POSSIBLY... KNOW ALL THIS...?
ISN'T THAT STRANGE?
SHE TOLD ME YOU WOULD SAY THAT...

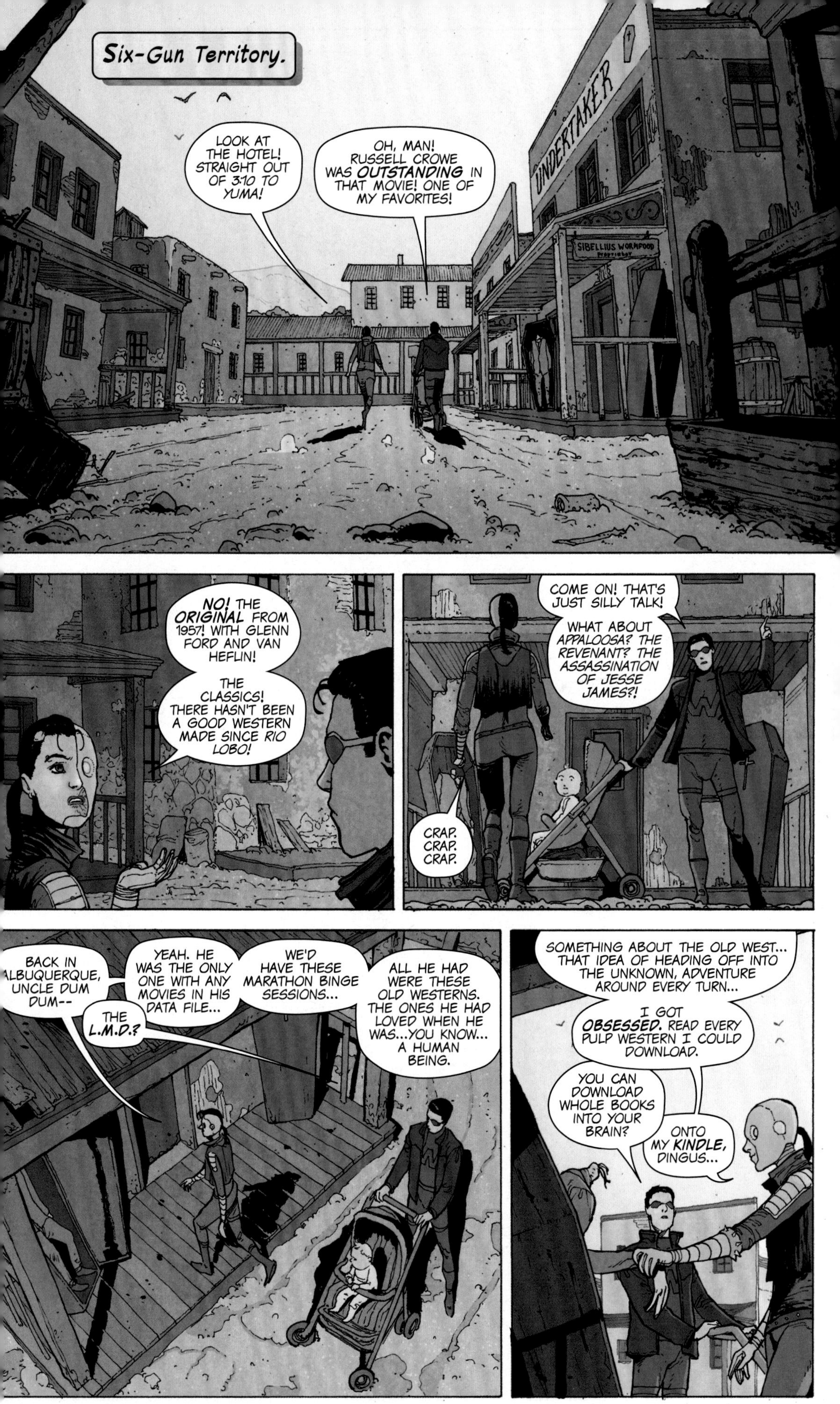

Six-Gun Territory.
LOOK AT THE HOTEL! STRAIGHT OUT OF 3:10 TO YUMA!
OH, MAN! RUSSELL CROWE WAS OUTSTANDING IN THAT MOVIE! ONE OF MY FAVORITES!
UNDERTAKER
SIBELLIUS WORMWOOD
NO! THE ORIGINAL FROM 1957! WITH GLENN FORD AND VAN HEFLIN!
THE CLASSICS! THERE HASN'T BEEN A GOOD WESTERN MADE SINCE RIO LOBO!
COME ON! THAT'S JUST SILLY TALK!
WHAT ABOUT APPALOOSA? THE REVENANT? THE ASSASSINATION OF JESSE JAMES?!
CRAP. CRAP. CRAP.
BACK IN ALBUQUERQUE, UNCLE DUM DUM--
THE L.M.D.?
YEAH. HE WAS THE ONLY ONE WITH ANY MOVIES IN HIS DATA FILE...
WE'D HAVE THESE MARATHON BINGE SESSIONS...
ALL HE HAD WERE THESE OLD WESTERNS. THE ONES HE HAD LOVED WHEN HE WAS...YOU KNOW... A HUMAN BEING.
SOMETHING ABOUT THE OLD WEST... THAT IDEA OF HEADING OFF INTO THE UNKNOWN, ADVENTURE AROUND EVERY TURN...
I GOT OBSESSED. READ EVERY PULP WESTERN I COULD DOWNLOAD.
YOU CAN DOWNLOAD WHOLE BOOKS INTO YOUR BRAIN?
ONTO MY KINDLE, DINGUS...

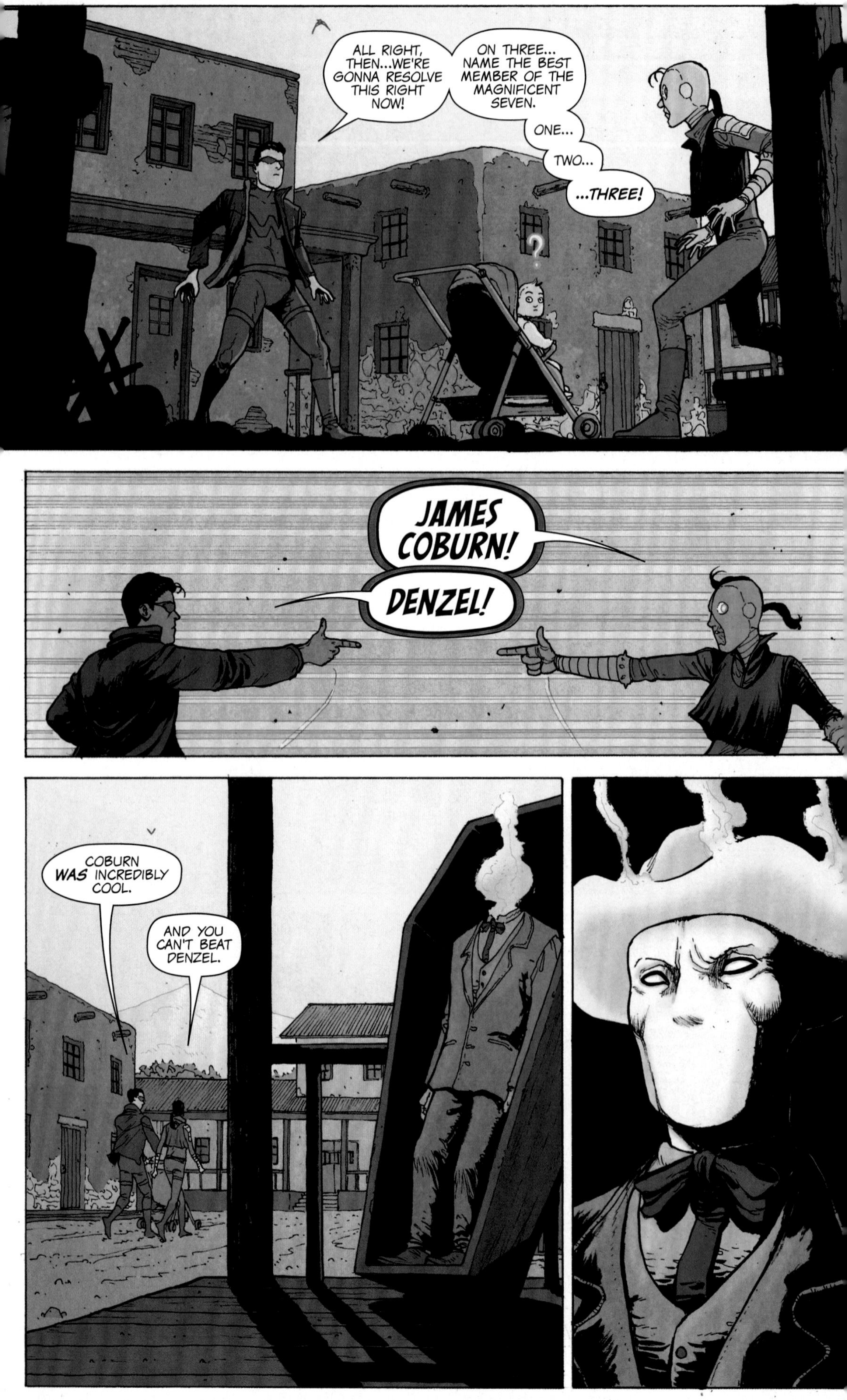
ALL RIGHT, THEN...WE'RE GONNA RESOLVE THIS RIGHT NOW!
ON THREE... NAME THE BEST MEMBER OF THE MAGNIFICENT SEVEN.
ONE...
TWO...
...THREE!
?
JAMES COBURN!
DENZEL!
COBURN WAS INCREDIBLY COOL.
AND YOU CAN'T BEAT DENZEL.

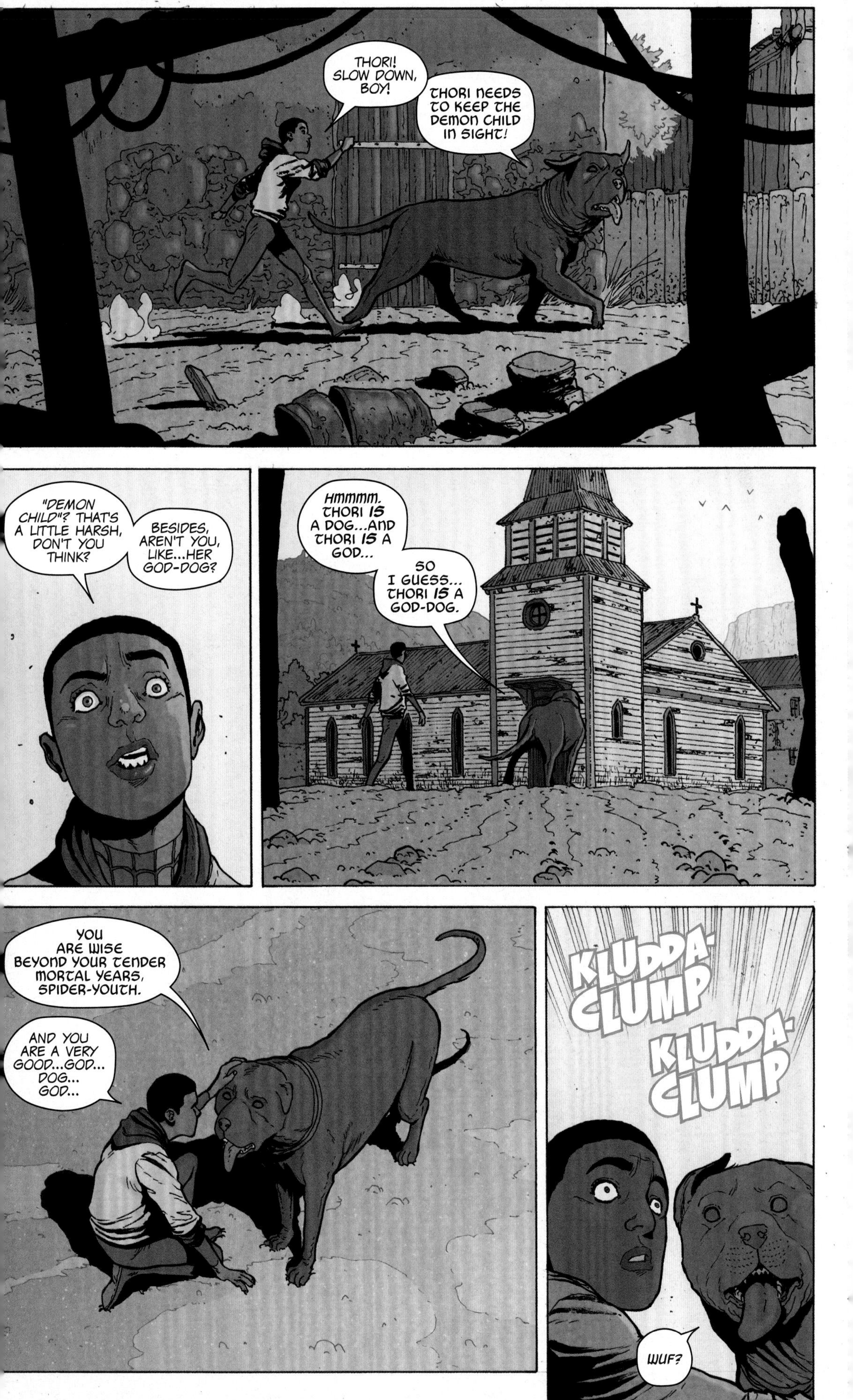
THORI! SLOW DOWN, BOY!
THORI NEEDS TO KEEP THE DEMON CHILD IN SIGHT!
"DEMON CHILD"? THAT'S A LITTLE HARSH, DON'T YOU THINK?
BESIDES, AREN'T YOU, LIKE...HER GOD-DOG?
HMMMM. THORI IS A DOG...AND THORI IS A GOD...
SO I GUESS... THORI IS A GOD-DOG.
YOU ARE WISE BEYOND YOUR TENDER MORTAL YEARS, SPIDER-YOUTH.
AND YOU ARE A VERY GOOD...GOD... DOG... GOD...
KLUDDA-CLUMP
KLUDDA-CLUMP
WUF?

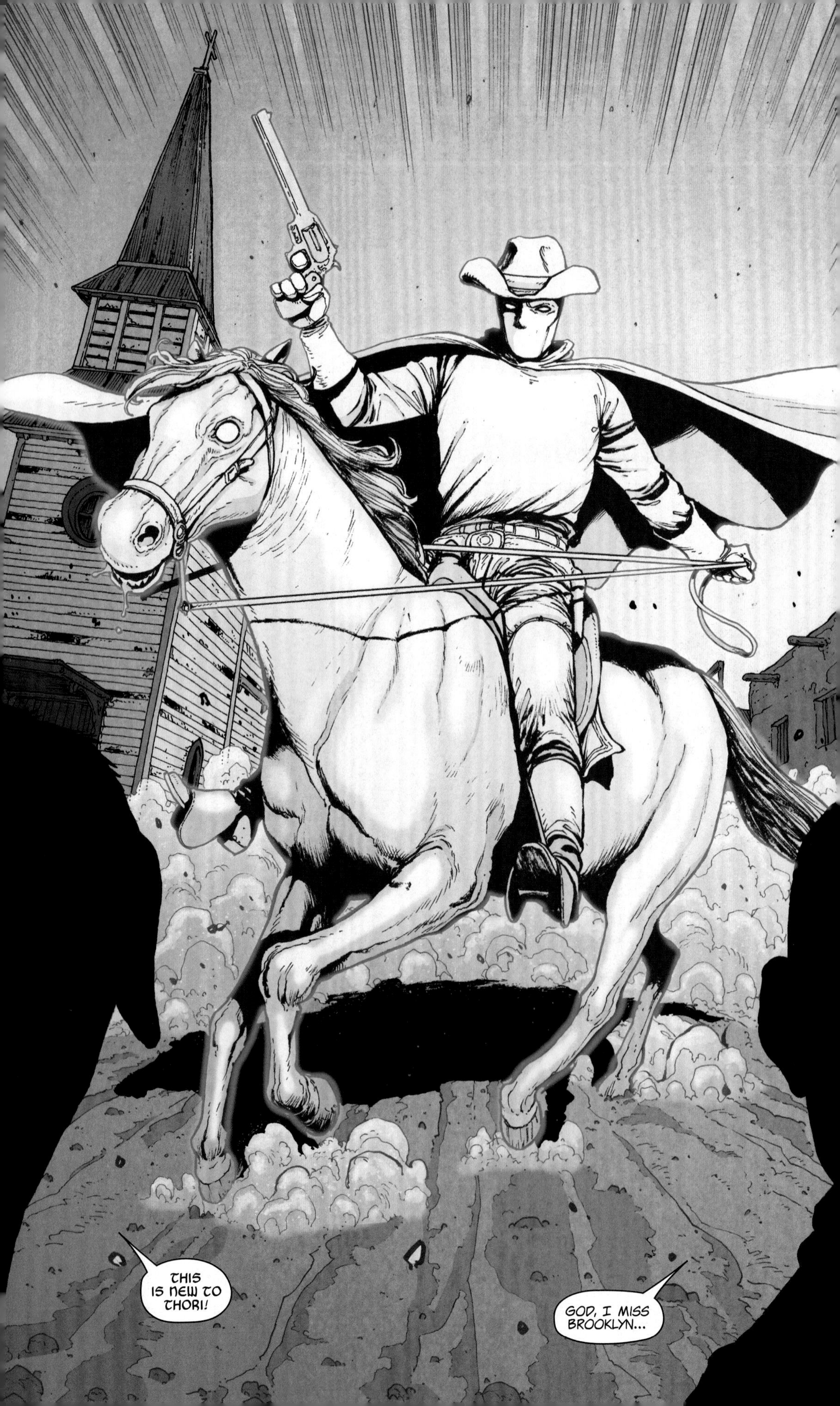
THIS IS NEW TO THORI!
GOD, I MISS BROOKLYN...

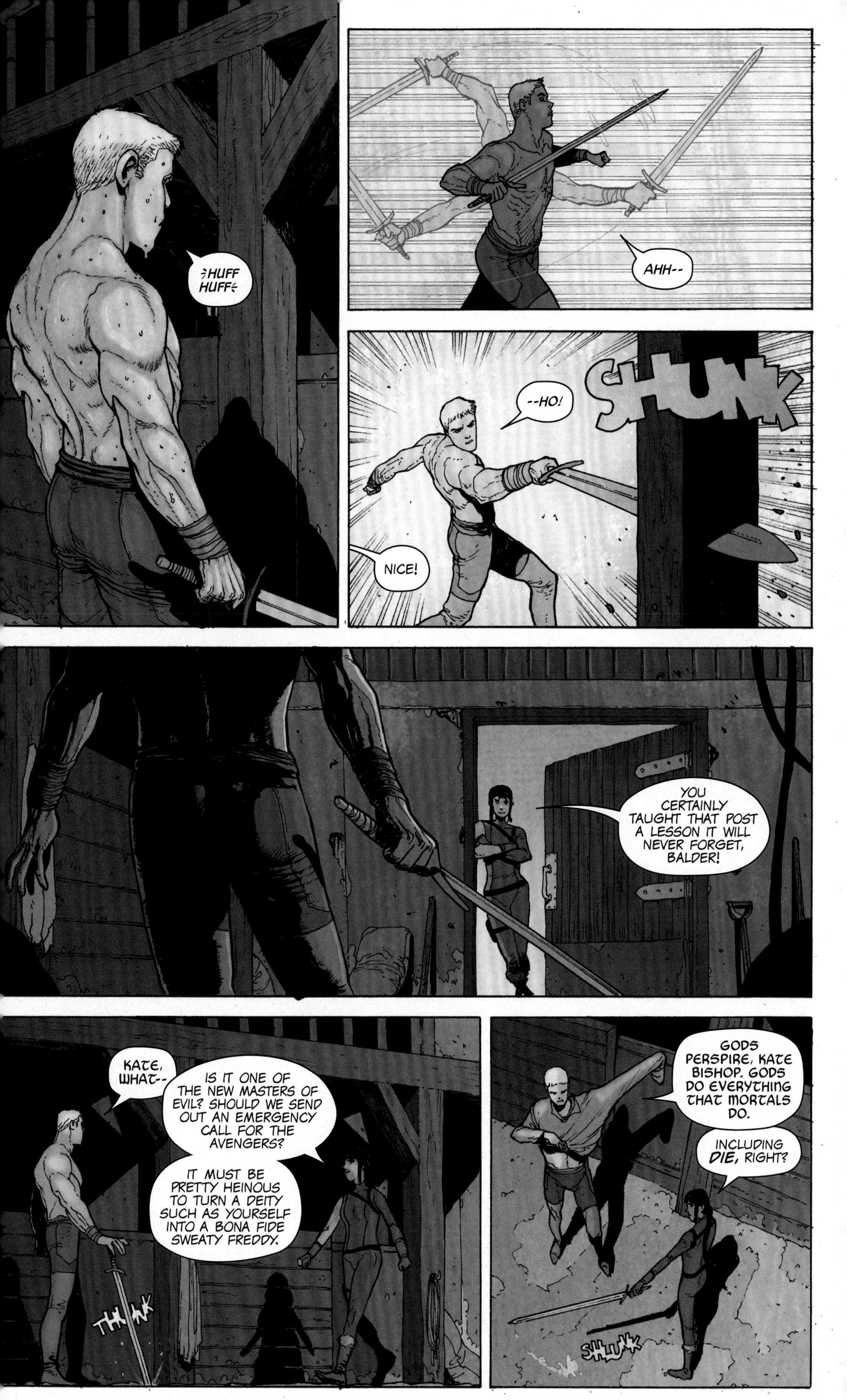
HUFF HUFF
AHH--
--HO!
SHUNK
NICE!
YOU CERTAINLY TAUGHT THAT POST A LESSON IT WILL NEVER FORGET, BALDER!
KATE, WHAT--
IS IT ONE OF THE NEW MASTERS OF EVIL? SHOULD WE SEND OUT AN EMERGENCY CALL FOR THE AVENGERS?
IT MUST BE PRETTY HEINOUS TO TURN A DEITY SUCH AS YOURSELF INTO A BONA FIDE SWEATY FREDDY.
GODS PERSPIRE, KATE BISHOP. GODS DO EVERYTHING THAT MORTALS DO.
INCLUDING DIE, RIGHT?
SHUNK

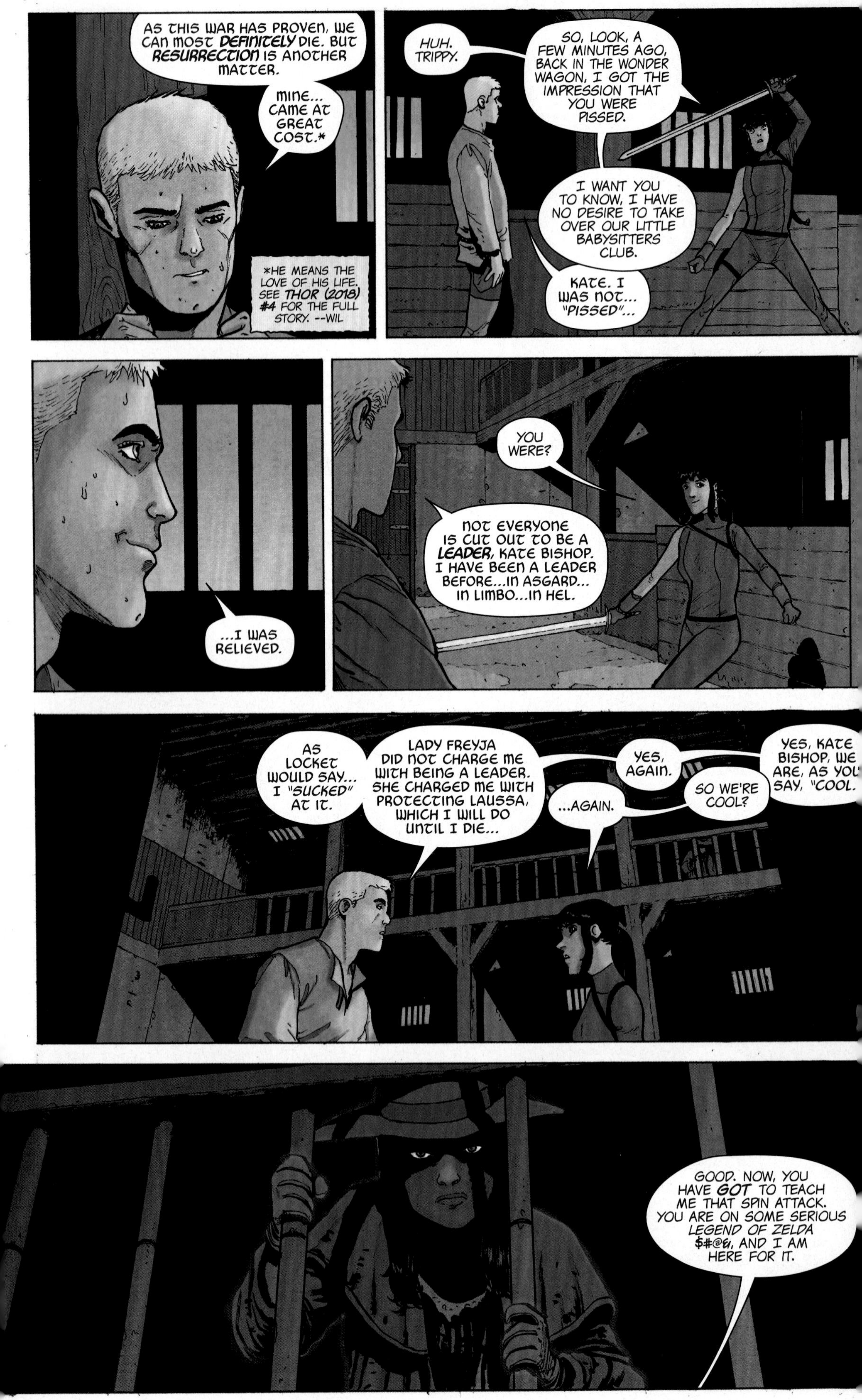
AS THIS WAR HAS PROVEN, WE CAN MOST DEFINITELY DIE. BUT RESURRECTION IS ANOTHER MATTER.
MINE... CAME AT GREAT COST.*
*HE MEANS THE LOVE OF HIS LIFE. SEE THOR (2018) #4 FOR THE FULL STORY. --WIL
HUH. TRIPPY.
SO, LOOK, A FEW MINUTES AGO, BACK IN THE WONDER WAGON, I GOT THE IMPRESSION THAT YOU WERE PISSED.
I WANT YOU TO KNOW, I HAVE NO DESIRE TO TAKE OVER OUR LITTLE BABYSITTERS CLUB.
KATE. I WAS NOT... "PISSED"...
...I WAS RELIEVED.
YOU WERE?
NOT EVERYONE IS CUT OUT TO BE A LEADER, KATE BISHOP. I HAVE BEEN A LEADER BEFORE...IN ASGARD... IN LIMBO...IN HEL.
AS LOCKET WOULD SAY... I "SUCKED" AT IT.
LADY FREYJA DID NOT CHARGE ME WITH BEING A LEADER. SHE CHARGED ME WITH PROTECTING LAUSSA, WHICH I WILL DO UNTIL I DIE...
...AGAIN.
YES, AGAIN.
SO WE'RE COOL?
YES, KATE BISHOP, WE ARE, AS YOU SAY, "COOL."
GOOD. NOW, YOU HAVE GOT TO TEACH ME THAT SPIN ATTACK. YOU ARE ON SOME SERIOUS LEGEND OF ZELDA $#@&, AND I AM HERE FOR IT.

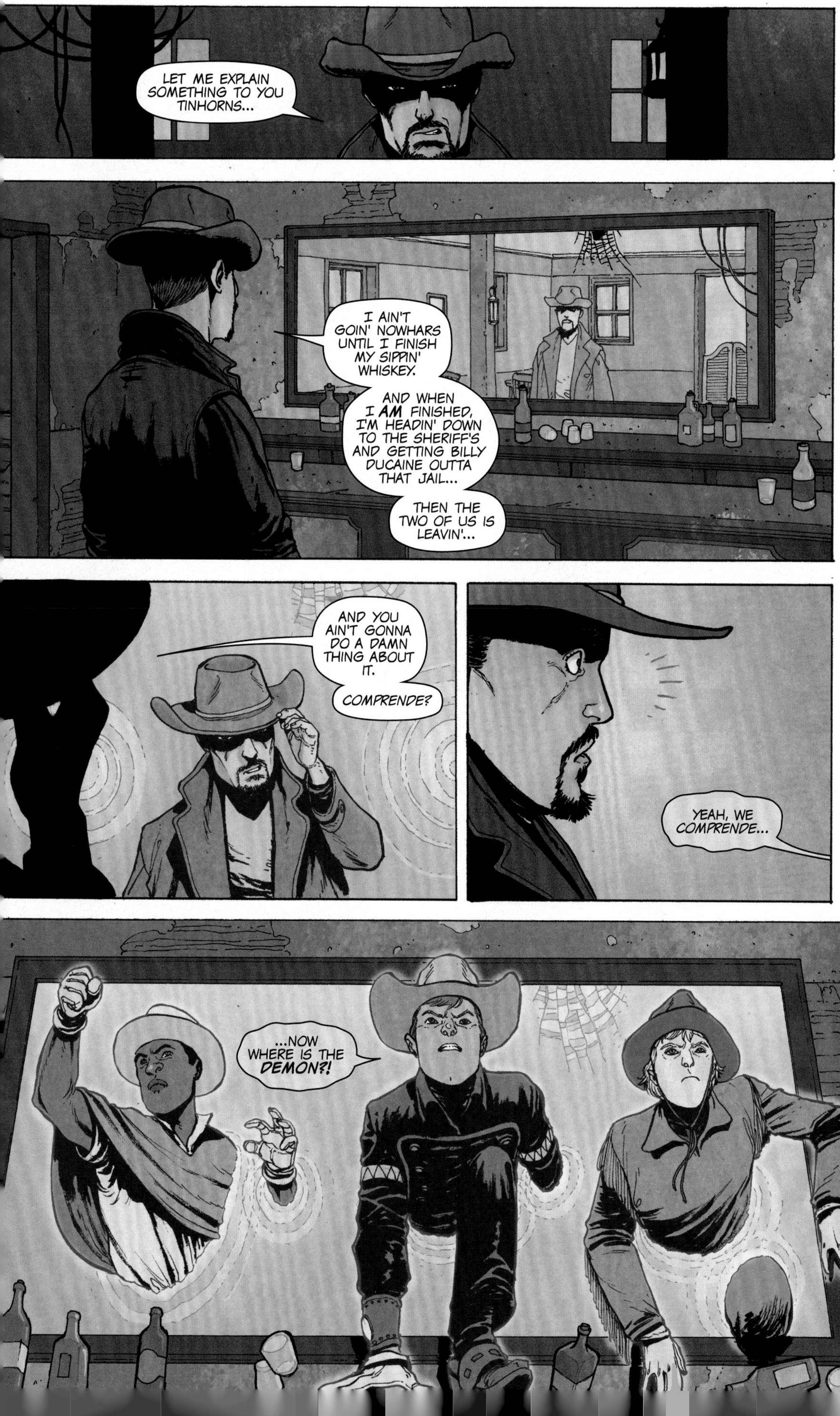
LET ME EXPLAIN SOMETHING TO YOU TINHORNS...
I AIN'T GOIN' NOWHARS UNTIL I FINISH MY SIPPIN' WHISKEY.
AND WHEN I AM FINISHED, I'M HEADIN' DOWN TO THE SHERIFF'S AND GETTING BILLY DUCAINE OUTTA THAT JAIL...
THEN THE TWO OF US IS LEAVIN'...
AND YOU AIN'T GONNA DO A DAMN THING ABOUT IT.
COMPRENDE?
YEAH, WE COMPRENDE...
...NOW WHERE IS THE DEMON?!

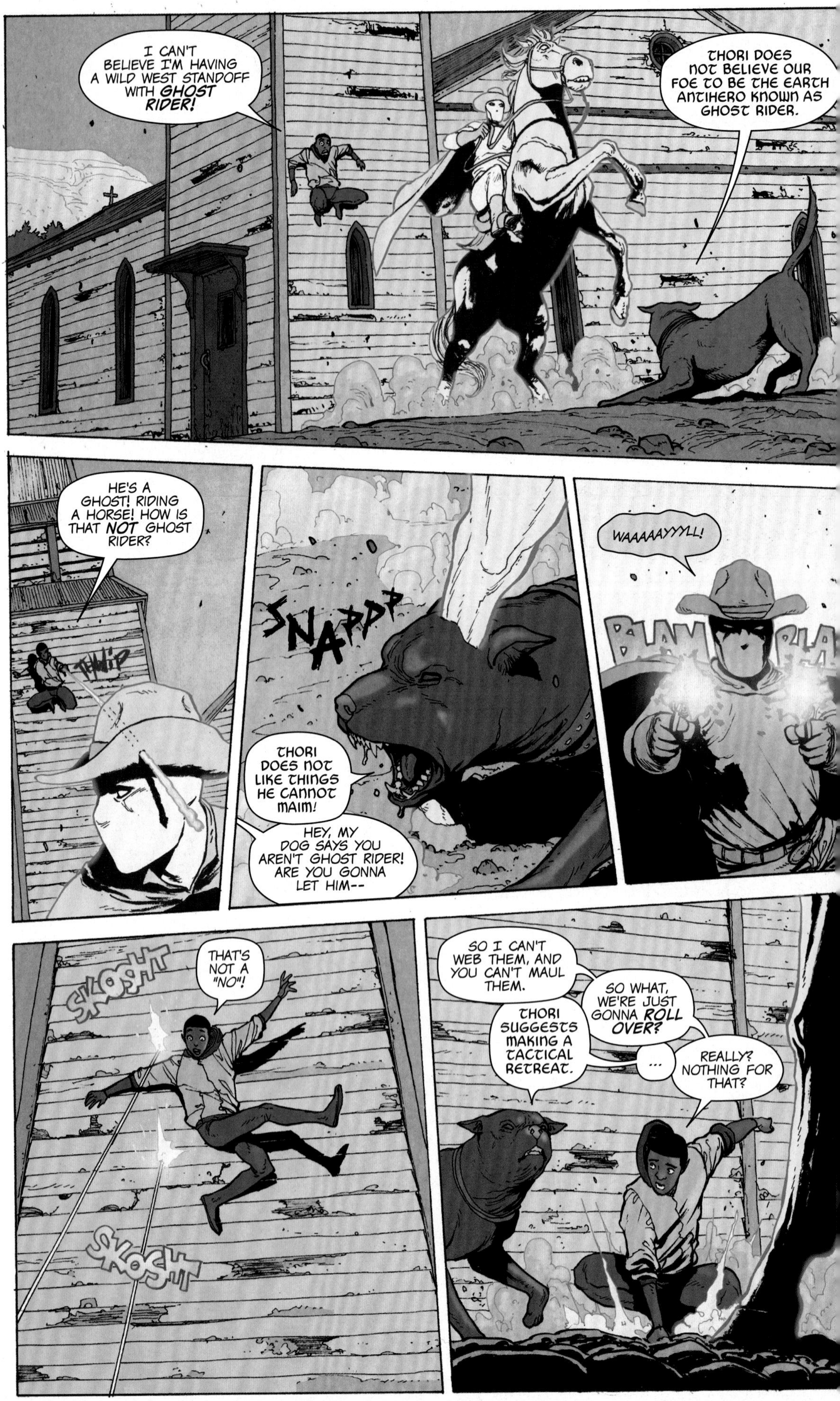

I CAN'T BELIEVE I'M HAVING A WILD WEST STANDOFF WITH GHOST RIDER!
THORI DOES NOT BELIEVE OUR FOE TO BE THE EARTH ANTIHERO KNOWN AS GHOST RIDER.
HE'S A GHOST! RIDING A HORSE! HOW IS THAT NOT GHOST RIDER?
TWHIP
SNAPP
THORI DOES NOT LIKE THINGS HE CANNOT MAIM!
HEY, MY DOG SAYS YOU AREN'T GHOST RIDER! ARE YOU GONNA LET HIM--
WAAAAAYYYLL!
THAT'S NOT A "NO"!
SKLOSH
SKLOSH
SO I CAN'T WEB THEM, AND YOU CAN'T MAUL THEM.
SO WHAT, WE'RE JUST GONNA ROLL OVER?
THORI SUGGESTS MAKING A TACTICAL RETREAT.
...
REALLY? NOTHING FOR THAT?

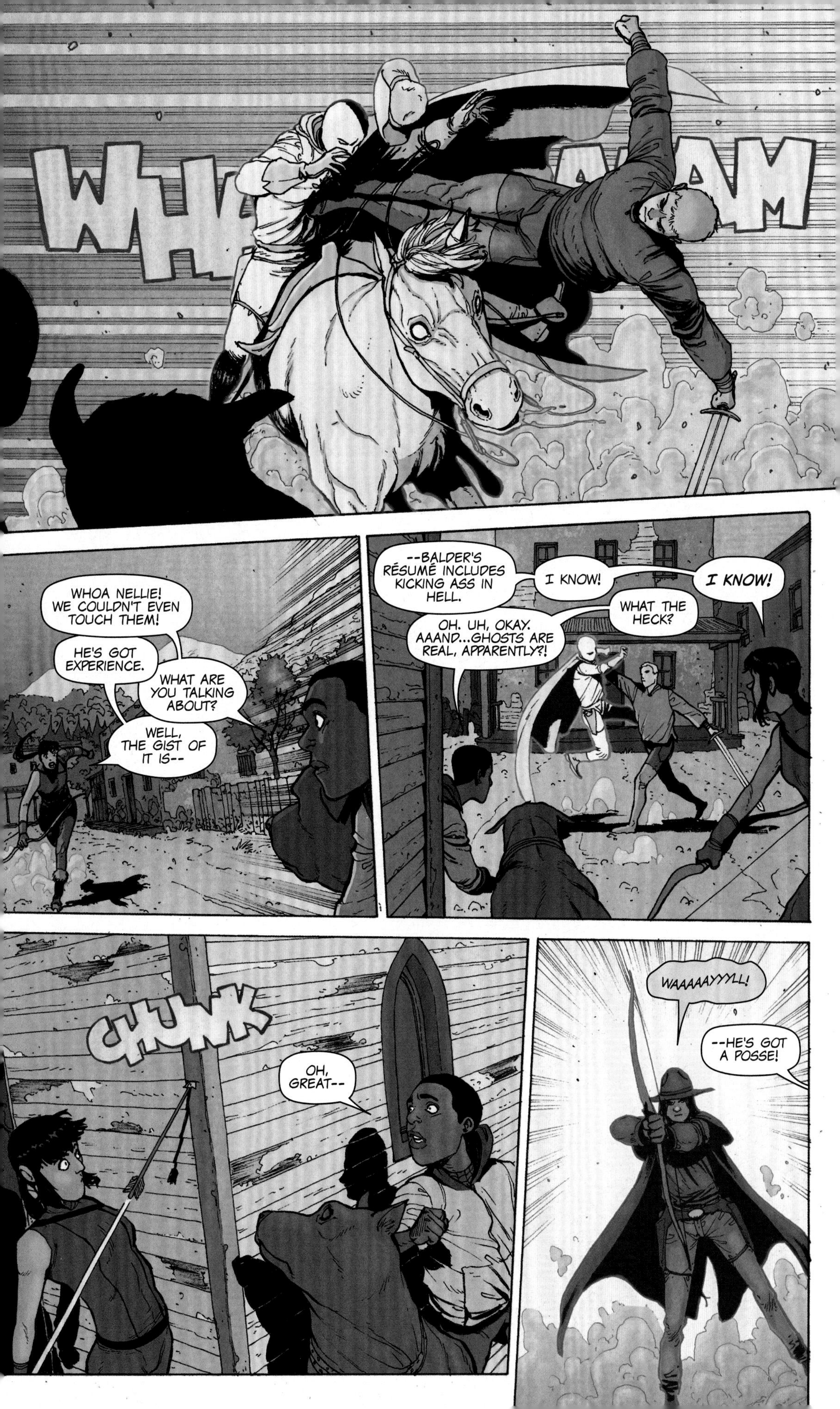
WHAM
WHOA NELLIE! WE COULDN'T EVEN TOUCH THEM!
HE'S GOT EXPERIENCE.
WHAT ARE YOU TALKING ABOUT?
WELL, THE GIST OF IT IS--
--BALDER'S RÉSUMÉ INCLUDES KICKING ASS IN HELL.
OH. UH, OKAY. AAAND...GHOSTS ARE REAL, APPARENTLY?!
I KNOW!
WHAT THE HECK?
I KNOW!
CHUNK
OH, GREAT--
WAAAAAYYYLL!
--HE'S GOT A POSSE!

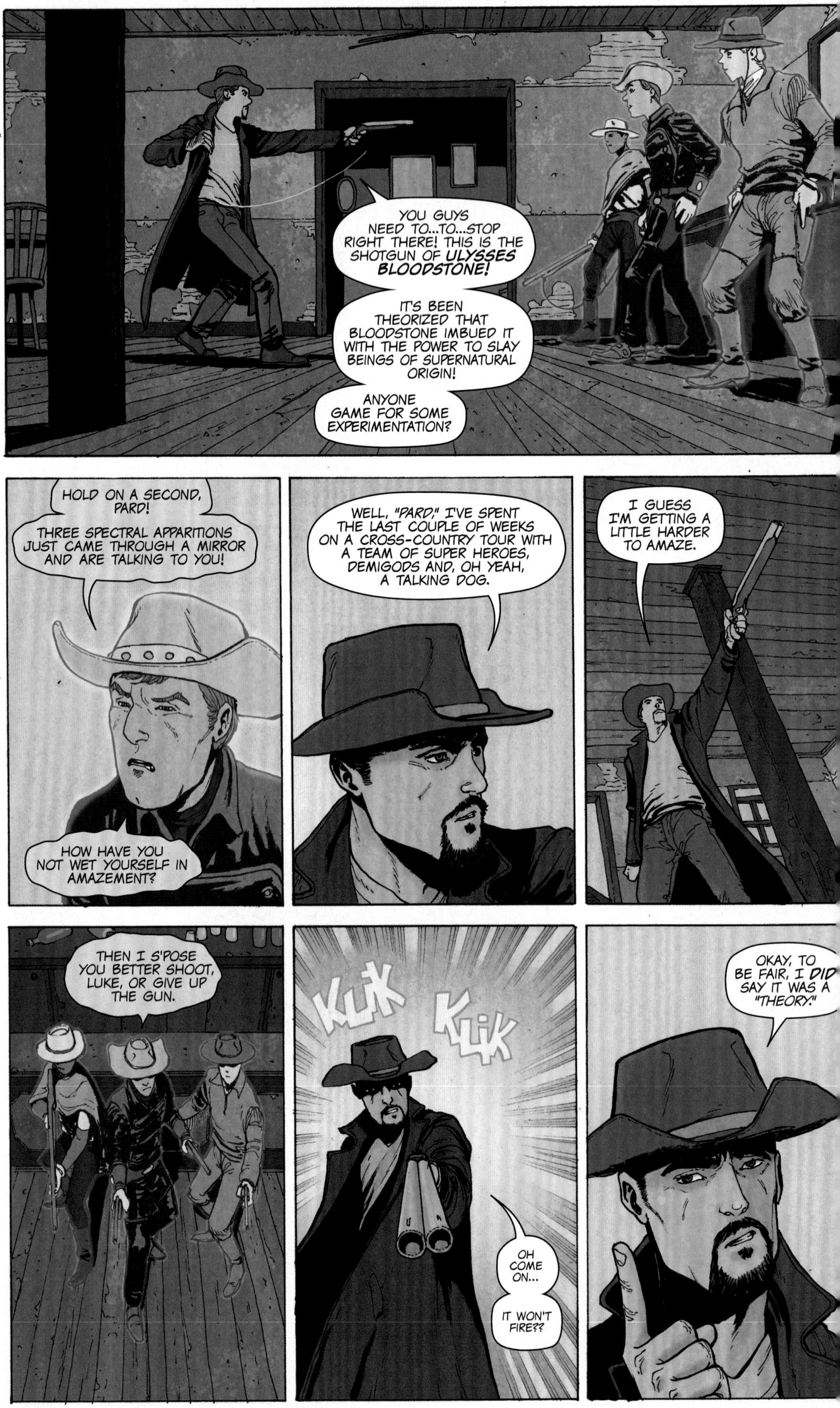
YOU GUYS NEED TO...TO...STOP RIGHT THERE! THIS IS THE SHOTGUN OF ULYSSES BLOODSTONE!
IT'S BEEN THEORIZED THAT BLOODSTONE IMBUED IT WITH THE POWER TO SLAY BEINGS OF SUPERNATURAL ORIGIN!
ANYONE GAME FOR SOME EXPERIMENTATION?
HOLD ON A SECOND, PARD!
THREE SPECTRAL APPARITIONS JUST CAME THROUGH A MIRROR AND ARE TALKING TO YOU!
HOW HAVE YOU NOT WET YOURSELF IN AMAZEMENT?
WELL, "PARD," I'VE SPENT THE LAST COUPLE OF WEEKS ON A CROSS-COUNTRY TOUR WITH A TEAM OF SUPER HEROES, DEMIGODS AND, OH YEAH, A TALKING DOG.
I GUESS I'M GETTING A LITTLE HARDER TO AMAZE.
THEN I S'POSE YOU BETTER SHOOT, LUKE, OR GIVE UP THE GUN.
KLIK
KLIK
OH COME ON...
IT WON'T FIRE??
OKAY, TO BE FAIR, I DID SAY IT WAS A "THEORY."

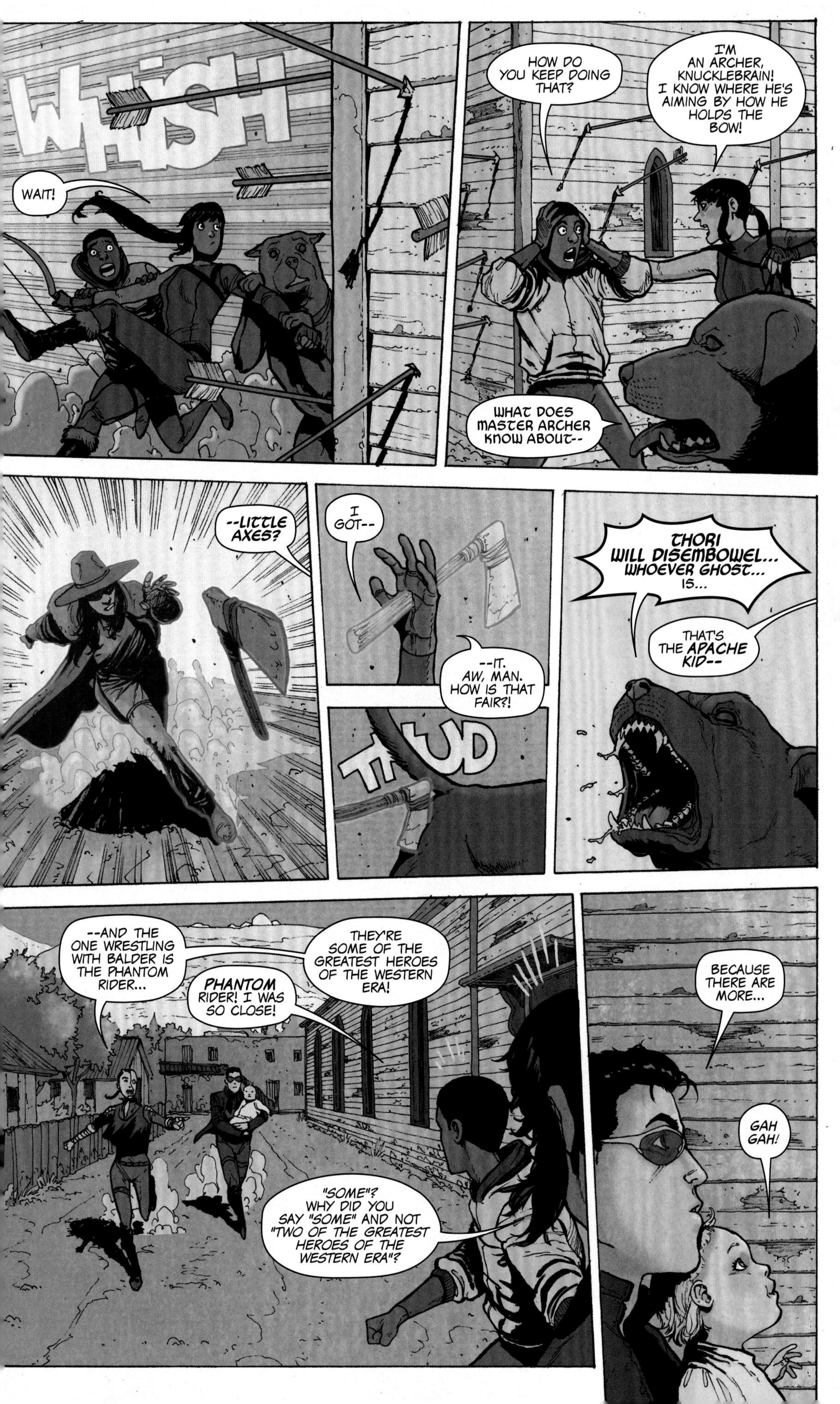
WHISH
WAIT!
HOW DO YOU KEEP DOING THAT?
I'M AN ARCHER, KNUCKLEBRAIN! I KNOW WHERE HE'S AIMING BY HOW HE HOLDS THE BOW!
WHAT DOES MASTER ARCHER KNOW ABOUT--
--LITTLE AXES?
I GOT--
--IT. AW, MAN. HOW IS THAT FAIR?!
THUD
THORI WILL DISEMBOWEL... WHOEVER GHOST... IS...
THAT'S THE APACHE KID--
--AND THE ONE WRESTLING WITH BALDER IS THE PHANTOM RIDER...
THEY'RE SOME OF THE GREATEST HEROES OF THE WESTERN ERA!
PHANTOM RIDER! I WAS SO CLOSE!
"SOME"? WHY DID YOU SAY "SOME" AND NOT "TWO OF THE GREATEST HEROES OF THE WESTERN ERA"?
BECAUSE THERE ARE MORE...
GAH GAH!

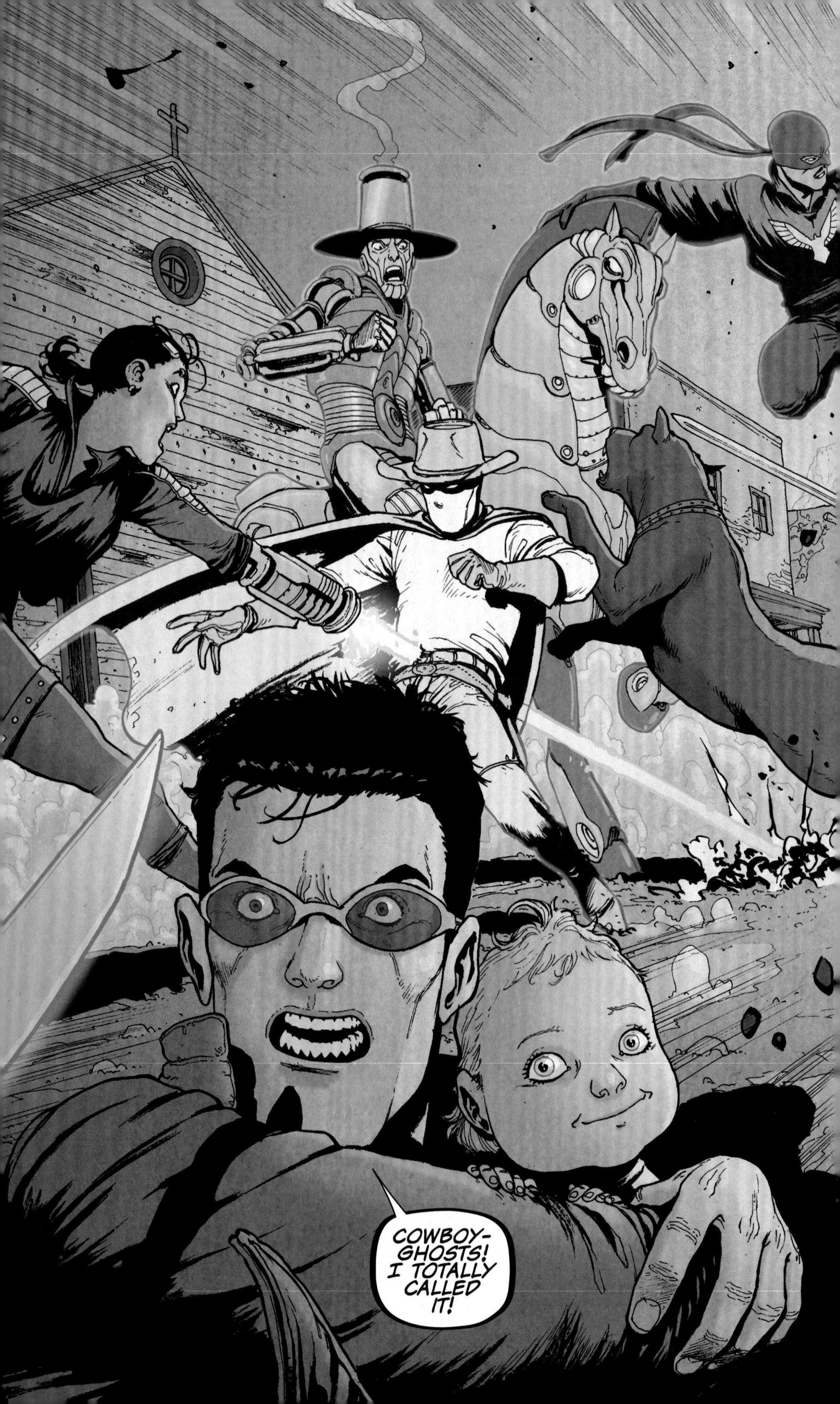
COWBOY-GHOSTS! I TOTALLY CALLED IT!

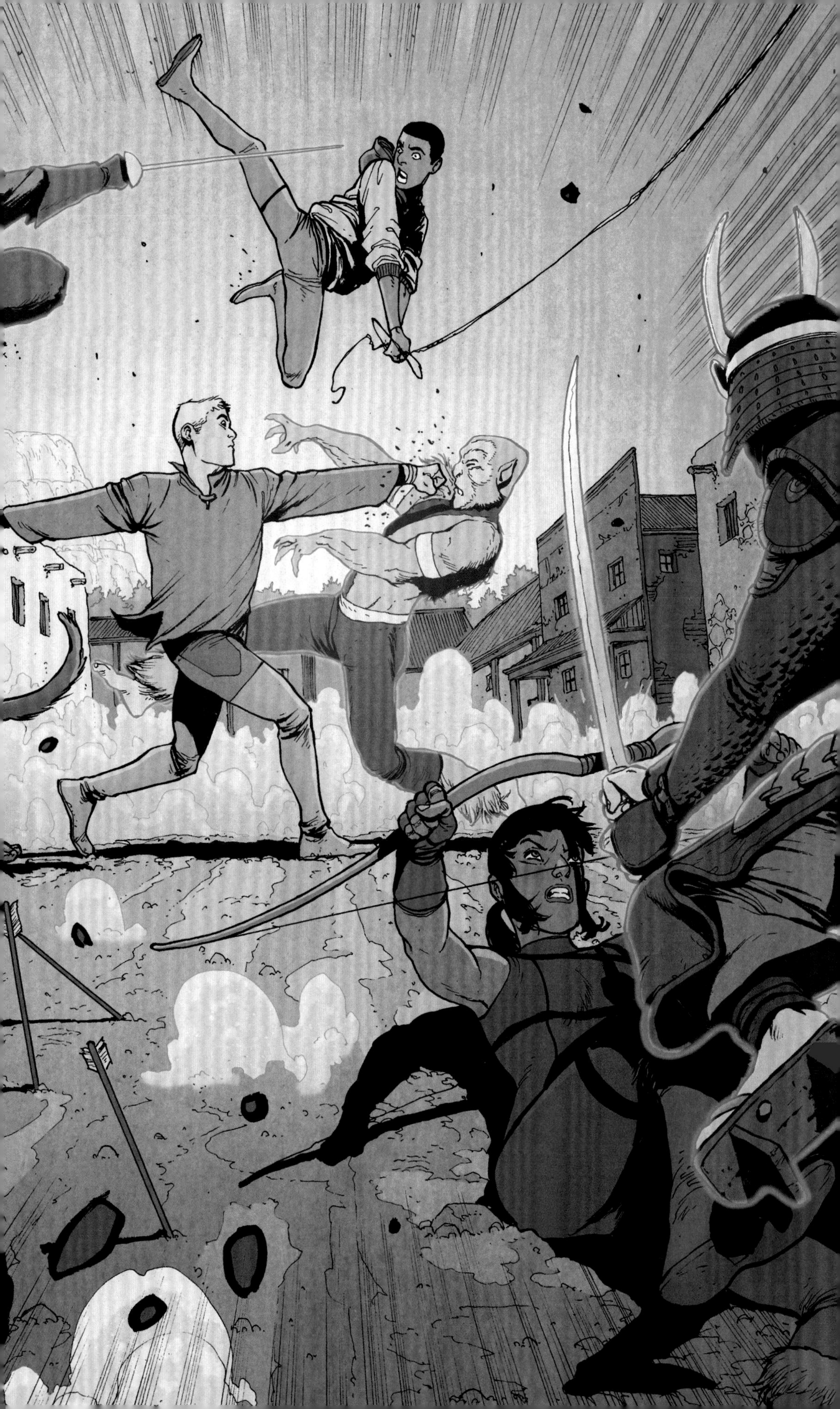

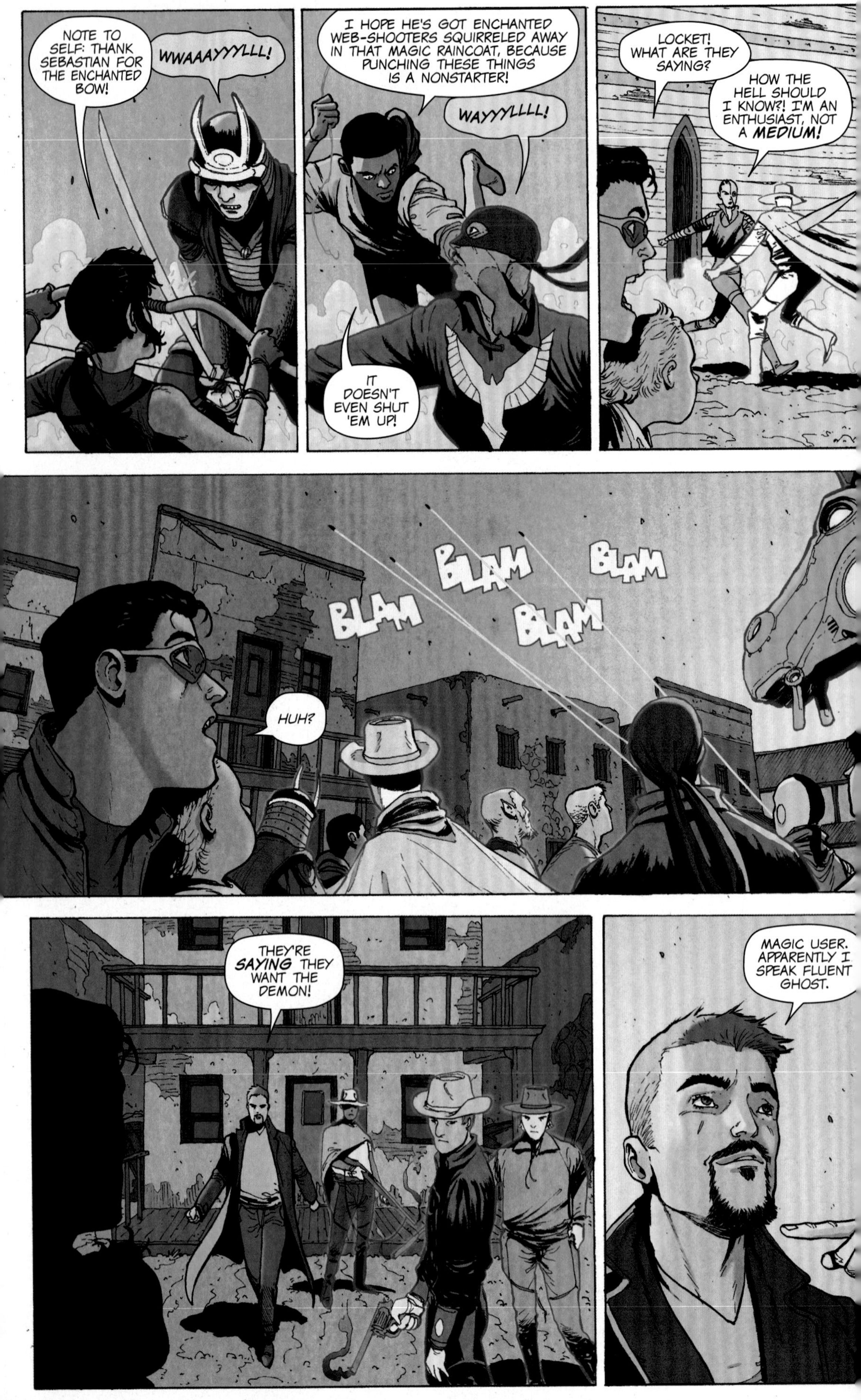

NOTE TO SELF: THANK SEBASTIAN FOR THE ENCHANTED BOW!
WWAAAYYYLLL!
I HOPE HE'S GOT ENCHANTED WEB-SHOOTERS SQUIRRELED AWAY IN THAT MAGIC RAINCOAT, BECAUSE PUNCHING THESE THINGS IS A NONSTARTER!
WAYYYLLLL!
IT DOESN'T EVEN SHUT 'EM UP!
LOCKET! WHAT ARE THEY SAYING?
HOW THE HELL SHOULD I KNOW?! I'M AN ENTHUSIAST, NOT A MEDIUM!
BLAM
BLAM
BLAM
BLAM
HUH?
THEY'RE SAYING THEY WANT THE DEMON!
MAGIC USER. APPARENTLY I SPEAK FLUENT GHOST.

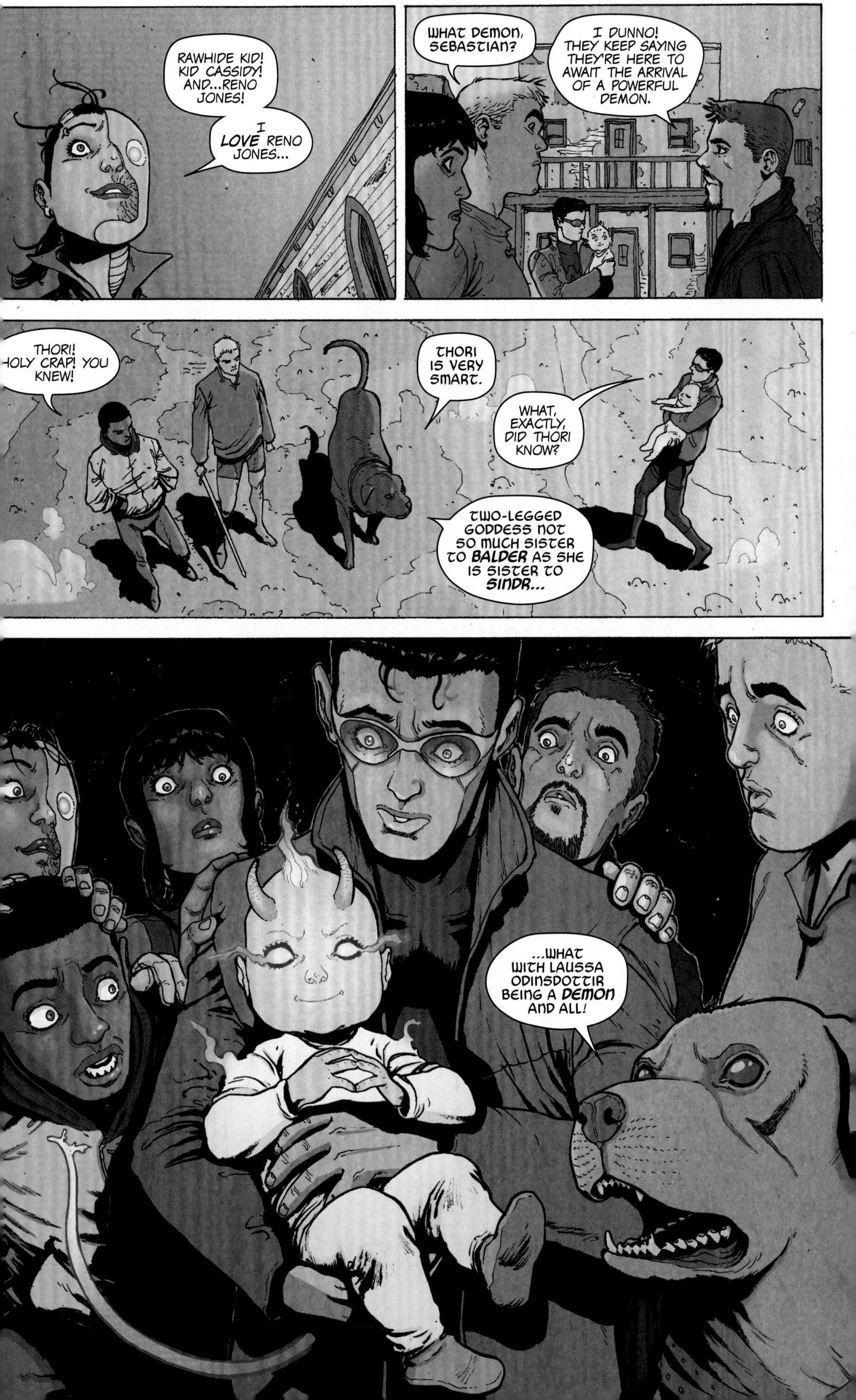

RAWHIDE KID! KID CASSIDY! AND...RENO JONES!
I LOVE RENO JONES...
WHAT DEMON, SEBASTIAN?
I DUNNO! THEY KEEP SAYING THEY'RE HERE TO AWAIT THE ARRIVAL OF A POWERFUL DEMON.
THORI! HOLY CRAP! YOU KNEW!
THORI IS VERY SMART.
WHAT, EXACTLY, DID THORI KNOW?
TWO-LEGGED GODDESS NOT SO MUCH SISTER TO BALDER AS SHE IS SISTER TO SINDR...
...WHAT WITH LAUSSA ODINSDOTTIR BEING A DEMON AND ALL!

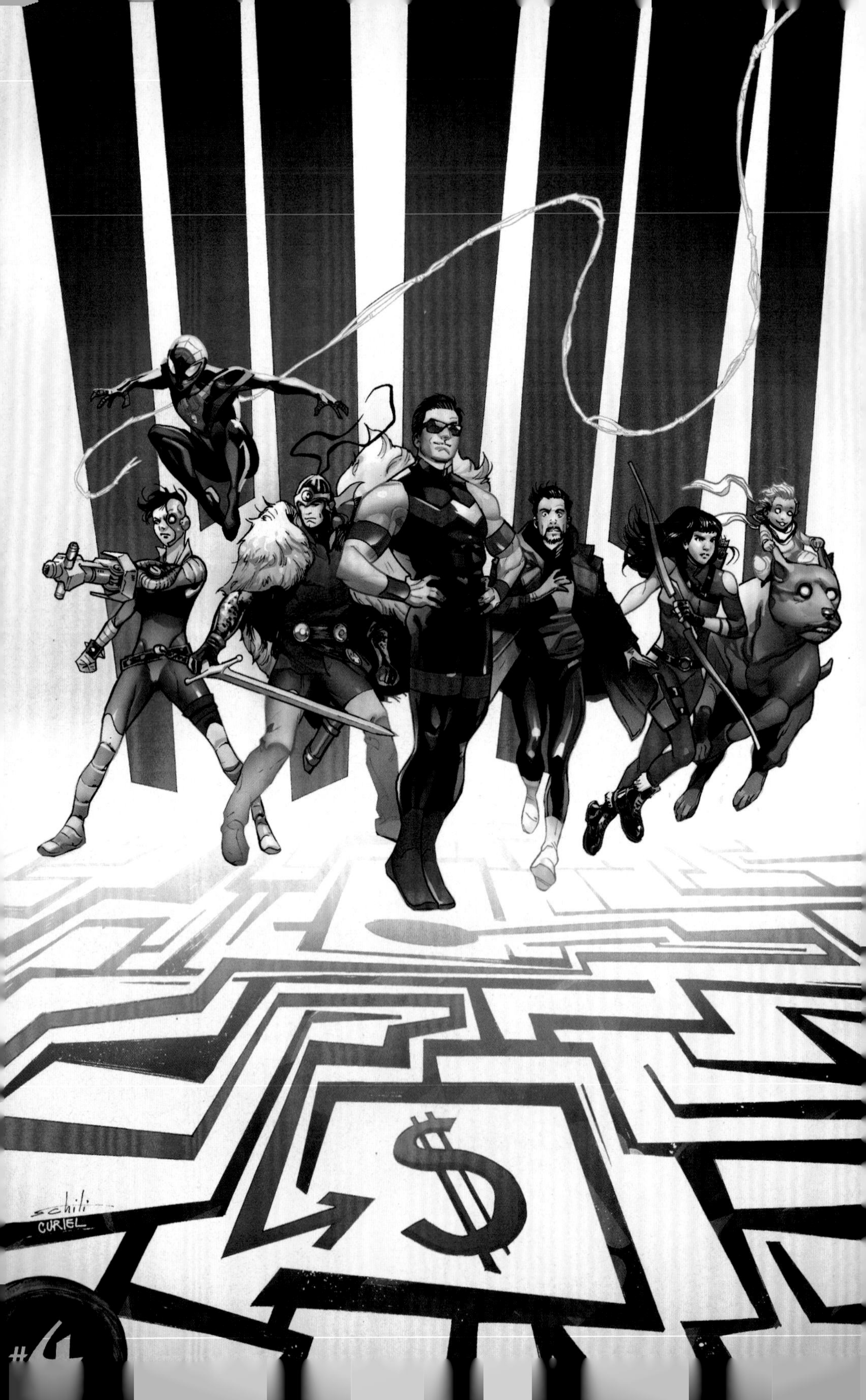

Schiti
CURIEL

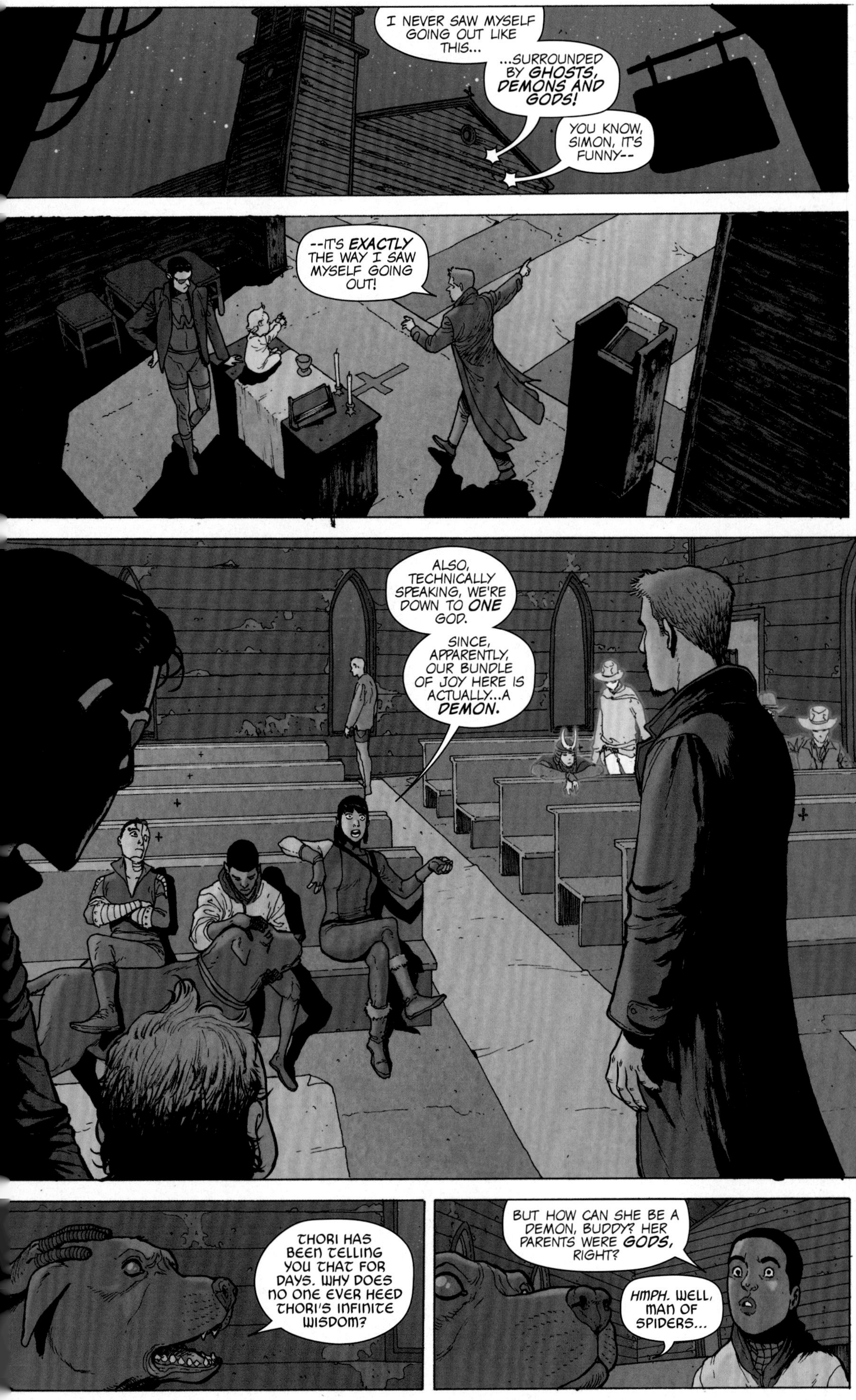

I NEVER SAW MYSELF GOING OUT LIKE THIS...
...SURROUNDED BY GHOSTS, DEMONS AND GODS!
YOU KNOW, SIMON, IT'S FUNNY--
--IT'S EXACTLY THE WAY I SAW MYSELF GOING OUT!
ALSO, TECHNICALLY SPEAKING, WE'RE DOWN TO ONE GOD.
SINCE, APPARENTLY, OUR BUNDLE OF JOY HERE IS ACTUALLY...A DEMON.
THORI HAS BEEN TELLING YOU THAT FOR DAYS. WHY DOES NO ONE EVER HEED THORI'S INFINITE WISDOM?
BUT HOW CAN SHE BE A DEMON, BUDDY? HER PARENTS WERE GODS, RIGHT?
HMPH. WELL, MAN OF SPIDERS...

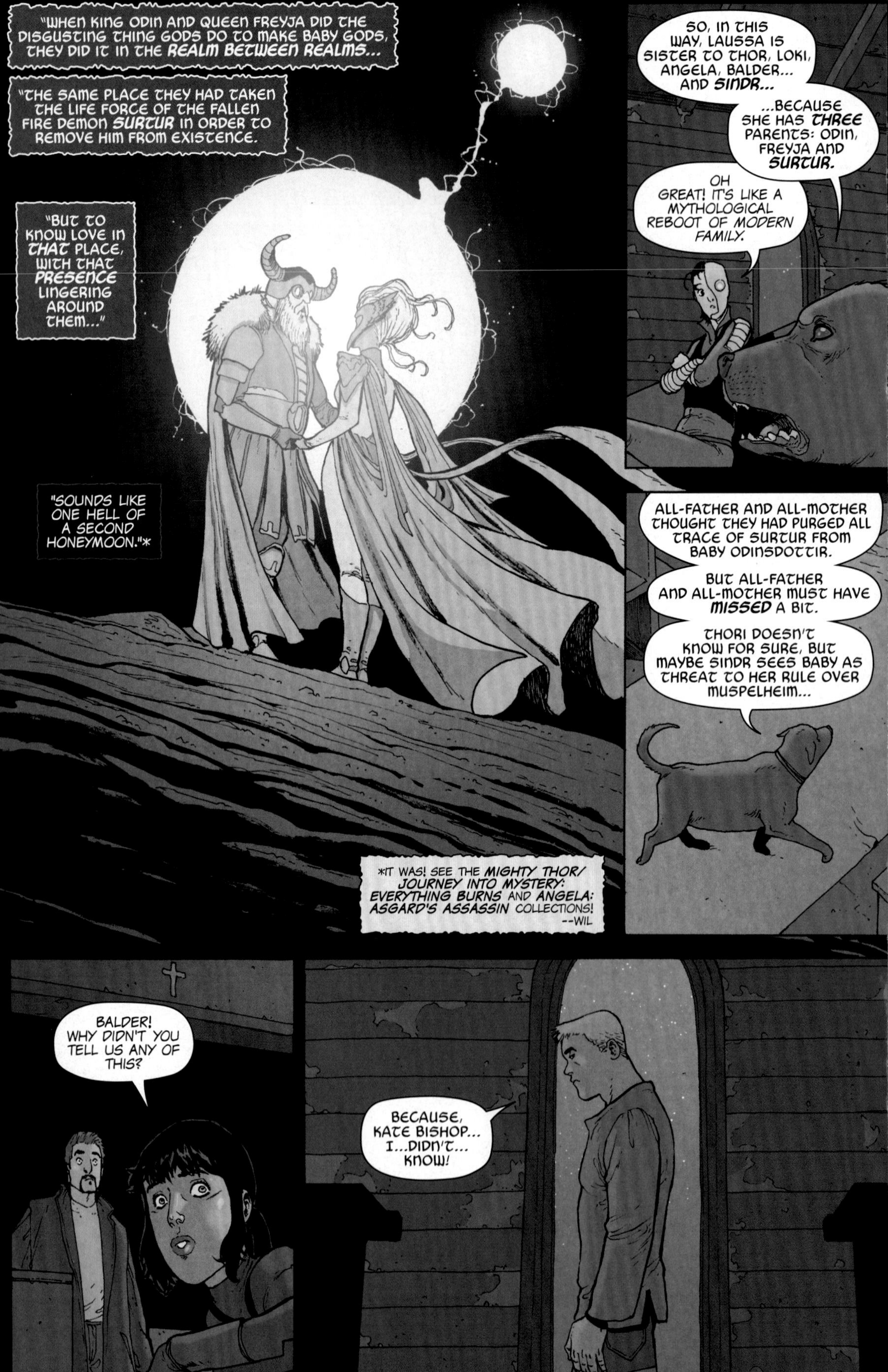
"WHEN KING ODIN AND QUEEN FREYJA DID THE DISGUSTING THING GODS DO TO MAKE BABY GODS, THEY DID IT IN THE REALM BETWEEN REALMS...
"THE SAME PLACE THEY HAD TAKEN THE LIFE FORCE OF THE FALLEN FIRE DEMON SURTUR IN ORDER TO REMOVE HIM FROM EXISTENCE.
"BUT TO KNOW LOVE IN THAT PLACE, WITH THAT PRESENCE LINGERING AROUND THEM..."
"SOUNDS LIKE ONE HELL OF A SECOND HONEYMOON."*
*IT WAS! SEE THE MIGHTY THOR/ JOURNEY INTO MYSTERY: EVERYTHING BURNS AND ANGELA: ASGARD'S ASSASSIN COLLECTIONS! --WIL
SO, IN THIS WAY, LAUSSA IS SISTER TO THOR, LOKI, ANGELA, BALDER... AND SINDR...
...BECAUSE SHE HAS THREE PARENTS: ODIN, FREYJA AND SURTUR.
OH GREAT! IT'S LIKE A MYTHOLOGICAL REBOOT OF MODERN FAMILY.
ALL-FATHER AND ALL-MOTHER THOUGHT THEY HAD PURGED ALL TRACE OF SURTUR FROM BABY ODINSDOTTIR.
BUT ALL-FATHER AND ALL-MOTHER MUST HAVE MISSED A BIT.
THORI DOESN'T KNOW FOR SURE, BUT MAYBE SINDR SEES BABY AS THREAT TO HER RULE OVER MUSPELHEIM...
BALDER! WHY DIDN'T YOU TELL US ANY OF THIS?
BECAUSE, KATE BISHOP... I...DIDN'T... KNOW!

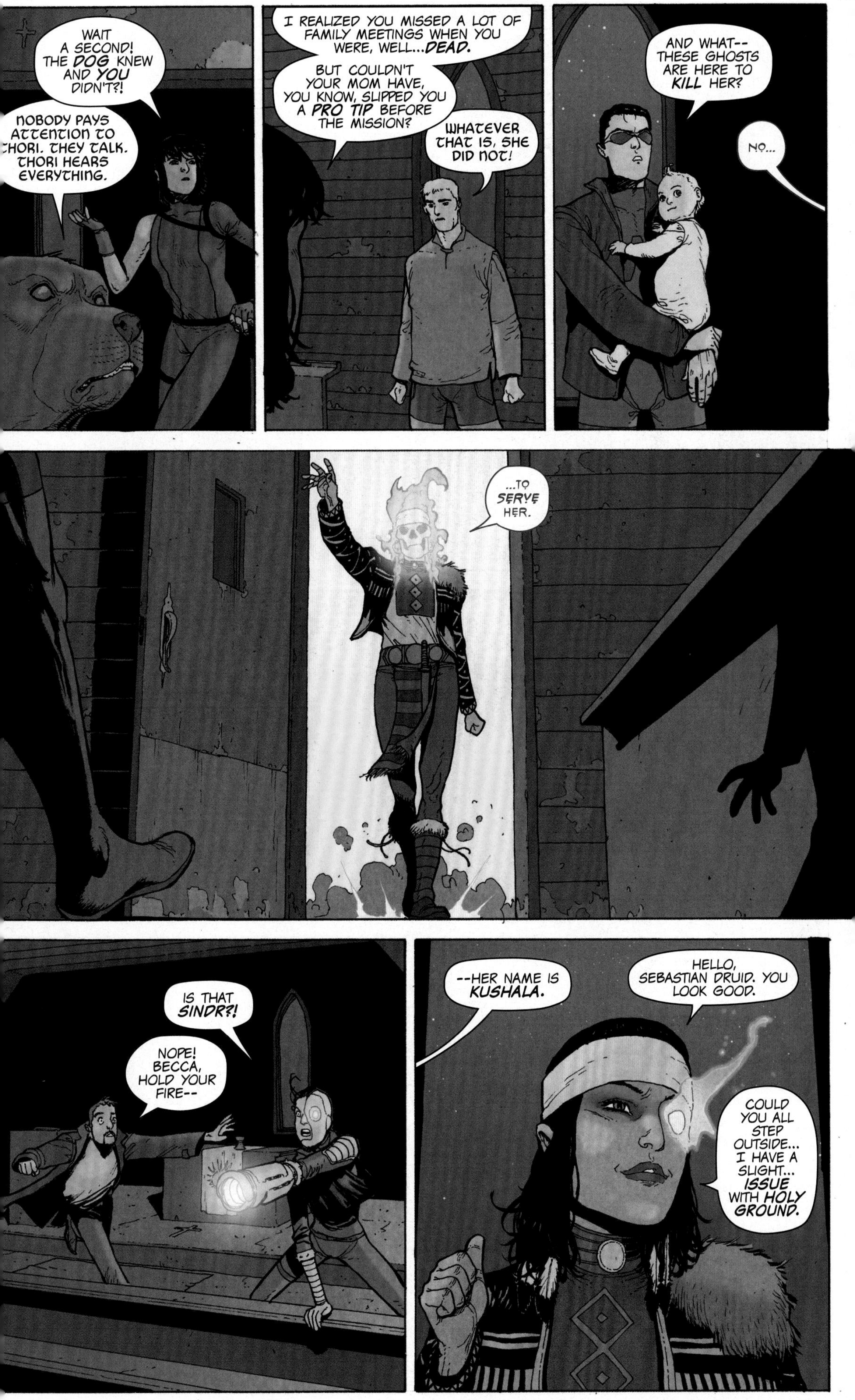
WAIT A SECOND! THE DOG KNEW AND YOU DIDN'T?!
NOBODY PAYS ATTENTION TO THORI. THEY TALK. THORI HEARS EVERYTHING.
I REALIZED YOU MISSED A LOT OF FAMILY MEETINGS WHEN YOU WERE, WELL...DEAD.
BUT COULDN'T YOUR MOM HAVE, YOU KNOW, SLIPPED YOU A PRO TIP BEFORE THE MISSION?
WHATEVER THAT IS, SHE DID NOT!
AND WHAT--THESE GHOSTS ARE HERE TO KILL HER?
NO...
...TO SERVE HER.
IS THAT SINDR?!
NOPE! BECCA, HOLD YOUR FIRE--
--HER NAME IS KUSHALA.
HELLO, SEBASTIAN DRUID. YOU LOOK GOOD.
COULD YOU ALL STEP OUTSIDE... I HAVE A SLIGHT... ISSUE WITH HOLY GROUND.

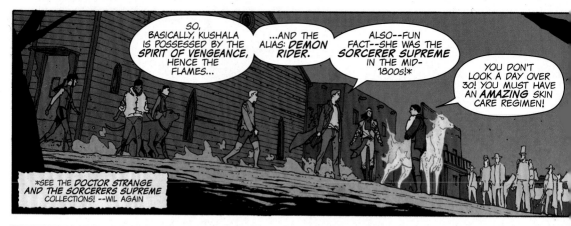

SO, BASICALLY, KUSHALA IS POSSESSED BY THE *SPIRIT OF VENGEANCE*, HENCE THE FLAMES...

...AND THE ALIAS: *DEMON RIDER.*

ALSO--FUN FACT--SHE WAS THE *SORCERER SUPREME* IN THE MID-1800s!*

YOU DON'T LOOK A DAY OVER 30! YOU MUST HAVE AN *AMAZING* SKIN CARE REGIMEN!

*SEE THE *DOCTOR STRANGE AND THE SORCERERS SUPREME* COLLECTIONS! --WIL AGAIN

NO, SIMON WILLIAMS. I CAME TO YOUR TIME AND FOUGHT SIDE BY SIDE WITH STEPHEN STRANGE AGAINST A GREAT EVIL.

NOW I HAVE SUMMONED THESE POWERFUL WARRIORS FROM MY ERA TO FIGHT AN EVEN GREATER ONE.

WE PLEDGE OUR SERVICE TO THE GODDESS *LAUSSA* AND THE HOUSE OF ODIN AND FREYJA IN THIS WAR OF THE REALMS!

I STILL DO NOT UNDERSTAND WHY.

‹BECAUSE INVADERS ARE STILL INVADERS.›*

‹AND EVIL IS STILL EVIL.›

‹BESIDES...WE FOUGHT FOR JUSTICE WHEN WE WAS ALIVE. FIGGERED WHY STOP NOW JEST 'CAUSE WE'RE DEAD?›

THEY SAID--

YEAH, I THINK WE GOT TH GIST OF IT!

*TRANSLATED FROM GHOST. --CLAYTON

WE RIDE! TO THIS WAR'S *FINAL BATTLE!*

AND YOU SHOULD LEAVE SOON TOO, FOR HE WHO PURSUES YOU IS NOT FAR BEHIND!

HOW DID SHE KNOW THAT...?

THANKS, OLD WEST GHOSTS! SORRY WE TRIED TO KILL YOU! AGAIN!

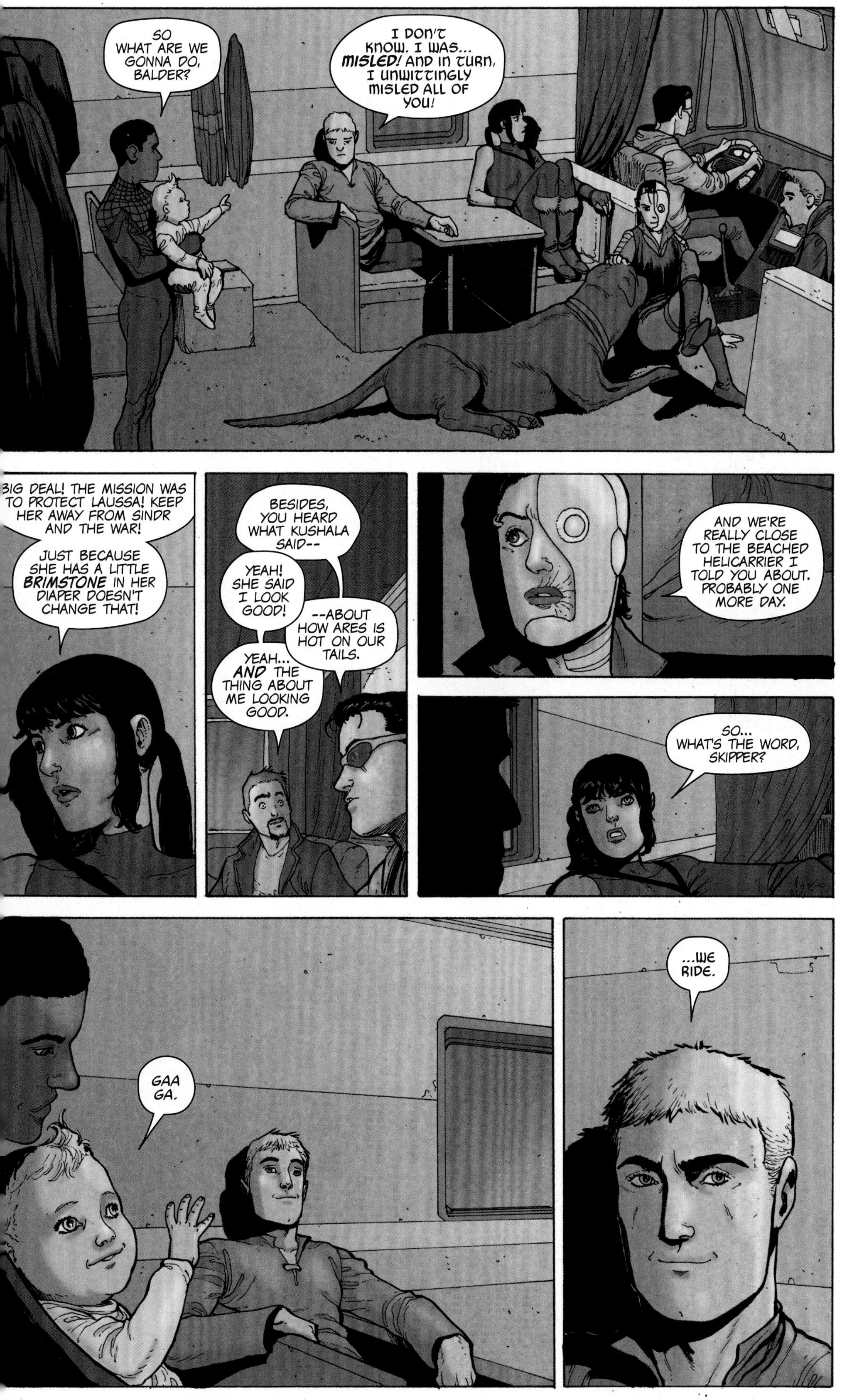
SO WHAT ARE WE GONNA DO, BALDER?
I DON'T KNOW. I WAS... MISLED! AND IN TURN, I UNWITTINGLY MISLED ALL OF YOU!
BIG DEAL! THE MISSION WAS TO PROTECT LAUSSA! KEEP HER AWAY FROM SINDR AND THE WAR!
JUST BECAUSE SHE HAS A LITTLE BRIMSTONE IN HER DIAPER DOESN'T CHANGE THAT!
BESIDES, YOU HEARD WHAT KUSHALA SAID--
YEAH! SHE SAID I LOOK GOOD!
--ABOUT HOW ARES IS HOT ON OUR TAILS.
YEAH... AND THE THING ABOUT ME LOOKING GOOD.
AND WE'RE REALLY CLOSE TO THE BEACHED HELICARRIER I TOLD YOU ABOUT. PROBABLY ONE MORE DAY.
SO... WHAT'S THE WORD, SKIPPER?
GAA GA.
...WE RIDE.

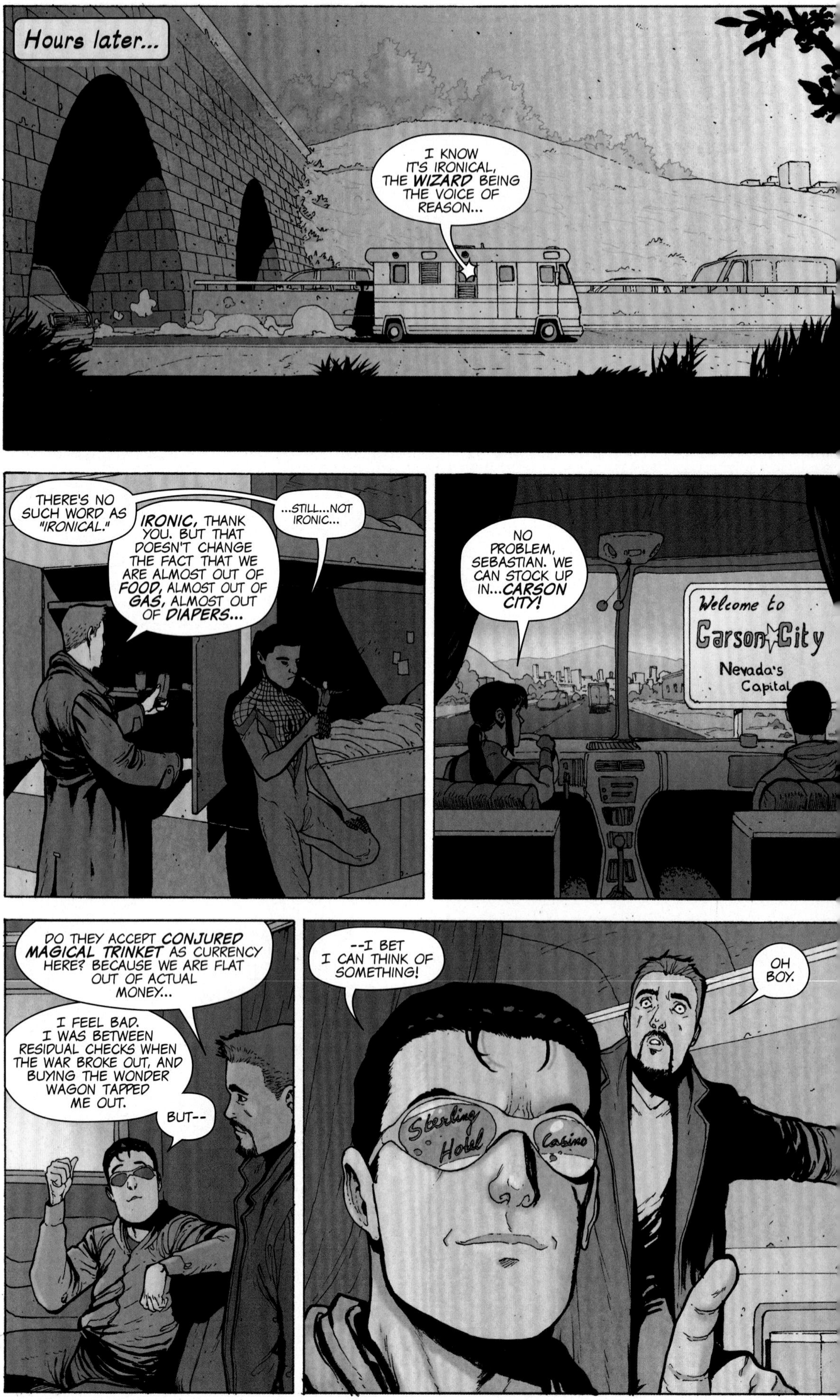
Hours later...
I KNOW IT'S IRONICAL, THE WIZARD BEING THE VOICE OF REASON...
THERE'S NO SUCH WORD AS "IRONICAL."
IRONIC, THANK YOU. BUT THAT DOESN'T CHANGE THE FACT THAT WE ARE ALMOST OUT OF FOOD, ALMOST OUT OF GAS, ALMOST OUT OF DIAPERS...
...STILL...NOT IRONIC...
NO PROBLEM, SEBASTIAN. WE CAN STOCK UP IN...CARSON CITY!
Welcome to
Carson City
Nevada's
Capital
DO THEY ACCEPT CONJURED MAGICAL TRINKET AS CURRENCY HERE? BECAUSE WE ARE FLAT OUT OF ACTUAL MONEY...
I FEEL BAD. I WAS BETWEEN RESIDUAL CHECKS WHEN THE WAR BROKE OUT, AND BUYING THE WONDER WAGON TAPPED ME OUT.
BUT--
--I BET I CAN THINK OF SOMETHING!
Sterling Hotel
Casino
OH BOY.

SO THE "SOMETHING" YOU THOUGHT OF WAS...THROW ON DISGUISES AND **WIN A BUNCH OF MONEY?**

YES! I'M GONNA HIT THE CRAPS TABLE. I HAVE A NEVER-FAIL SYSTEM!

SAID EVERY SOON-TO-BE-BROKE GAMBLER...

NO, LISTEN, I WAS IN THE TOP 30 FOR JAMES BOND!

WHICH MOVIE?

UM. THE VIDEO GAME. GOLDENEYE... **RELOADED.**

-:SIGH:- HERE. JUST PLAY **SMART,** OKAY? WE DON'T HAVE MUCH TO BET!

WAIT A SEC! THIS IS BAD! LOOK AT... EVERYBODY!

THIS PLACE IS LOUSY WITH **SUPER VILLAINS!**

The Sterling Hotel & Casino SHC

IT'S **LOUSY** ALL RIGHT, BUT...NOT EXACTLY WITH **SUPER** VILLAINS...

The Sterling Hotel & Casino SHC
proudly welcomes you to:

HENCHFEST

"while the villains are away, the henches do play."

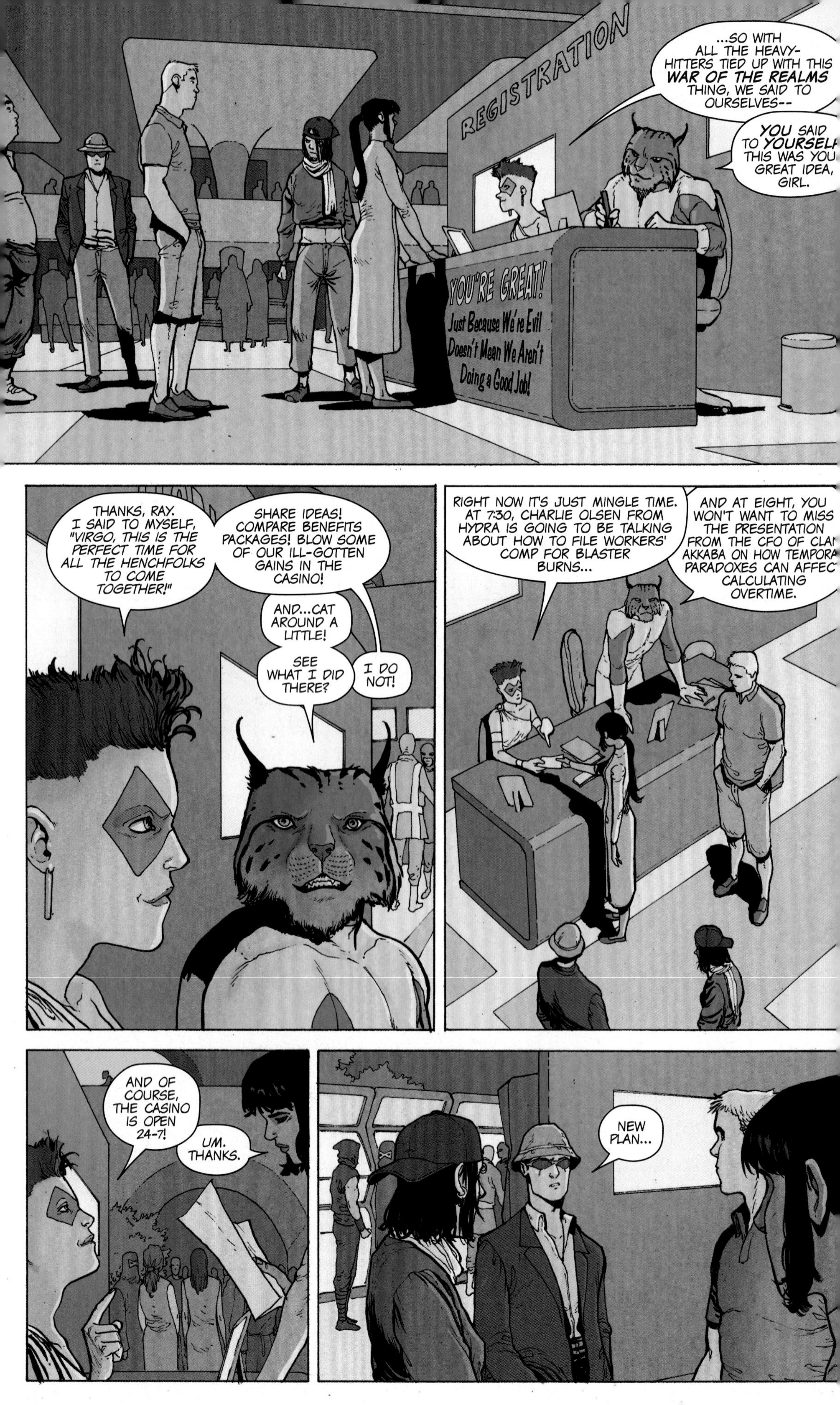
REGISTRATION
...SO WITH ALL THE HEAVY-HITTERS TIED UP WITH THIS WAR OF THE REALMS THING, WE SAID TO OURSELVES--
YOU SAID TO YOURSELF THIS WAS YOU GREAT IDEA, GIRL.
YOU'RE GREAT! Just Because We're Evil Doesn't Mean We Aren't Doing a Good Job!
THANKS, RAY. I SAID TO MYSELF, "VIRGO, THIS IS THE PERFECT TIME FOR ALL THE HENCHFOLKS TO COME TOGETHER!"
SHARE IDEAS! COMPARE BENEFITS PACKAGES! BLOW SOME OF OUR ILL-GOTTEN GAINS IN THE CASINO!
AND...CAT AROUND A LITTLE!
SEE WHAT I DID THERE?
I DO NOT!
RIGHT NOW IT'S JUST MINGLE TIME. AT 7:30, CHARLIE OLSEN FROM HYDRA IS GOING TO BE TALKING ABOUT HOW TO FILE WORKERS' COMP FOR BLASTER BURNS...
AND AT EIGHT, YOU WON'T WANT TO MISS THE PRESENTATION FROM THE CFO OF CLA AKKABA ON HOW TEMPORA PARADOXES CAN AFFEC CALCULATING OVERTIME.
AND OF COURSE, THE CASINO IS OPEN 24-7!
UM. THANKS.
NEW PLAN...

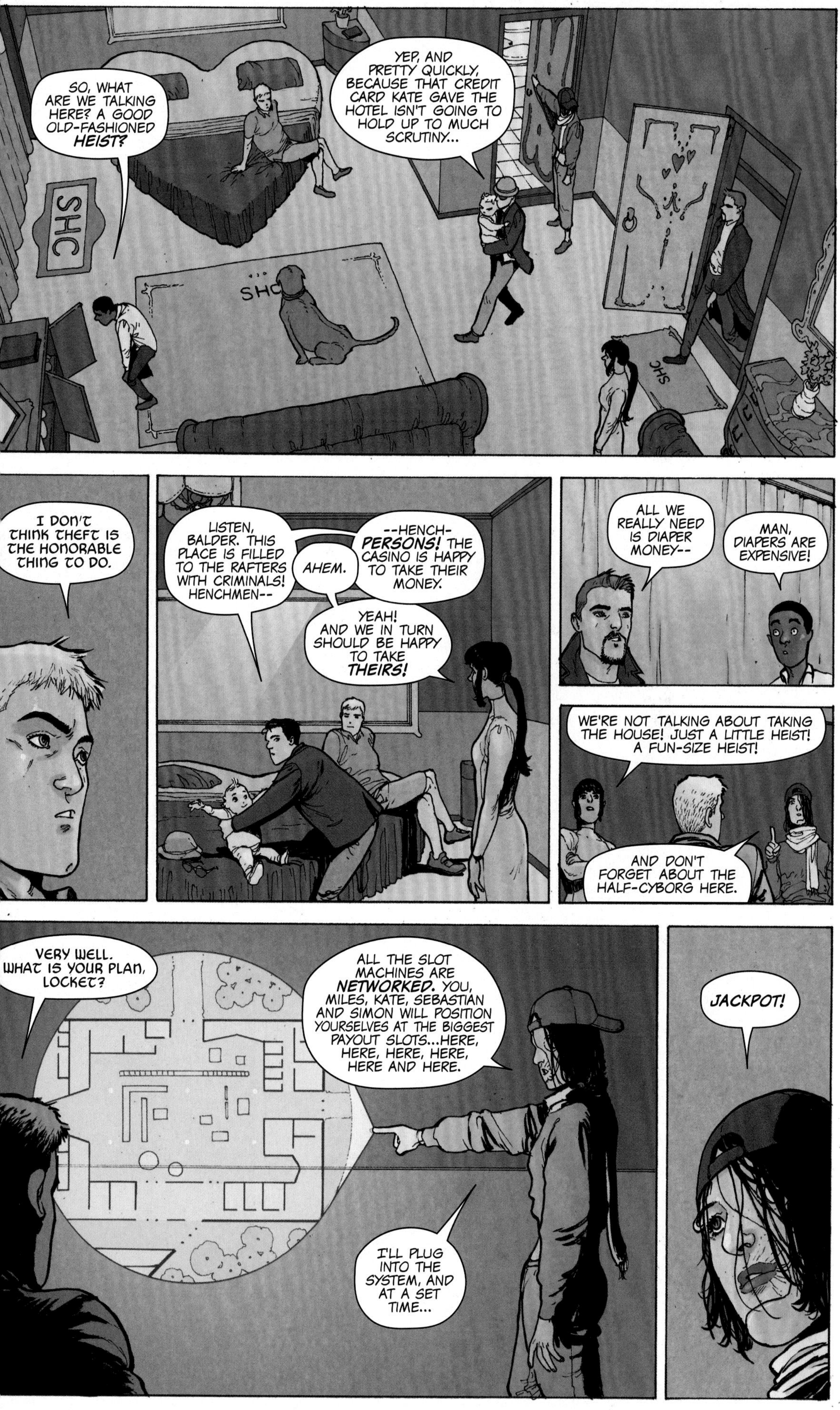

SO, WHAT ARE WE TALKING HERE? A GOOD OLD-FASHIONED **HEIST?**
SHC
YEP, AND PRETTY QUICKLY, BECAUSE THAT CREDIT CARD KATE GAVE THE HOTEL ISN'T GOING TO HOLD UP TO MUCH SCRUTINY...
SHC
SHC
I DON'T THINK THEFT IS THE HONORABLE THING TO DO.
LISTEN, BALDER. THIS PLACE IS FILLED TO THE RAFTERS WITH CRIMINALS! HENCHMEN--
AHEM.
--HENCH-**PERSONS!** THE CASINO IS HAPPY TO TAKE THEIR MONEY.
YEAH! AND WE IN TURN SHOULD BE HAPPY TO TAKE **THEIRS!**
ALL WE REALLY NEED IS DIAPER MONEY--
MAN, DIAPERS ARE EXPENSIVE!
WE'RE NOT TALKING ABOUT TAKING THE HOUSE! JUST A LITTLE HEIST! A FUN-SIZE HEIST!
AND DON'T FORGET ABOUT THE HALF-CYBORG HERE.
VERY WELL. WHAT IS YOUR PLAN, LOCKET?
ALL THE SLOT MACHINES ARE **NETWORKED.** YOU, MILES, KATE, SEBASTIAN AND SIMON WILL POSITION YOURSELVES AT THE BIGGEST PAYOUT SLOTS...HERE, HERE, HERE, HERE, HERE AND HERE.
I'LL PLUG INTO THE SYSTEM, AND AT A SET TIME...
JACKPOT!

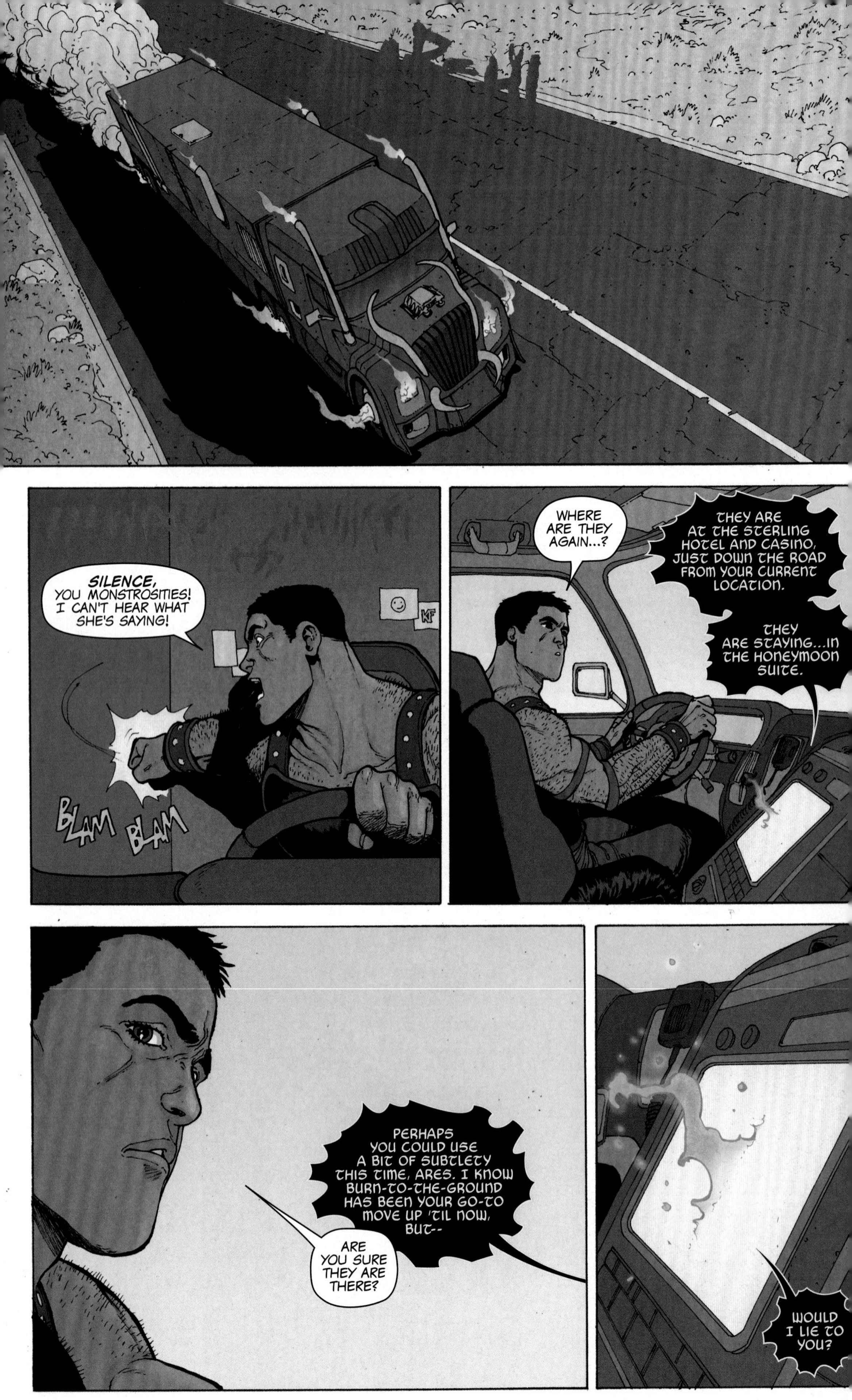
SILENCE, YOU MONSTROSITIES! I CAN'T HEAR WHAT SHE'S SAYING!
BLAM BLAM
WHERE ARE THEY AGAIN...?
THEY ARE AT THE STERLING HOTEL AND CASINO, JUST DOWN THE ROAD FROM YOUR CURRENT LOCATION.
THEY ARE STAYING...IN THE HONEYMOON SUITE.
ARE YOU SURE THEY ARE THERE?
PERHAPS YOU COULD USE A BIT OF SUBTLETY THIS TIME, ARES. I KNOW BURN-TO-THE-GROUND HAS BEEN YOUR GO-TO MOVE UP 'TIL NOW, BUT--
WOULD I LIE TO YOU?

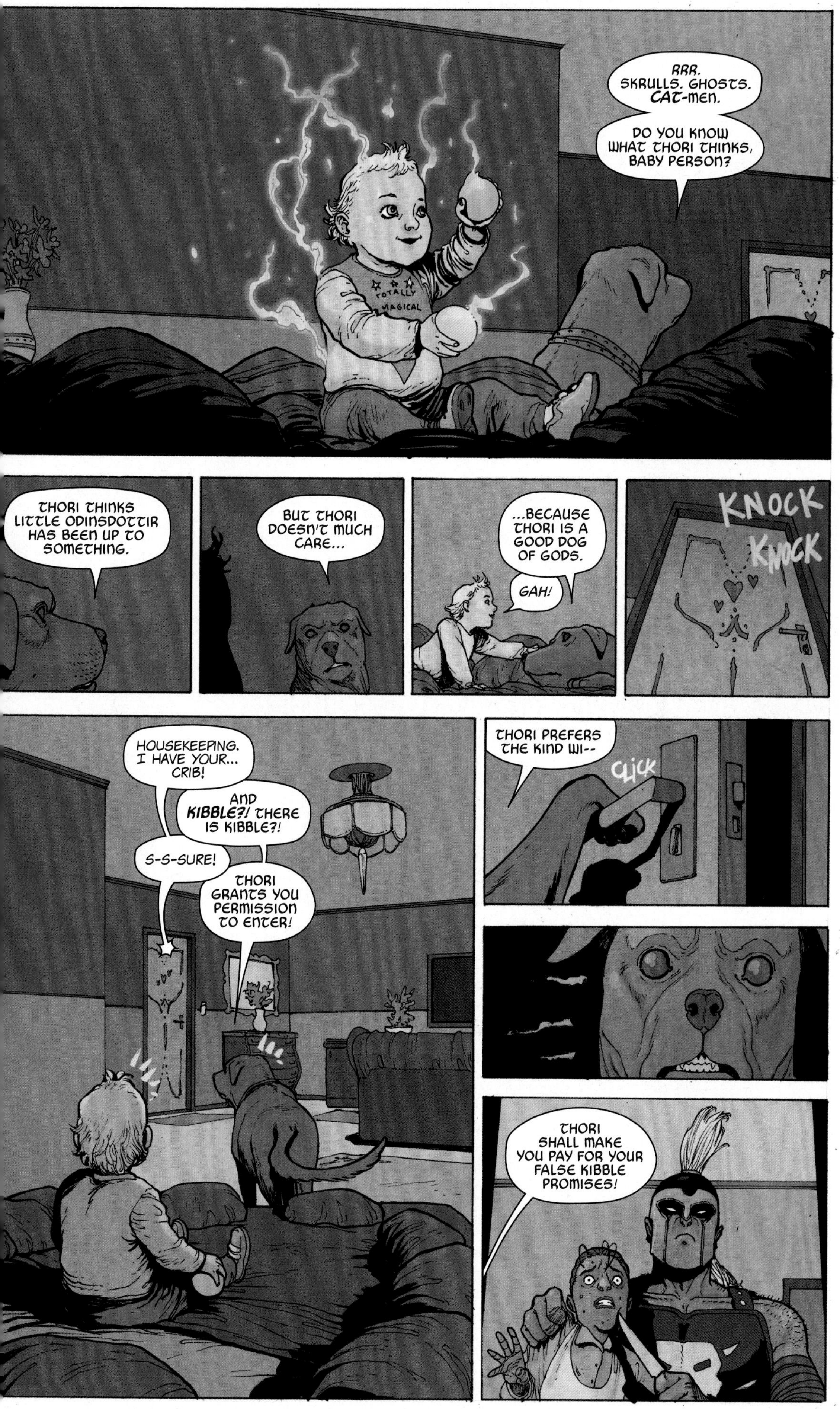
RRR.
SKRULLS. GHOSTS. CAT-men.
DO YOU KNOW WHAT THORI THINKS, BABY PERSON?
TOTALLY MAGICAL
THORI THINKS LITTLE ODINSDOTTIR HAS BEEN UP TO SOMETHING.
BUT THORI DOESN'T MUCH CARE...
...BECAUSE THORI IS A GOOD DOG OF GODS.
GAH!
KNOCK
KNOCK
HOUSEKEEPING. I HAVE YOUR... CRIB!
AND KIBBLE?! THERE IS KIBBLE?!
S-S-SURE!
THORI GRANTS YOU PERMISSION TO ENTER!
THORI PREFERS THE KIND WI--
CLICK
THORI SHALL MAKE YOU PAY FOR YOUR FALSE KIBBLE PROMISES!

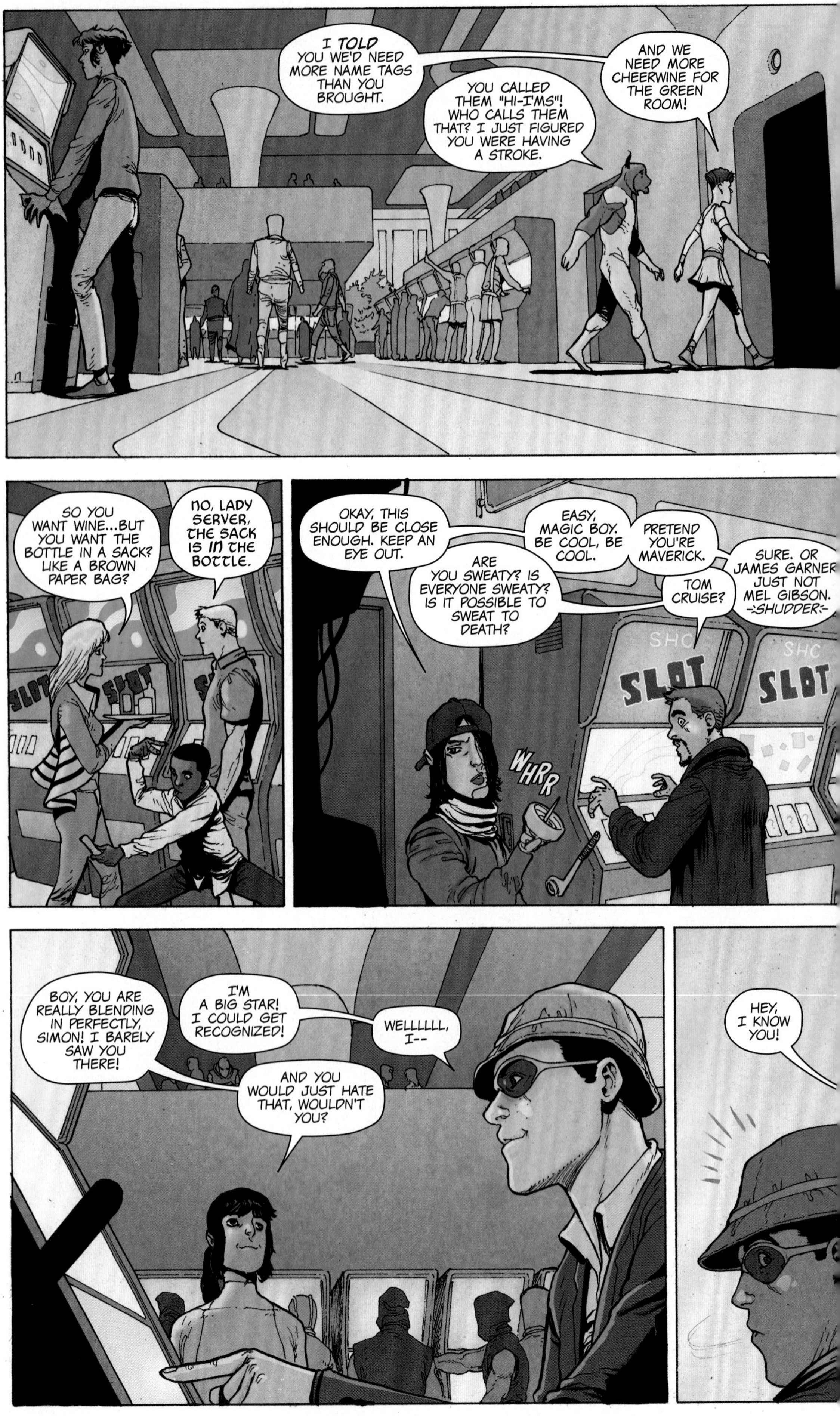
I TOLD YOU WE'D NEED MORE NAME TAGS THAN YOU BROUGHT.
YOU CALLED THEM "HI-I'MS"! WHO CALLS THEM THAT? I JUST FIGURED YOU WERE HAVING A STROKE.
AND WE NEED MORE CHEERWINE FOR THE GREEN ROOM!
SO YOU WANT WINE...BUT YOU WANT THE BOTTLE IN A SACK? LIKE A BROWN PAPER BAG?
NO, LADY SERVER, THE SACK IS IN THE BOTTLE.
OKAY, THIS SHOULD BE CLOSE ENOUGH. KEEP AN EYE OUT.
ARE YOU SWEATY? IS EVERYONE SWEATY? IS IT POSSIBLE TO SWEAT TO DEATH?
EASY, MAGIC BOY. BE COOL, BE COOL.
PRETEND YOU'RE MAVERICK.
TOM CRUISE?
SURE. OR JAMES GARNER JUST NOT MEL GIBSON. -SHUDDER-
SHC
SLOT
SHC
SLOT
SLOT
SLOT
WHRR
BOY, YOU ARE REALLY BLENDING IN PERFECTLY, SIMON! I BARELY SAW YOU THERE!
I'M A BIG STAR! I COULD GET RECOGNIZED!
AND YOU WOULD JUST HATE THAT, WOULDN'T YOU?
WELLLLLL, I--
HEY, I KNOW YOU!

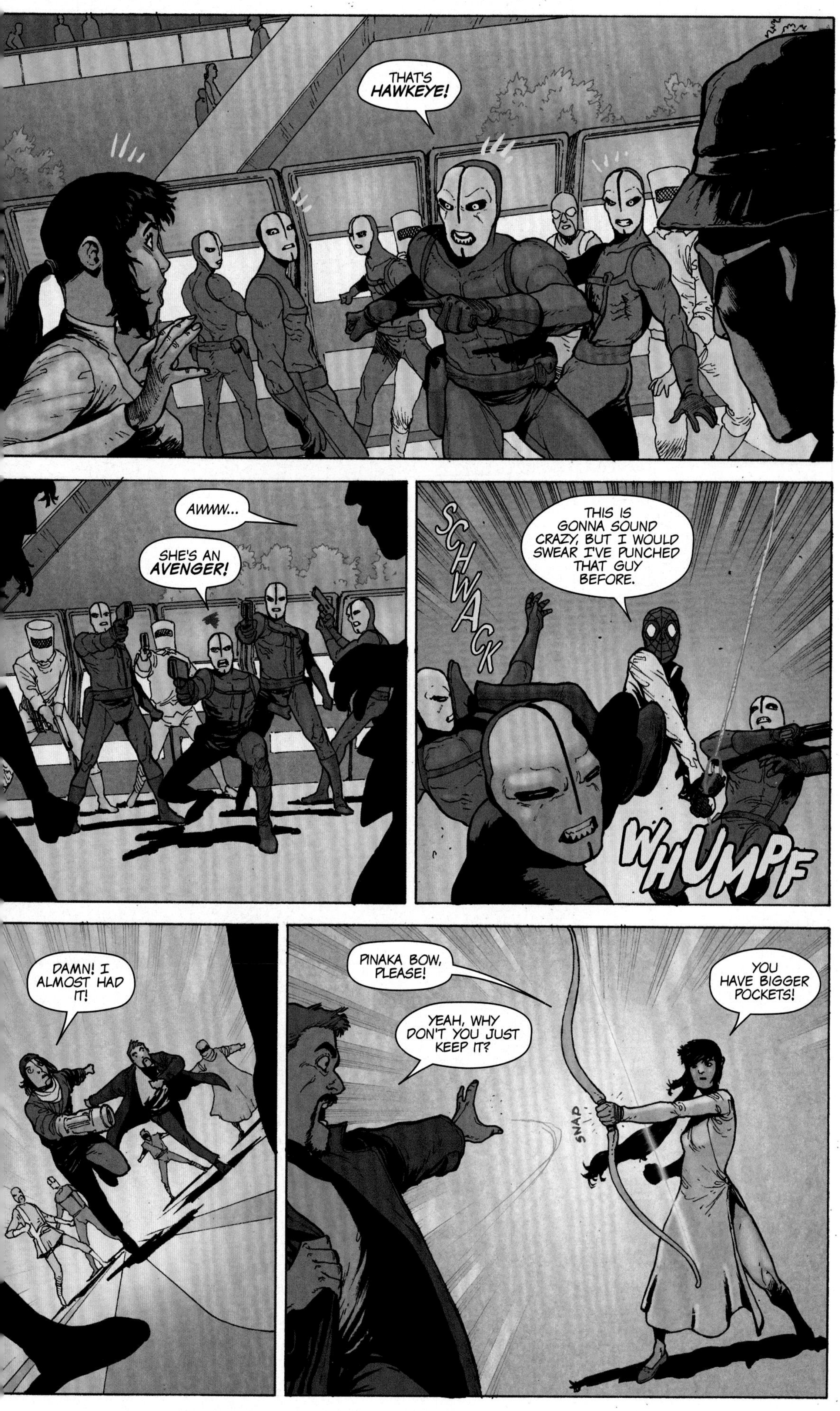
THAT'S HAWKEYE!
AWWW...
SHE'S AN AVENGER!
SCHWACK
THIS IS GONNA SOUND CRAZY, BUT I WOULD SWEAR I'VE PUNCHED THAT GUY BEFORE.
WHUMPF
DAMN! I ALMOST HAD IT!
PINAKA BOW, PLEASE!
YEAH, WHY DON'T YOU JUST KEEP IT?
YOU HAVE BIGGER POCKETS!
SNAP

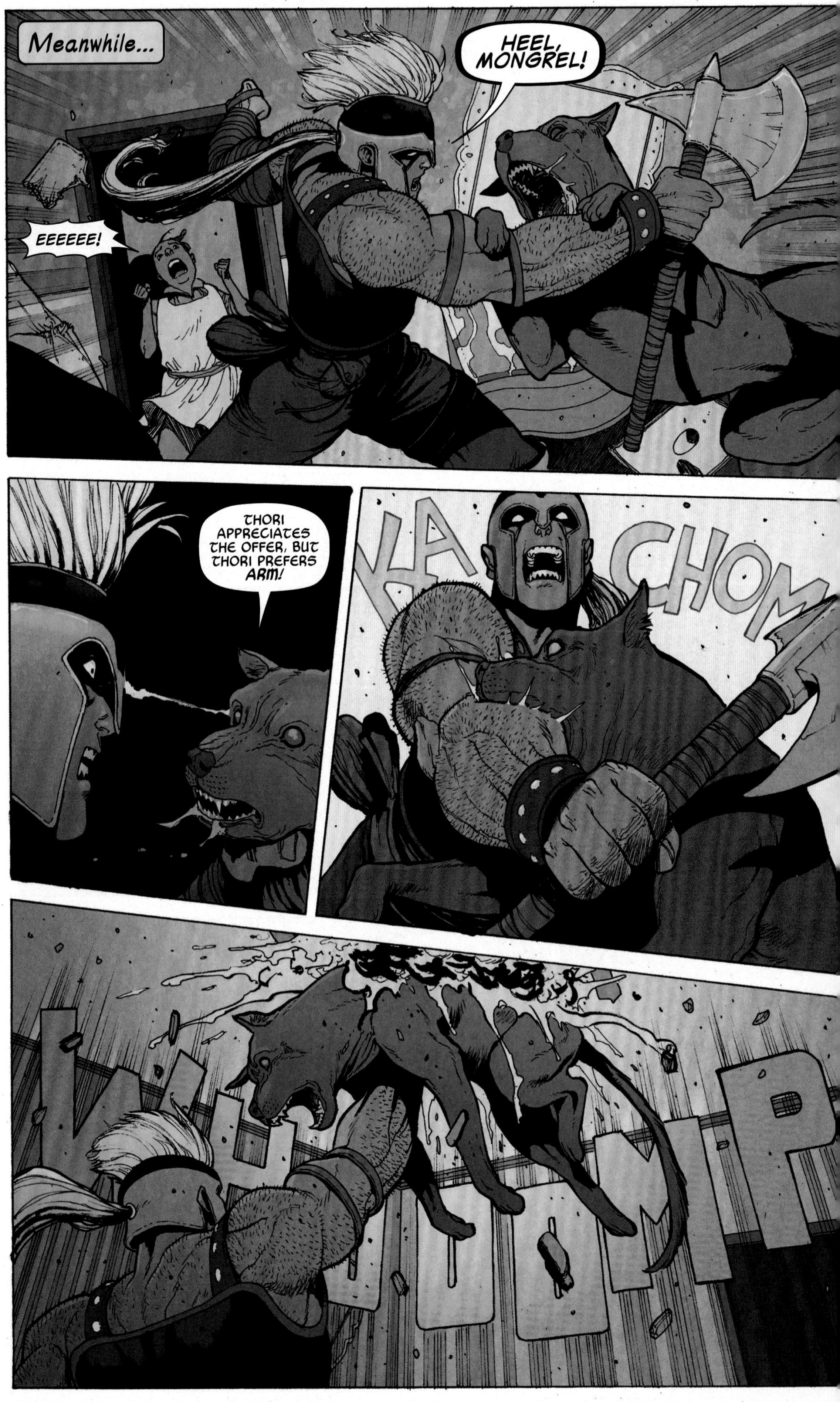

Meanwhile...
HEEL, MONGREL!
EEEEEE!
THORI APPRECIATES THE OFFER, BUT THORI PREFERS ARM!
KA-CHOM

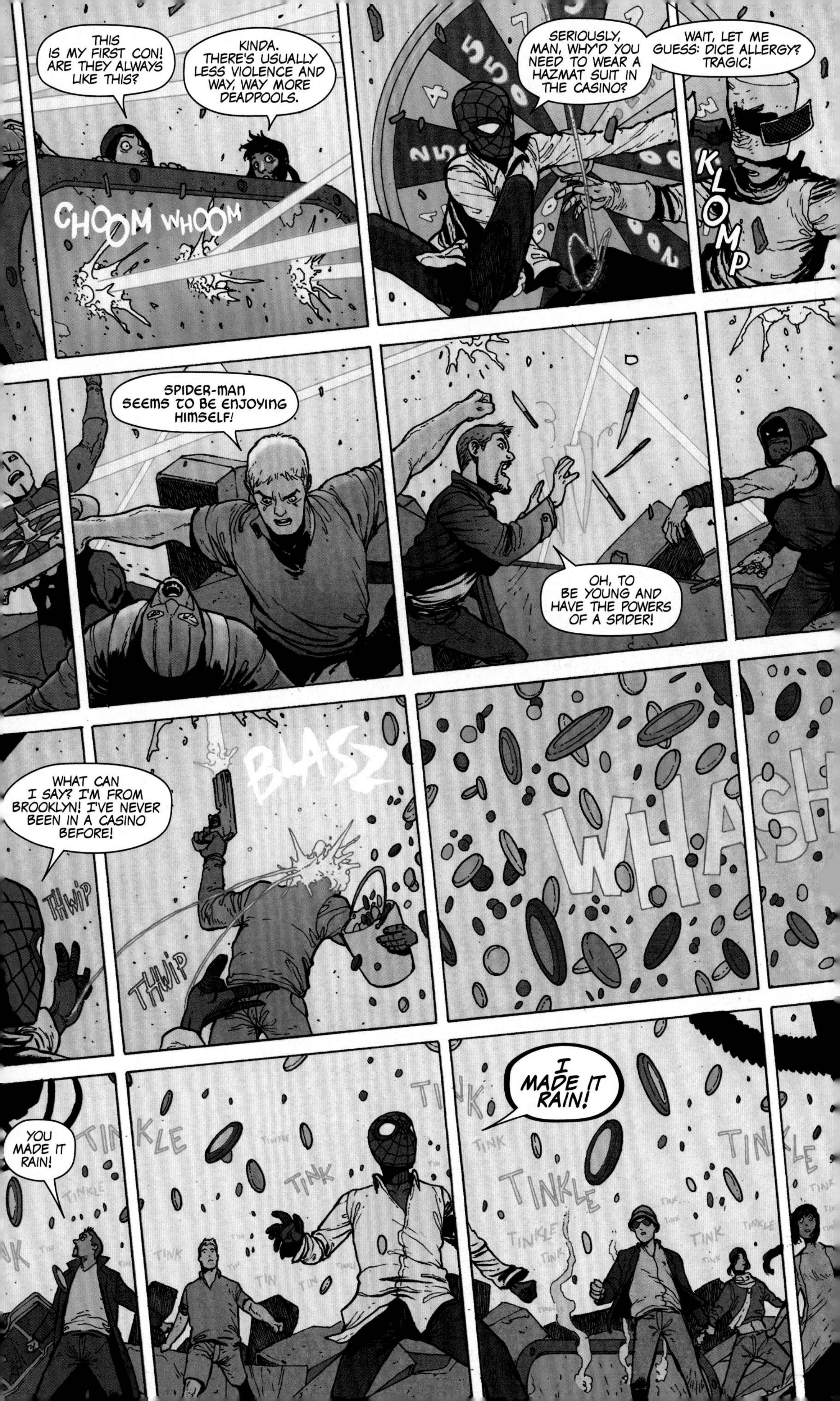
THIS IS MY FIRST CON! ARE THEY ALWAYS LIKE THIS?
KINDA. THERE'S USUALLY LESS VIOLENCE AND WAY, WAY MORE DEADPOOLS.
CHOOM WHOOM
SERIOUSLY, MAN, WHY'D YOU NEED TO WEAR A HAZMAT SUIT IN THE CASINO?
WAIT, LET ME GUESS: DICE ALLERGY? TRAGIC!
KLOMP
SPIDER-MAN SEEMS TO BE ENJOYING HIMSELF!
OH, TO BE YOUNG AND HAVE THE POWERS OF A SPIDER!
WHAT CAN I SAY? I'M FROM BROOKLYN! I'VE NEVER BEEN IN A CASINO BEFORE!
THWIP
THWIP
BLASZ
WHASH
YOU MADE IT RAIN!
I MADE IT RAIN!
TINKLE
TINK
TINKLE

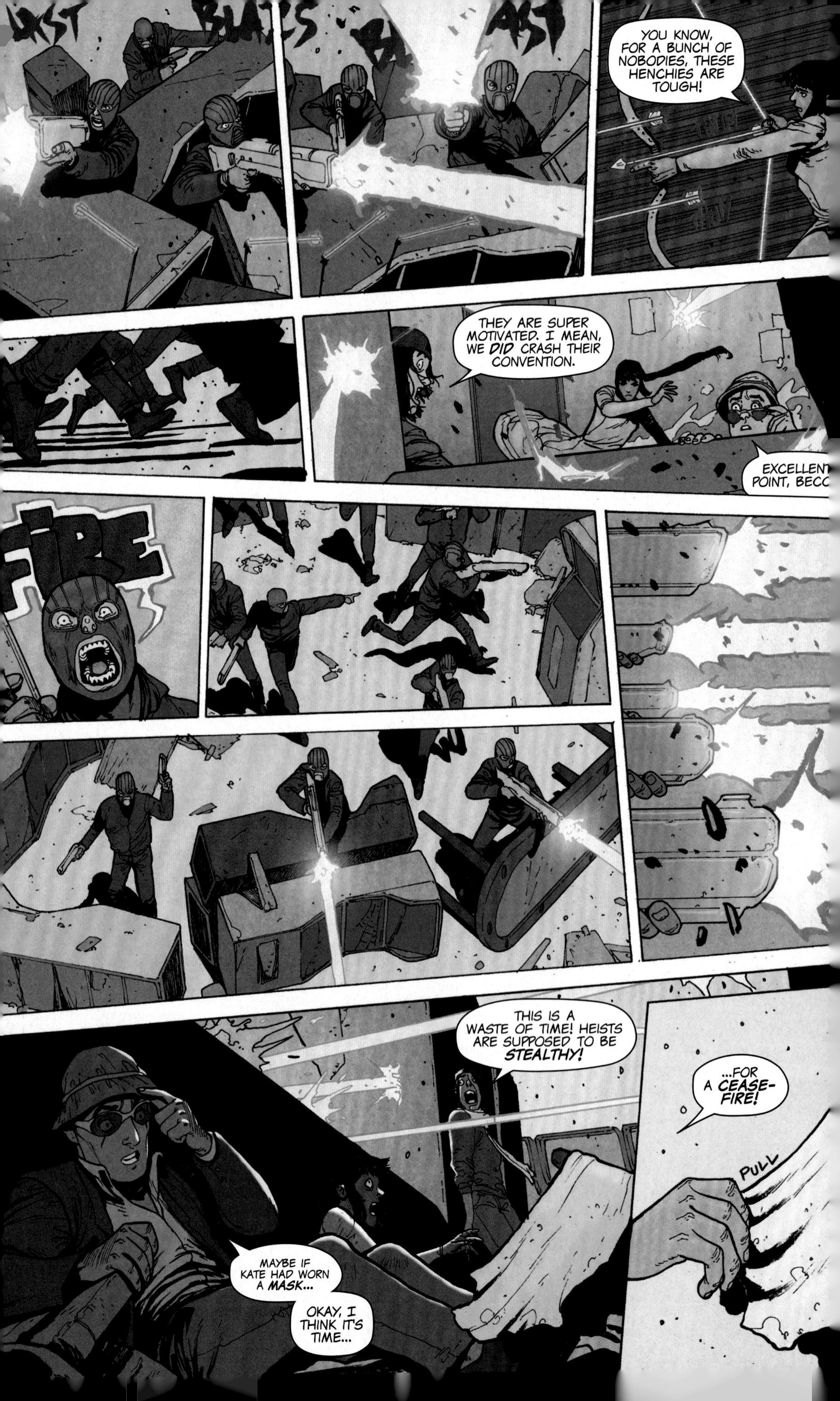
YOU KNOW, FOR A BUNCH OF NOBODIES, THESE HENCHIES ARE TOUGH!
THEY ARE SUPER MOTIVATED. I MEAN, WE *DID* CRASH THEIR CONVENTION.
EXCELLENT POINT, BECC
FIRE
THIS IS A WASTE OF TIME! HEISTS ARE SUPPOSED TO BE **STEALTHY!**
MAYBE IF KATE HAD WORN A **MASK...**
OKAY, I THINK IT'S TIME...
...FOR A **CEASE-FIRE!**
PULL

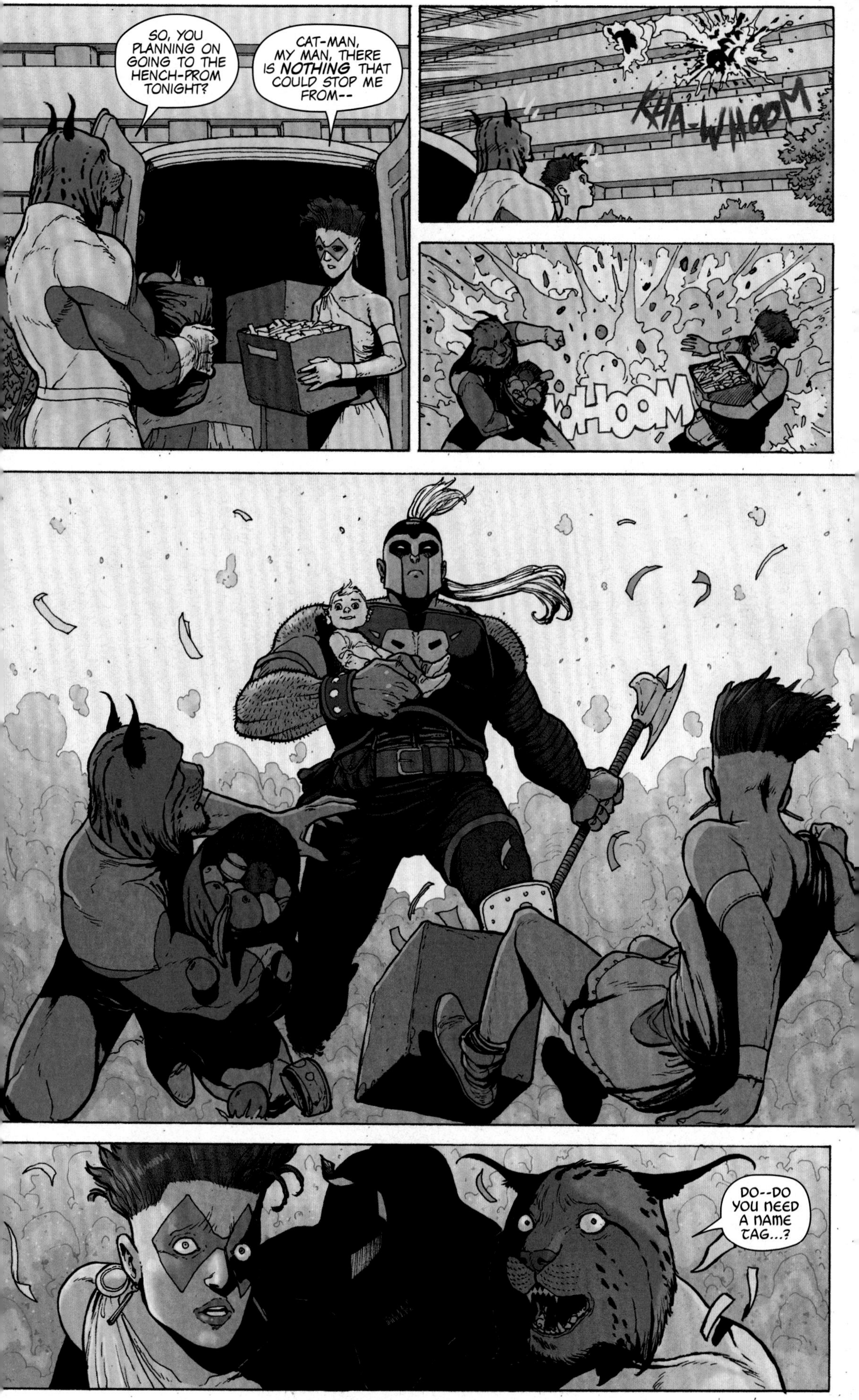
SO, YOU PLANNING ON GOING TO THE HENCH-PROM TONIGHT?
CAT-MAN, MY MAN, THERE IS **NOTHING** THAT COULD STOP ME FROM--
KHA-WHOOM
WHOOM
DO--DO YOU NEED A NAME TAG...?

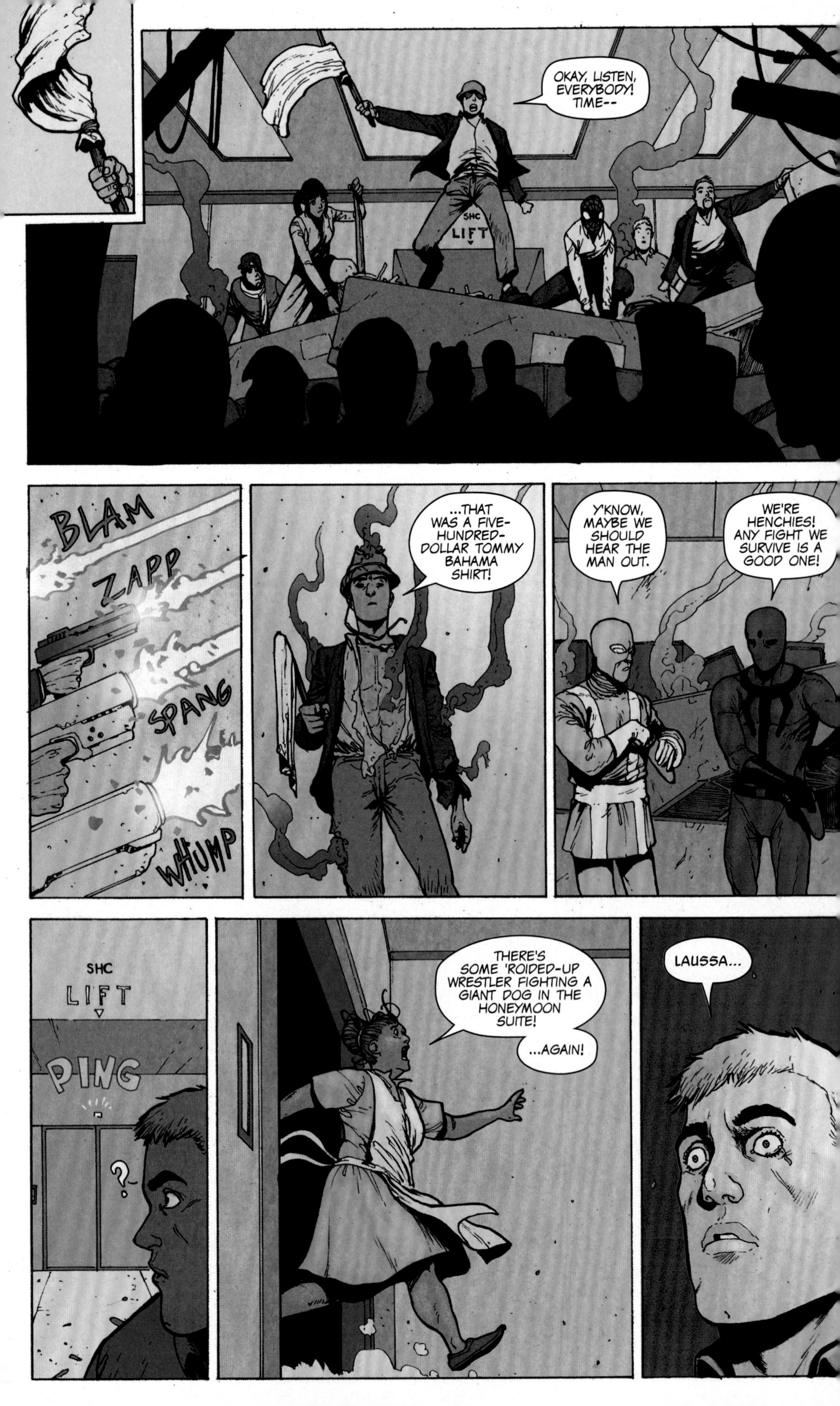

OKAY, LISTEN, EVERYBODY! TIME--
SHC
LIFT
BLAM
ZAPP
SPANG
WHUMP
...THAT WAS A FIVE-HUNDRED-DOLLAR TOMMY BAHAMA SHIRT!
Y'KNOW, MAYBE WE SHOULD HEAR THE MAN OUT.
WE'RE HENCHIES! ANY FIGHT WE SURVIVE IS A GOOD ONE!
SHC
LIFT
PING
?
THERE'S SOME 'ROIDED-UP WRESTLER FIGHTING A GIANT DOG IN THE HONEYMOON SUITE!
...AGAIN!
LAUSSA...

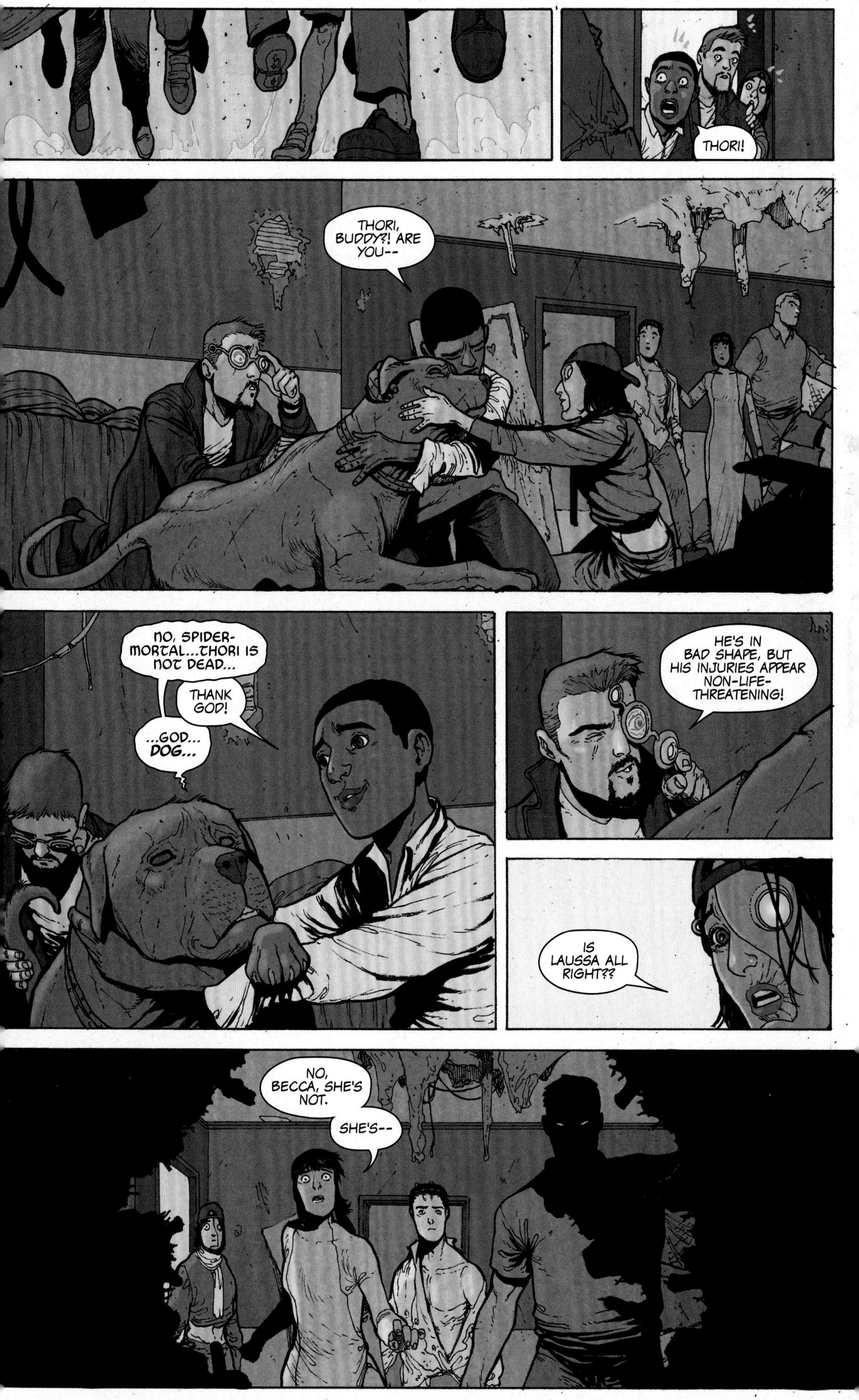

THORI!
THORI, BUDDY?! ARE YOU--
NO, SPIDER-MORTAL...THORI IS NOT DEAD...
THANK GOD!
...GOD... **DOG...**
HE'S IN BAD SHAPE, BUT HIS INJURIES APPEAR NON-LIFE-THREATENING!
IS LAUSSA ALL RIGHT??
NO, BECCA, SHE'S NOT.
SHE'S--

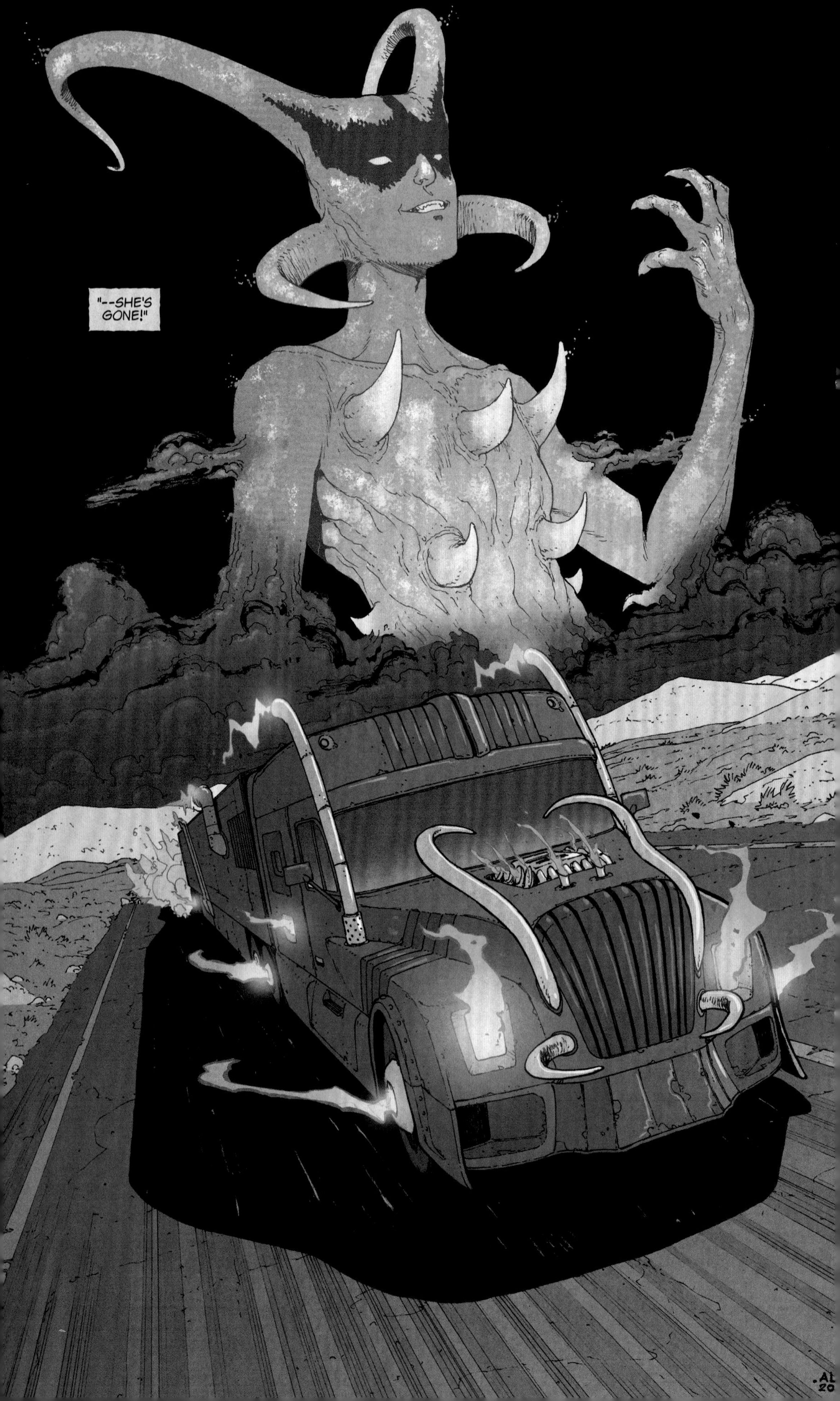
"--SHE'S GONE!"

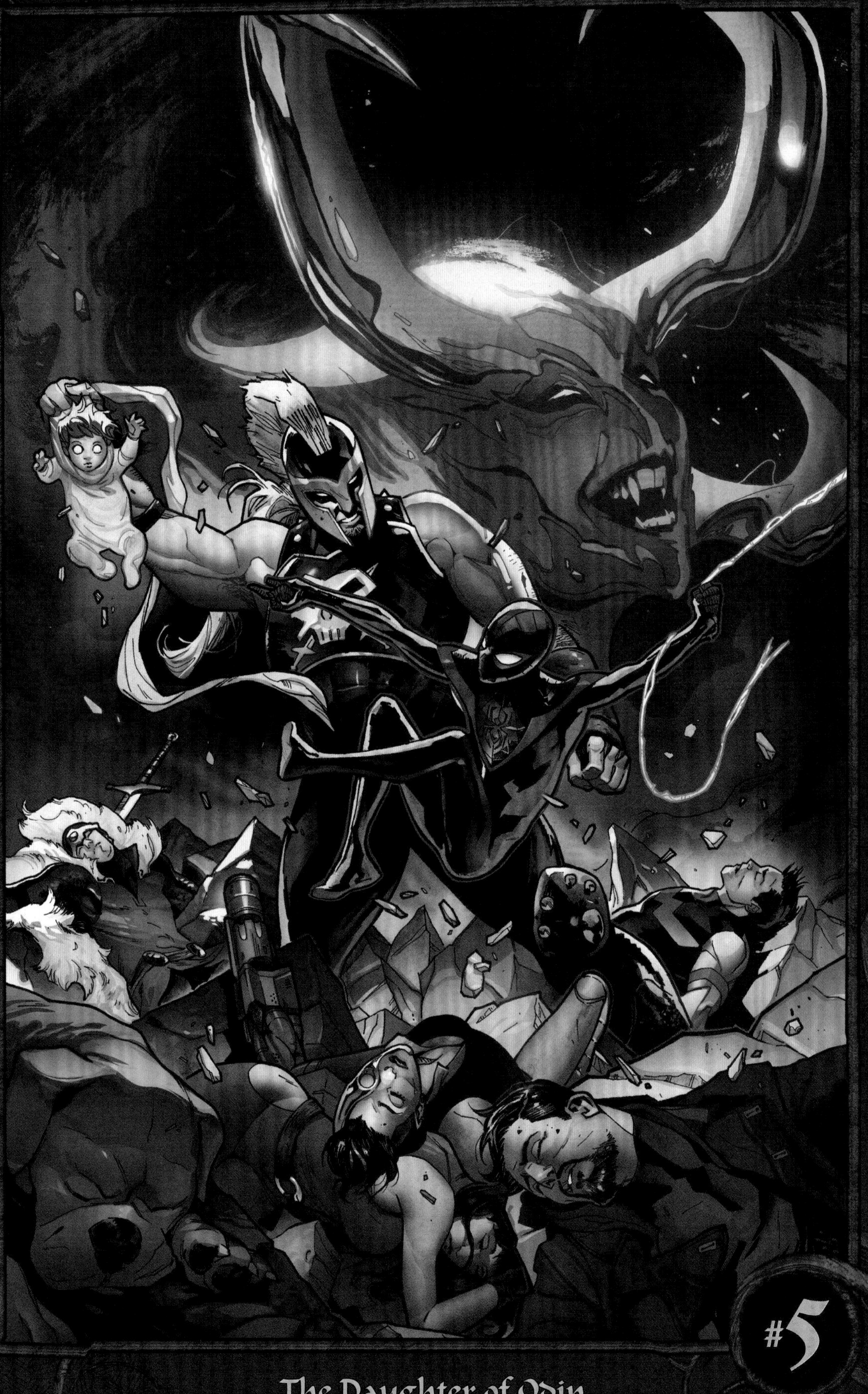
#5

The Daughter of Odin

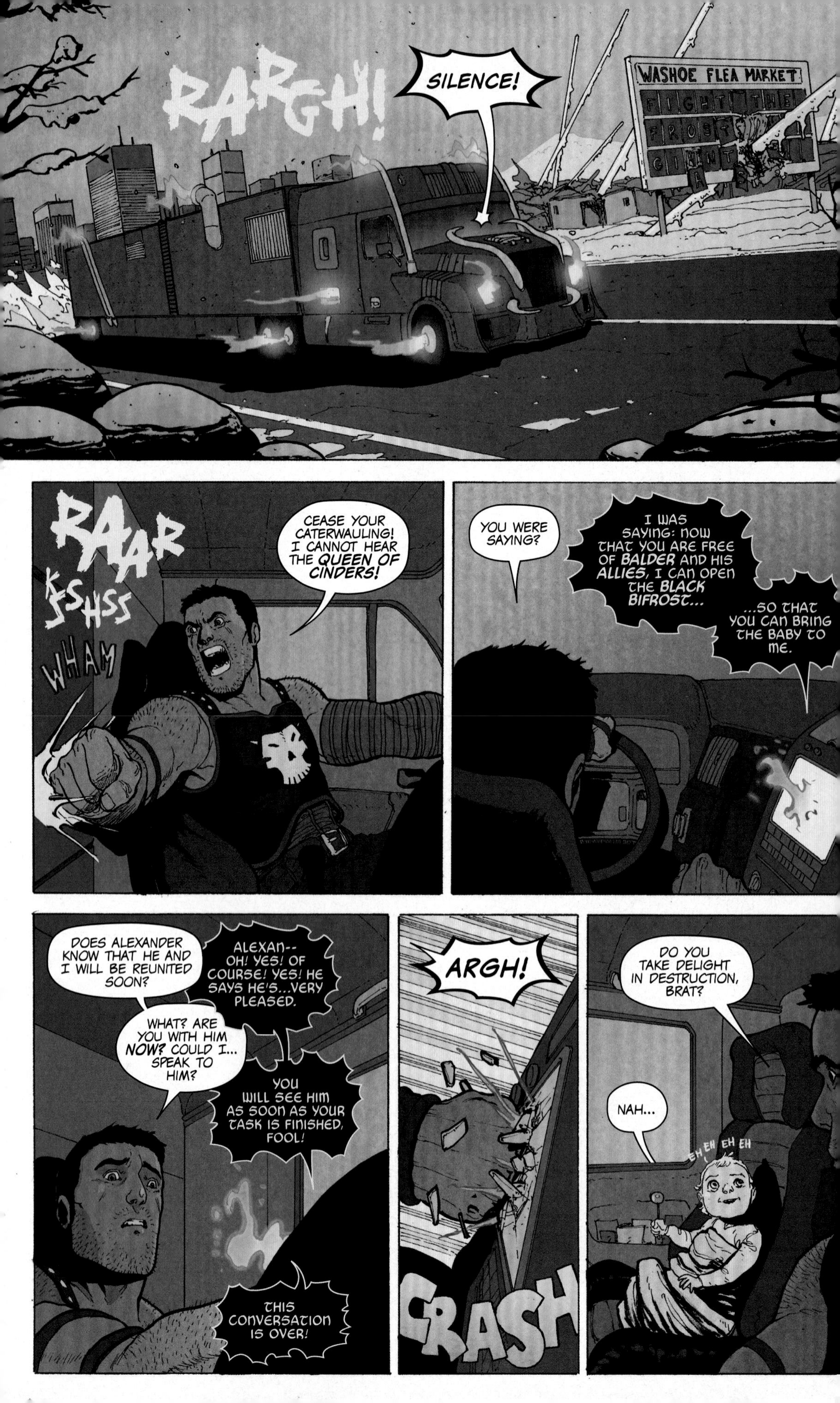
RARGH!
SILENCE!
WASHOE FLEA MARKET
FIGHT THE FROST GIANTS
RAAR
KSHSS
WHAM
CEASE YOUR CATERWAULING! I CANNOT HEAR THE QUEEN OF CINDERS!
YOU WERE SAYING?
I WAS SAYING: NOW THAT YOU ARE FREE OF BALDER AND HIS ALLIES, I CAN OPEN THE BLACK BIFROST...
...SO THAT YOU CAN BRING THE BABY TO ME.
DOES ALEXANDER KNOW THAT HE AND I WILL BE REUNITED SOON?
ALEXAN-- OH! YES! OF COURSE! YES! HE SAYS HE'S...VERY PLEASED.
WHAT? ARE YOU WITH HIM NOW? COULD I... SPEAK TO HIM?
YOU WILL SEE HIM AS SOON AS YOUR TASK IS FINISHED, FOOL!
THIS CONVERSATION IS OVER!
ARGH!
CRASH
DO YOU TAKE DELIGHT IN DESTRUCTION, BRAT?
NAH...
EH EH EH EH

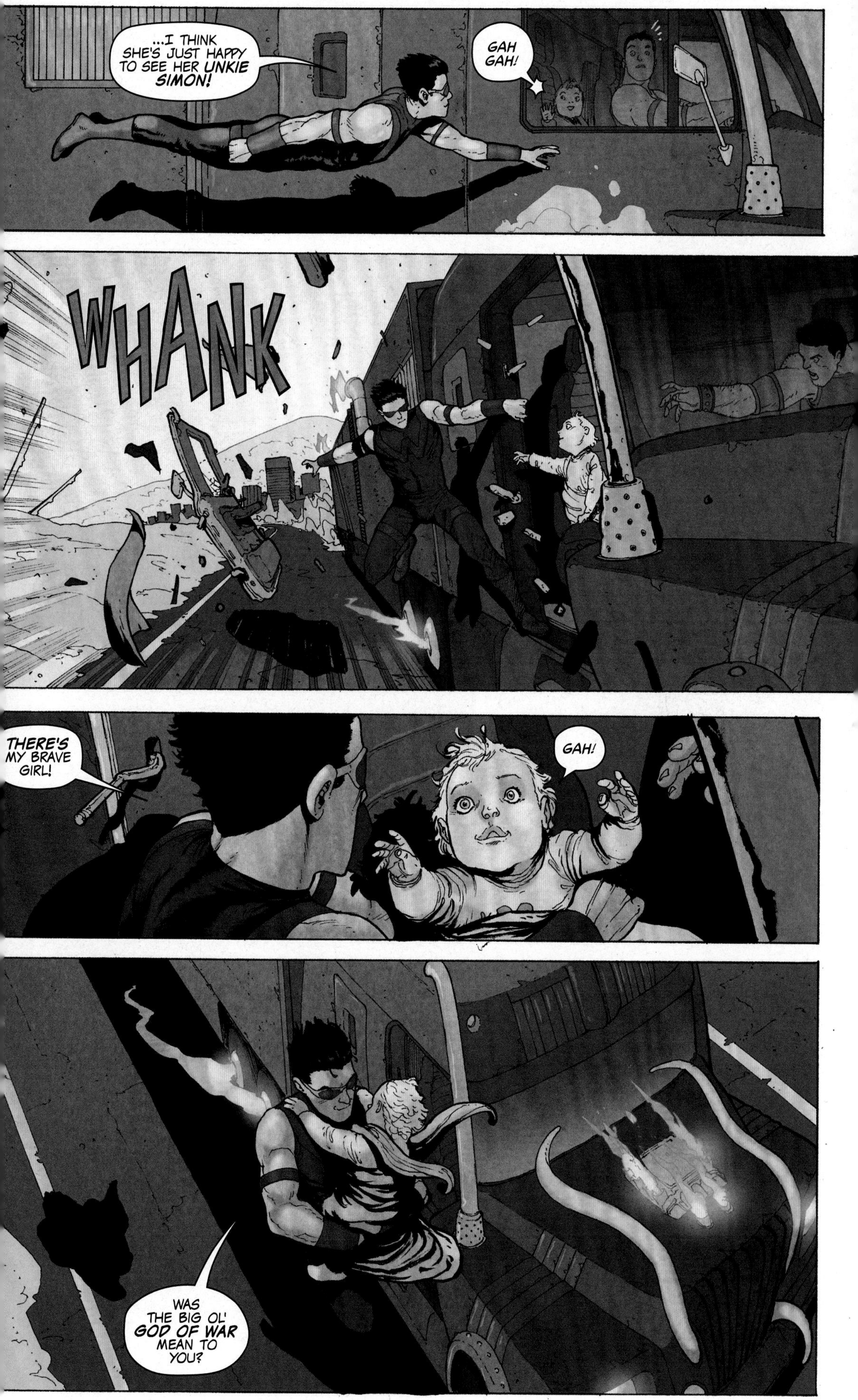
...I THINK SHE'S JUST HAPPY TO SEE HER UNKIE SIMON!
GAH GAH!
WHANK
THERE'S MY BRAVE GIRL!
GAH!
WAS THE BIG OL' GOD OF WAR MEAN TO YOU?

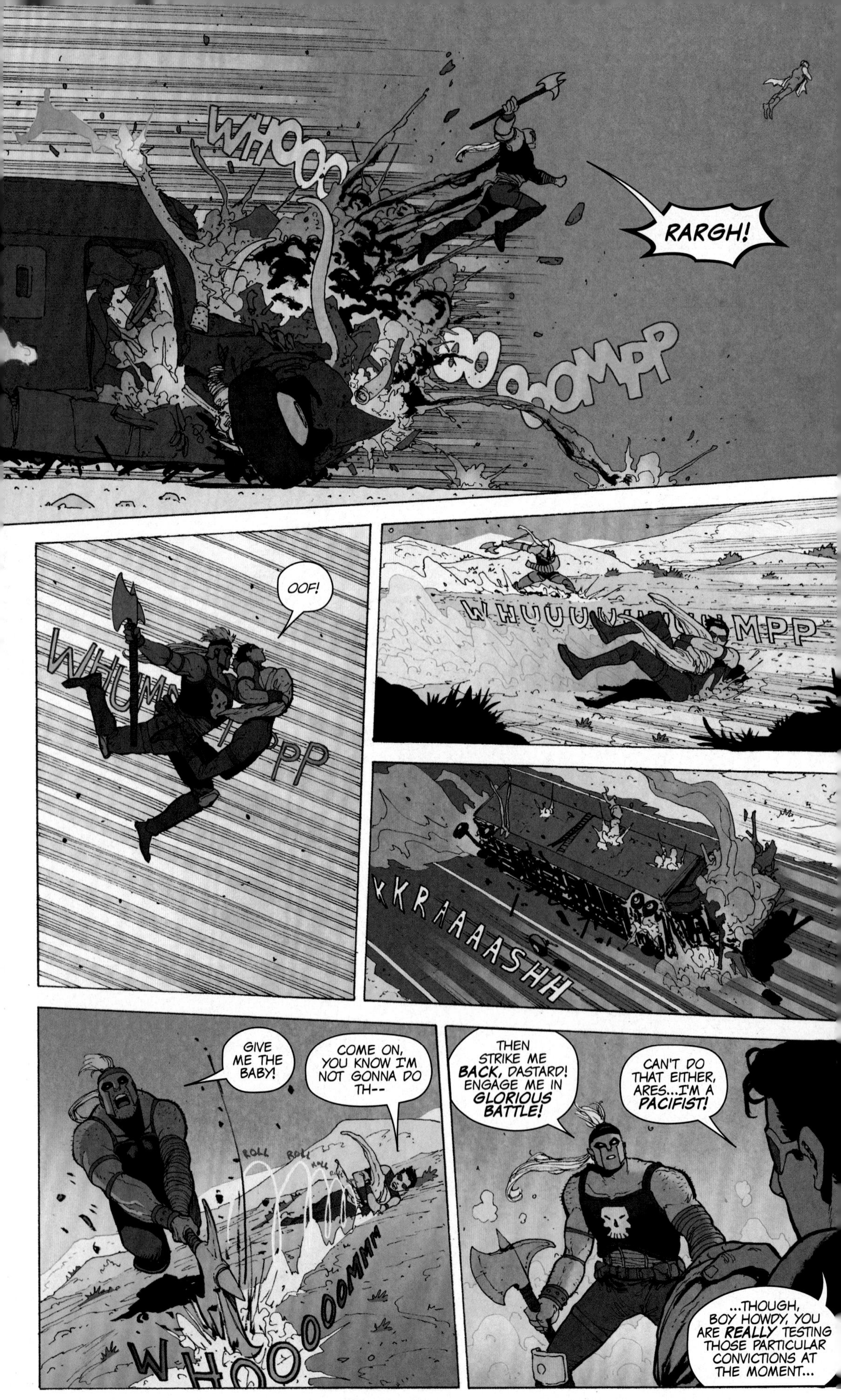
WHOOO
BOOOOMPP
RARGH!
WHUMPP
OOF!
WHUUUUUUUUUMPP
KKRAAAAASHH
GIVE ME THE BABY!
COME ON, YOU KNOW I'M NOT GONNA DO TH--
WHOOOOOOMMM
THEN STRIKE ME BACK, DASTARD! ENGAGE ME IN GLORIOUS BATTLE!
CAN'T DO THAT EITHER, ARES...I'M A PACIFIST!
...THOUGH, BOY HOWDY, YOU ARE REALLY TESTING THOSE PARTICULAR CONVICTIONS AT THE MOMENT...

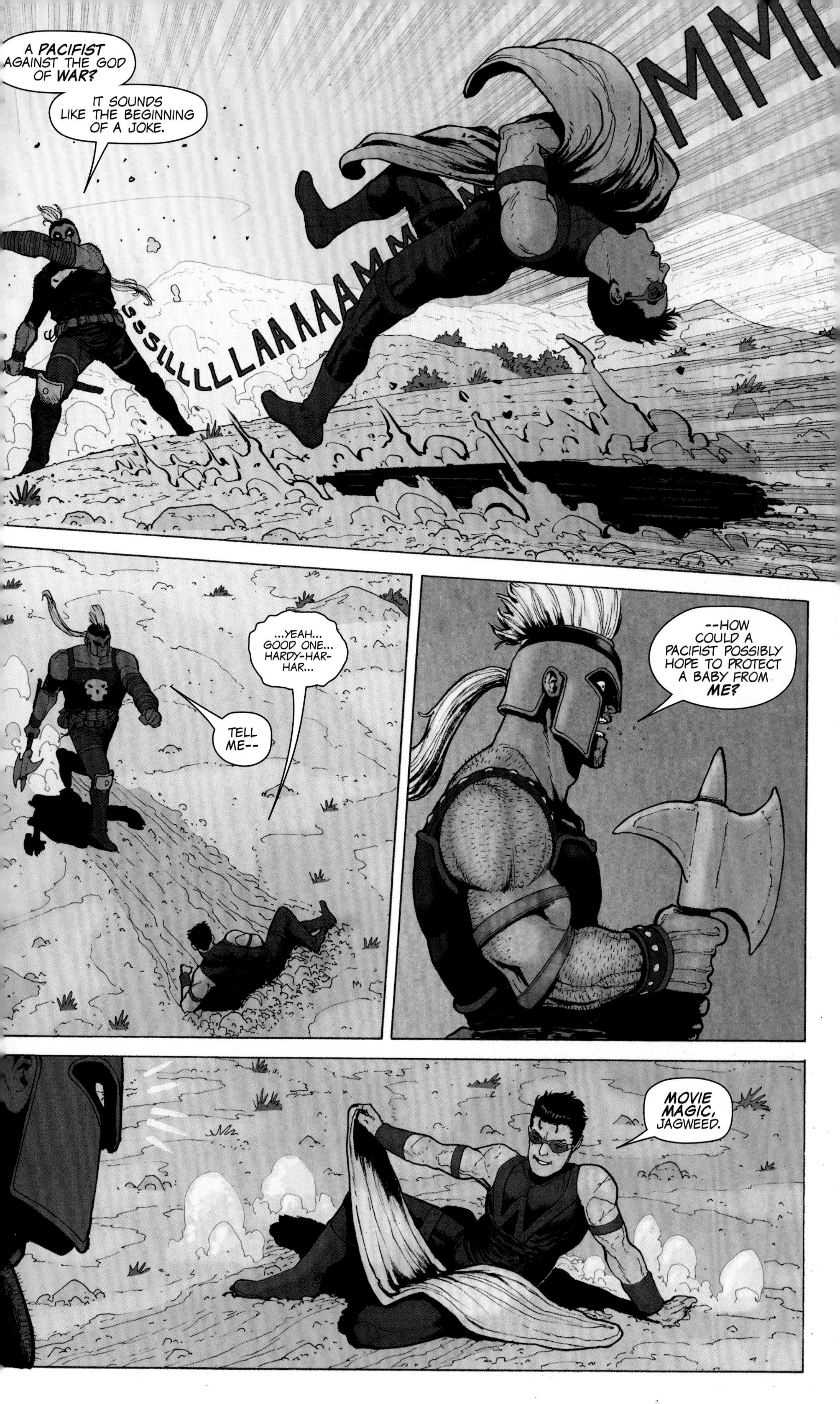
A PACIFIST AGAINST THE GOD OF WAR?
IT SOUNDS LIKE THE BEGINNING OF A JOKE.
SSSILLLLLLAAAAAAMMMMM
TELL ME--
...YEAH... GOOD ONE... HARDY-HAR-HAR...
--HOW COULD A PACIFIST POSSIBLY HOPE TO PROTECT A BABY FROM ME?
MOVIE MAGIC, JAGWEED.

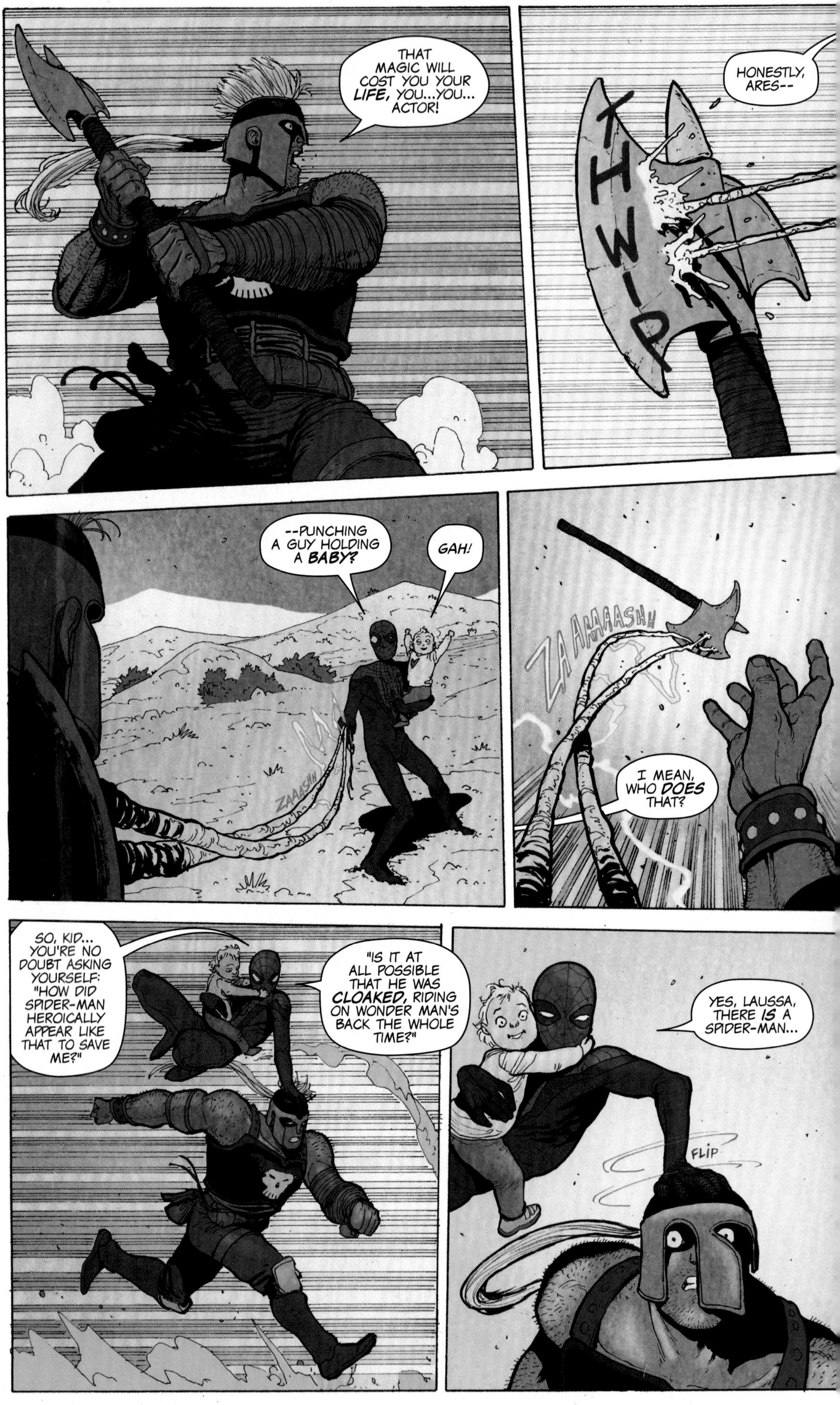
THAT MAGIC WILL COST YOU YOUR LIFE, YOU...YOU... ACTOR!
HONESTLY, ARES--
THWIP
--PUNCHING A GUY HOLDING A BABY?
GAH!
ZAAASHH
ZAAAAAASHH
I MEAN, WHO DOES THAT?
SO, KID... YOU'RE NO DOUBT ASKING YOURSELF: "HOW DID SPIDER-MAN HEROICALLY APPEAR LIKE THAT TO SAVE ME?"
"IS IT AT ALL POSSIBLE THAT HE WAS CLOAKED, RIDING ON WONDER MAN'S BACK THE WHOLE TIME?"
YES, LAUSSA, THERE IS A SPIDER-MAN...
FLIP

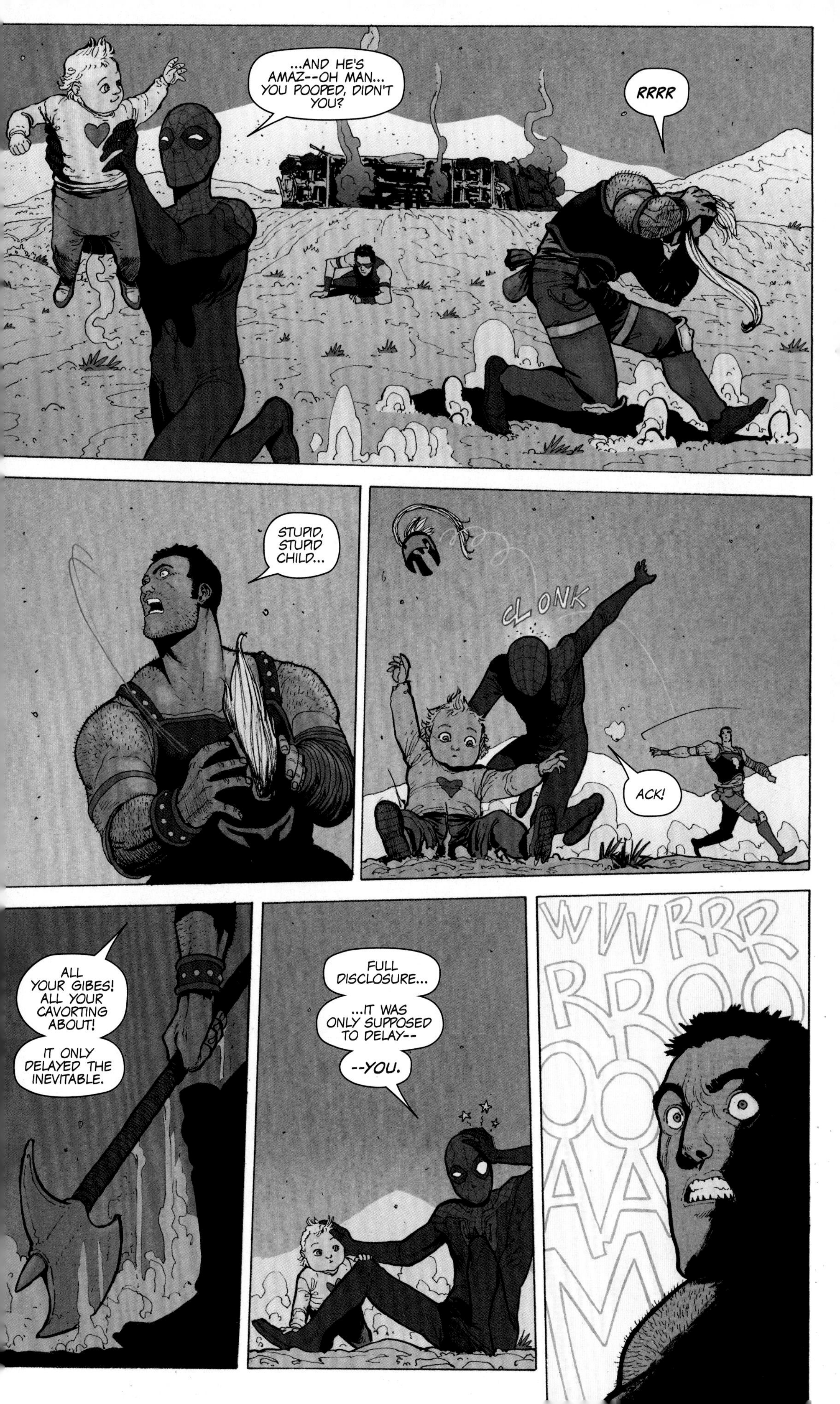
...AND HE'S AMAZ--OH MAN... YOU POOPED, DIDN'T YOU?
RRRR
STUPID, STUPID CHILD...
CLONK
ACK!
ALL YOUR GIBES! ALL YOUR CAVORTING ABOUT!
IT ONLY DELAYED THE INEVITABLE.
FULL DISCLOSURE...
...IT WAS ONLY SUPPOSED TO DELAY--
--YOU.
WVVRRR RROOOOAAM

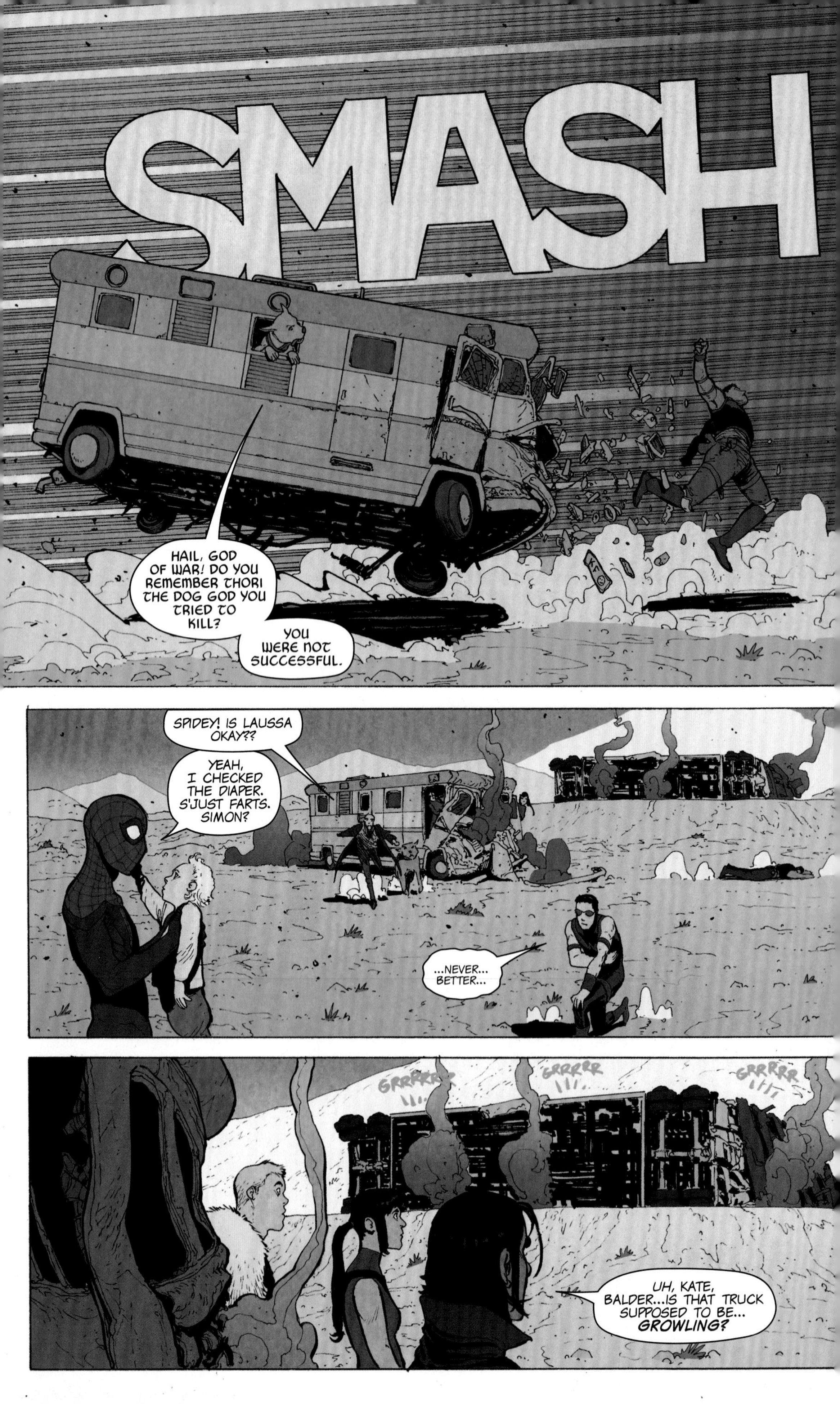
SMASH
HAIL, GOD OF WAR! DO YOU REMEMBER THORI THE DOG GOD YOU TRIED TO KILL?
YOU WERE NOT SUCCESSFUL.
SPIDEY! IS LAUSSA OKAY??
YEAH, I CHECKED THE DIAPER. S'JUST FARTS. SIMON?
...NEVER... BETTER...
GRRRRRR
GRRRRR
GRRRRRR
UH, KATE, BALDER...IS THAT TRUCK SUPPOSED TO BE... **GROWLING?**

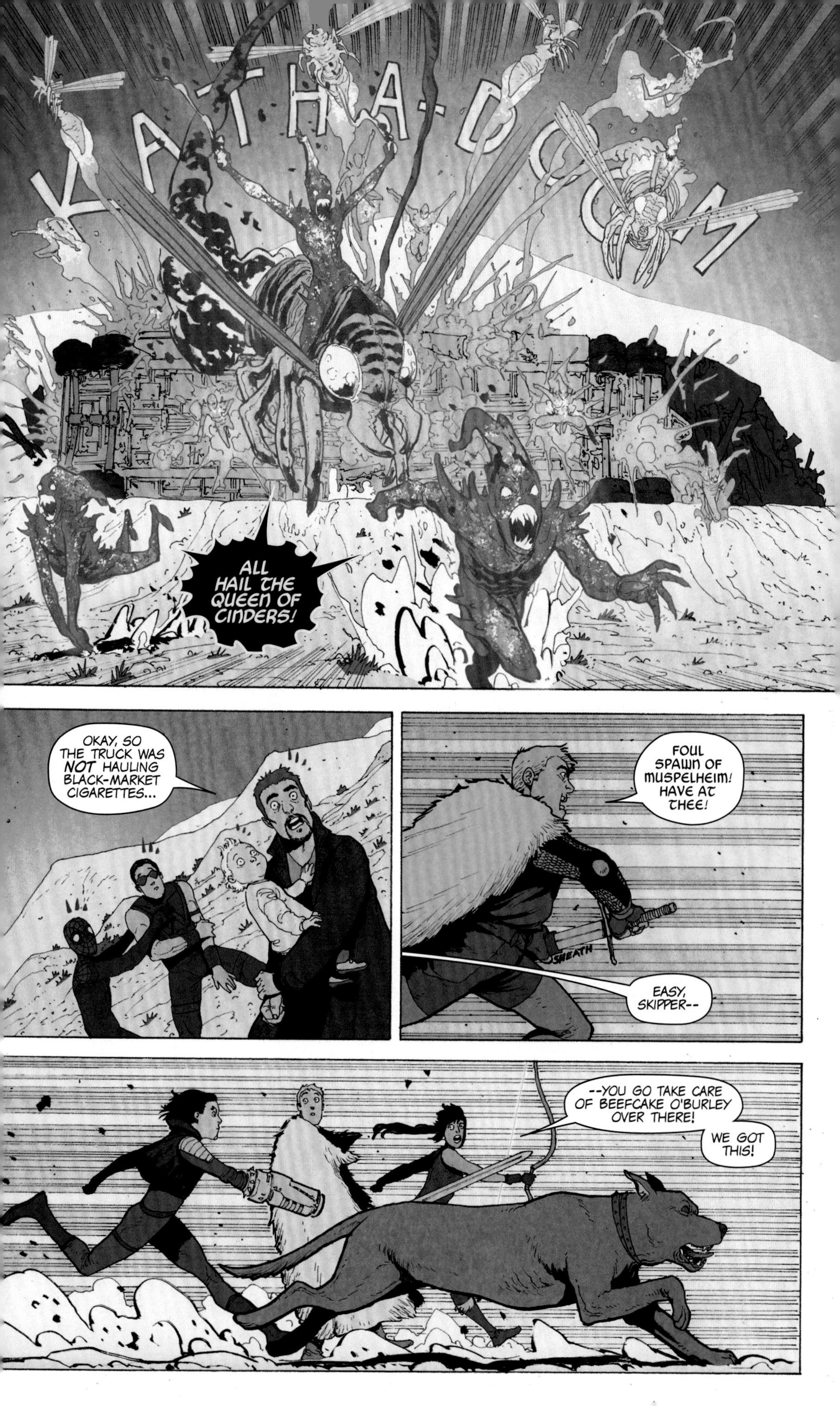

KATHADOOM
ALL HAIL THE QUEEN OF CINDERS!
OKAY, SO THE TRUCK WAS NOT HAULING BLACK-MARKET CIGARETTES...
FOUL SPAWN OF MUSPELHEIM! HAVE AT THEE!
SHEATH
EASY, SKIPPER--
--YOU GO TAKE CARE OF BEEFCAKE O'BURLEY OVER THERE!
WE GOT THIS!

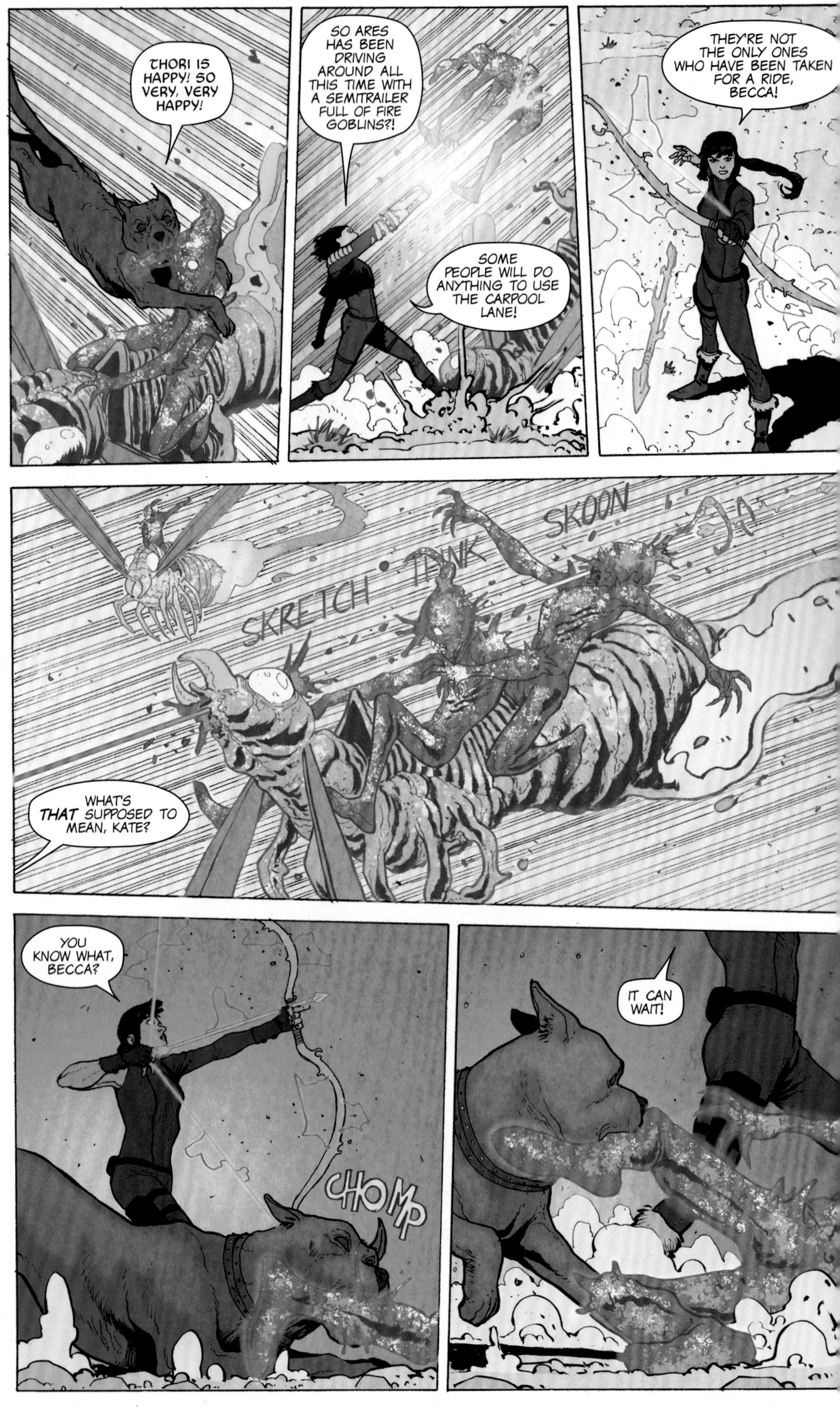
THORI IS HAPPY! SO VERY, VERY HAPPY!
SO ARES HAS BEEN DRIVING AROUND ALL THIS TIME WITH A SEMITRAILER FULL OF FIRE GOBLINS?!
SOME PEOPLE WILL DO ANYTHING TO USE THE CARPOOL LANE!
THEY'RE NOT THE ONLY ONES WHO HAVE BEEN TAKEN FOR A RIDE, BECCA!
SKOON
TINK
SKRETCH
WHAT'S THAT SUPPOSED TO MEAN, KATE?
YOU KNOW WHAT, BECCA?
CHOMP
IT CAN WAIT!

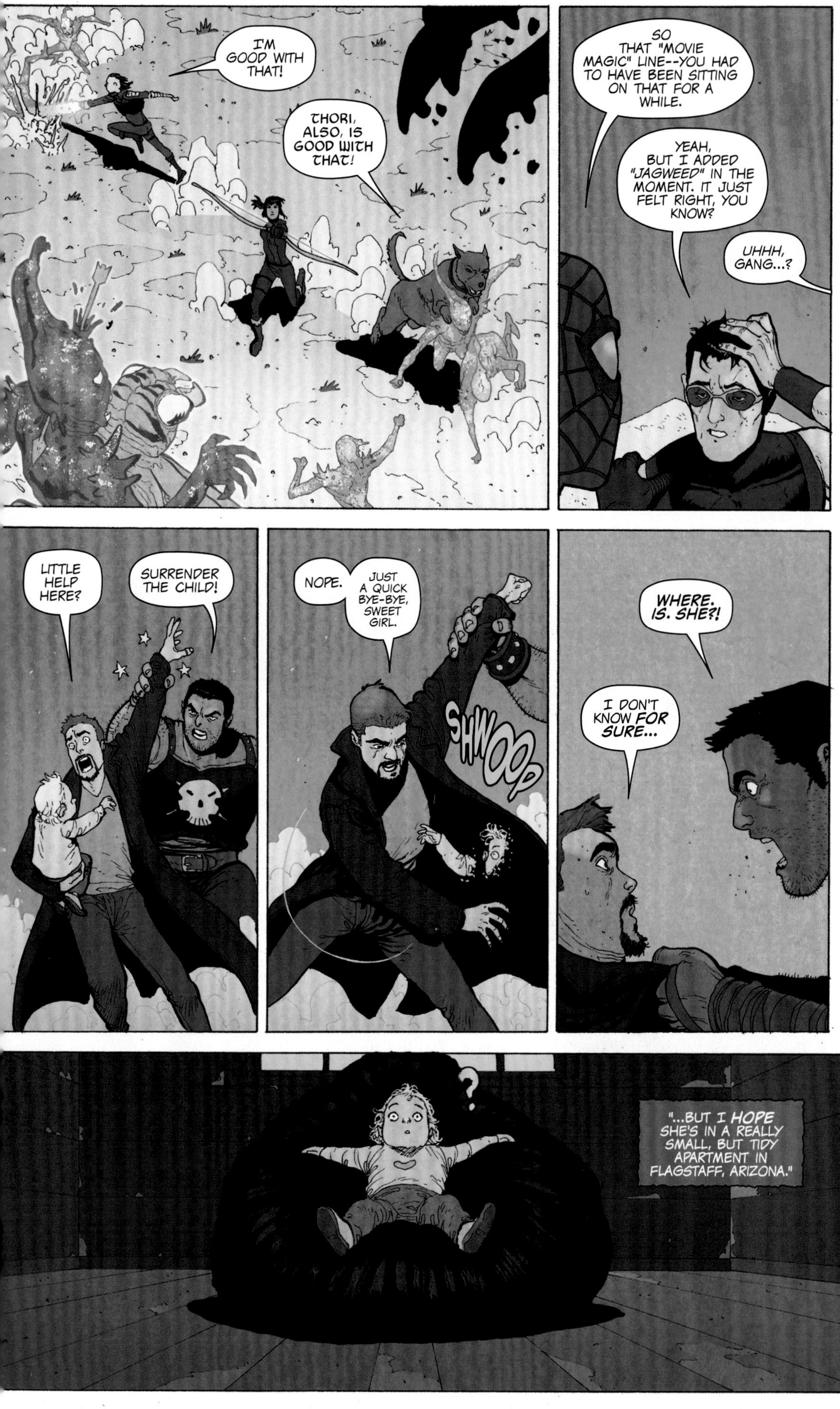
I'M GOOD WITH THAT!
THORI, ALSO, IS GOOD WITH THAT!
SO THAT "MOVIE MAGIC" LINE--YOU HAD TO HAVE BEEN SITTING ON THAT FOR A WHILE.
YEAH, BUT I ADDED "JAGWEED" IN THE MOMENT. IT JUST FELT RIGHT, YOU KNOW?
UHHH, GANG...?
LITTLE HELP HERE?
SURRENDER THE CHILD!
NOPE.
JUST A QUICK BYE-BYE, SWEET GIRL.
SHWOOP
WHERE. IS. SHE?!
I DON'T KNOW FOR SURE...
"...BUT I HOPE SHE'S IN A REALLY SMALL, BUT TIDY APARTMENT IN FLAGSTAFF, ARIZONA."

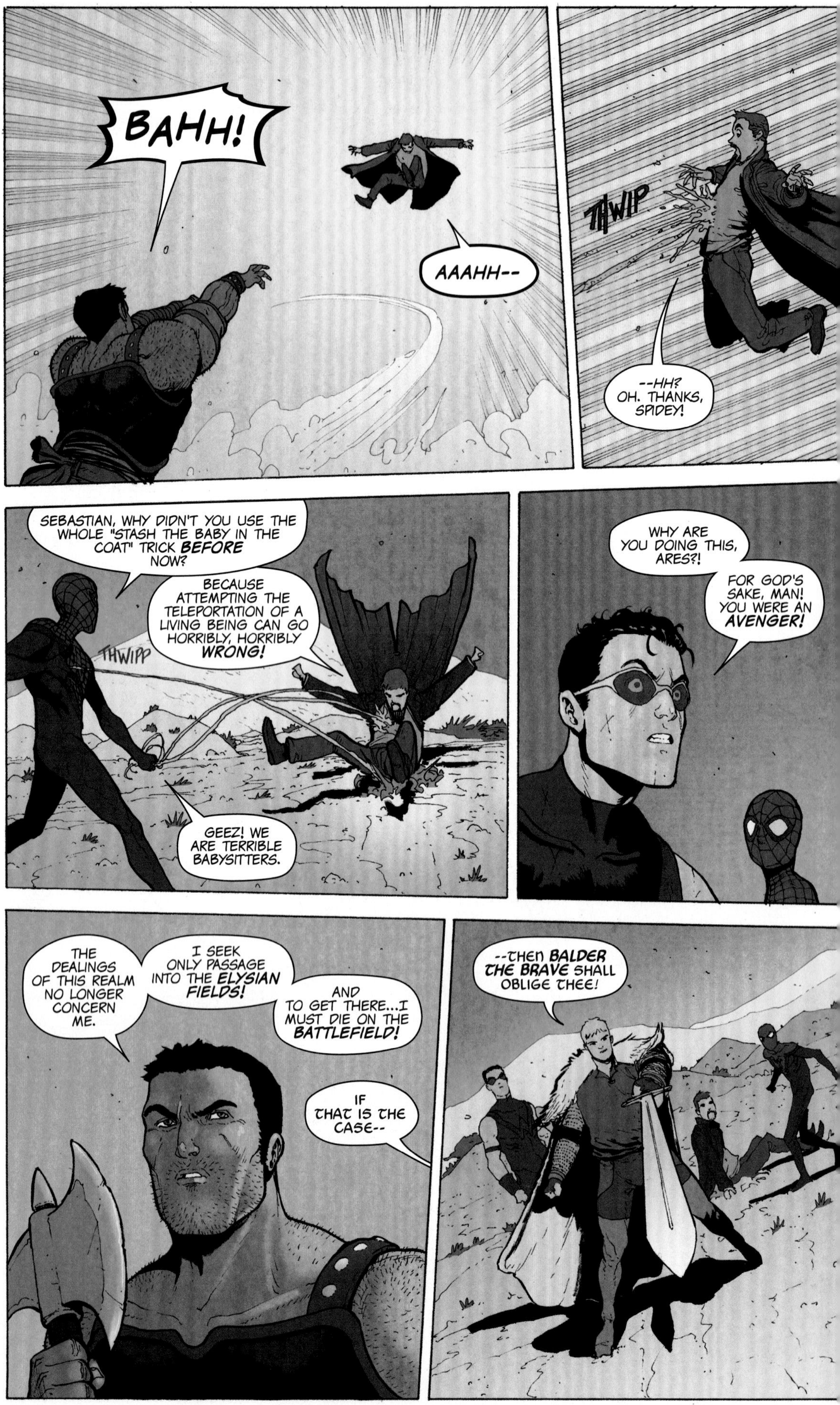

BAHH!
AAAHH--
THWIP
--HH? OH. THANKS, SPIDEY!
SEBASTIAN, WHY DIDN'T YOU USE THE WHOLE "STASH THE BABY IN THE COAT" TRICK BEFORE NOW?
BECAUSE ATTEMPTING THE TELEPORTATION OF A LIVING BEING CAN GO HORRIBLY, HORRIBLY WRONG!
THWIPP
GEEZ! WE ARE TERRIBLE BABYSITTERS.
WHY ARE YOU DOING THIS, ARES?!
FOR GOD'S SAKE, MAN! YOU WERE AN AVENGER!
THE DEALINGS OF THIS REALM NO LONGER CONCERN ME.
I SEEK ONLY PASSAGE INTO THE ELYSIAN FIELDS!
AND TO GET THERE...I MUST DIE ON THE BATTLEFIELD!
IF THAT IS THE CASE--
--THEN BALDER THE BRAVE SHALL OBLIGE THEE!

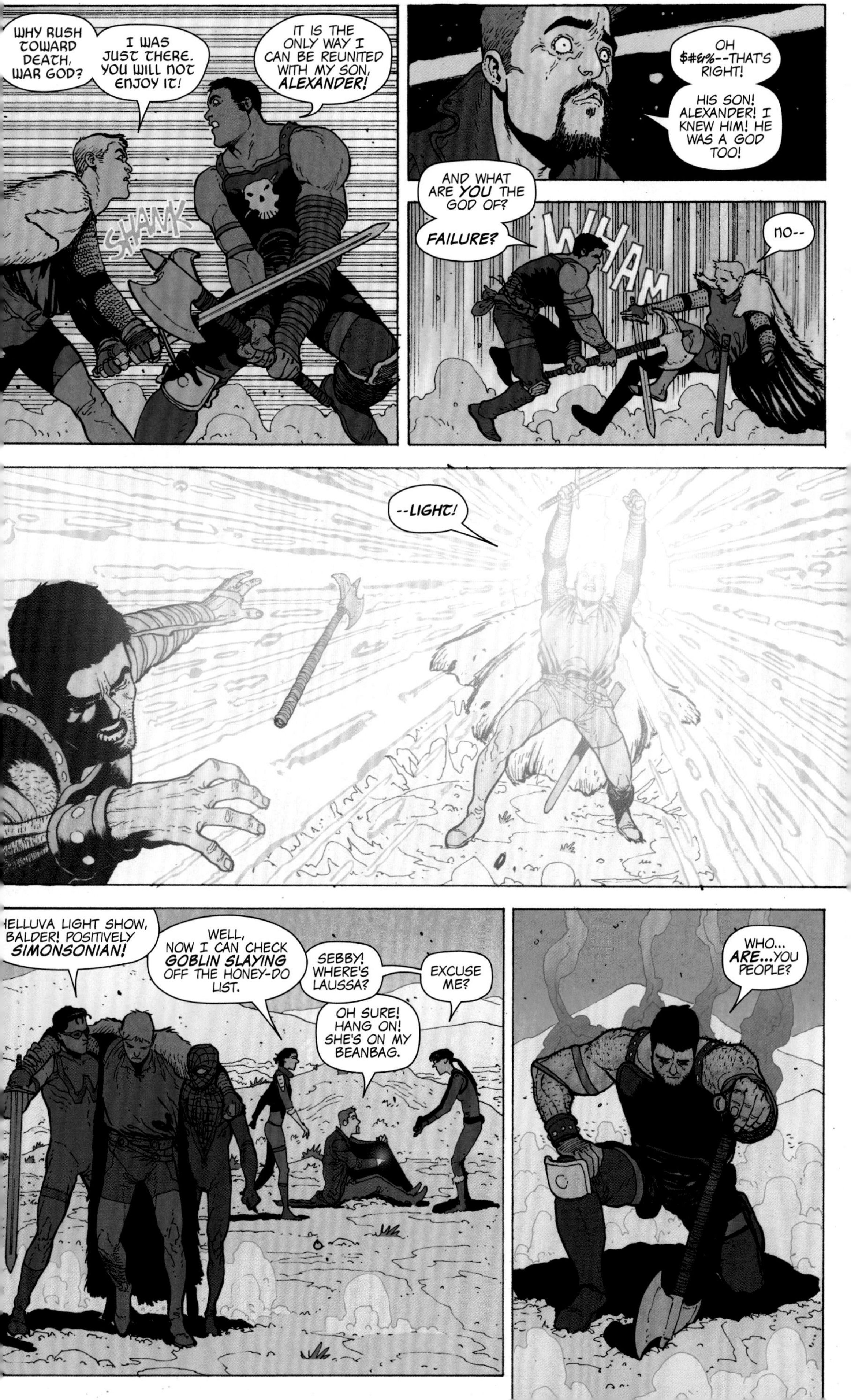
WHY RUSH TOWARD DEATH, WAR GOD?
I WAS JUST THERE. YOU WILL NOT ENJOY IT!
IT IS THE ONLY WAY I CAN BE REUNITED WITH MY SON, ALEXANDER!
SHANK
OH $#£!%--THAT'S RIGHT!
HIS SON! ALEXANDER! I KNEW HIM! HE WAS A GOD TOO!
AND WHAT ARE YOU THE GOD OF?
FAILURE?
WHAM
no--
--LIGHT!
HELLUVA LIGHT SHOW, BALDER! POSITIVELY SIMONSONIAN!
WELL, NOW I CAN CHECK GOBLIN SLAYING OFF THE HONEY-DO LIST.
SEBBY! WHERE'S LAUSSA?
EXCUSE ME?
OH SURE! HANG ON! SHE'S ON MY BEANBAG.
WHO... ARE...YOU PEOPLE?

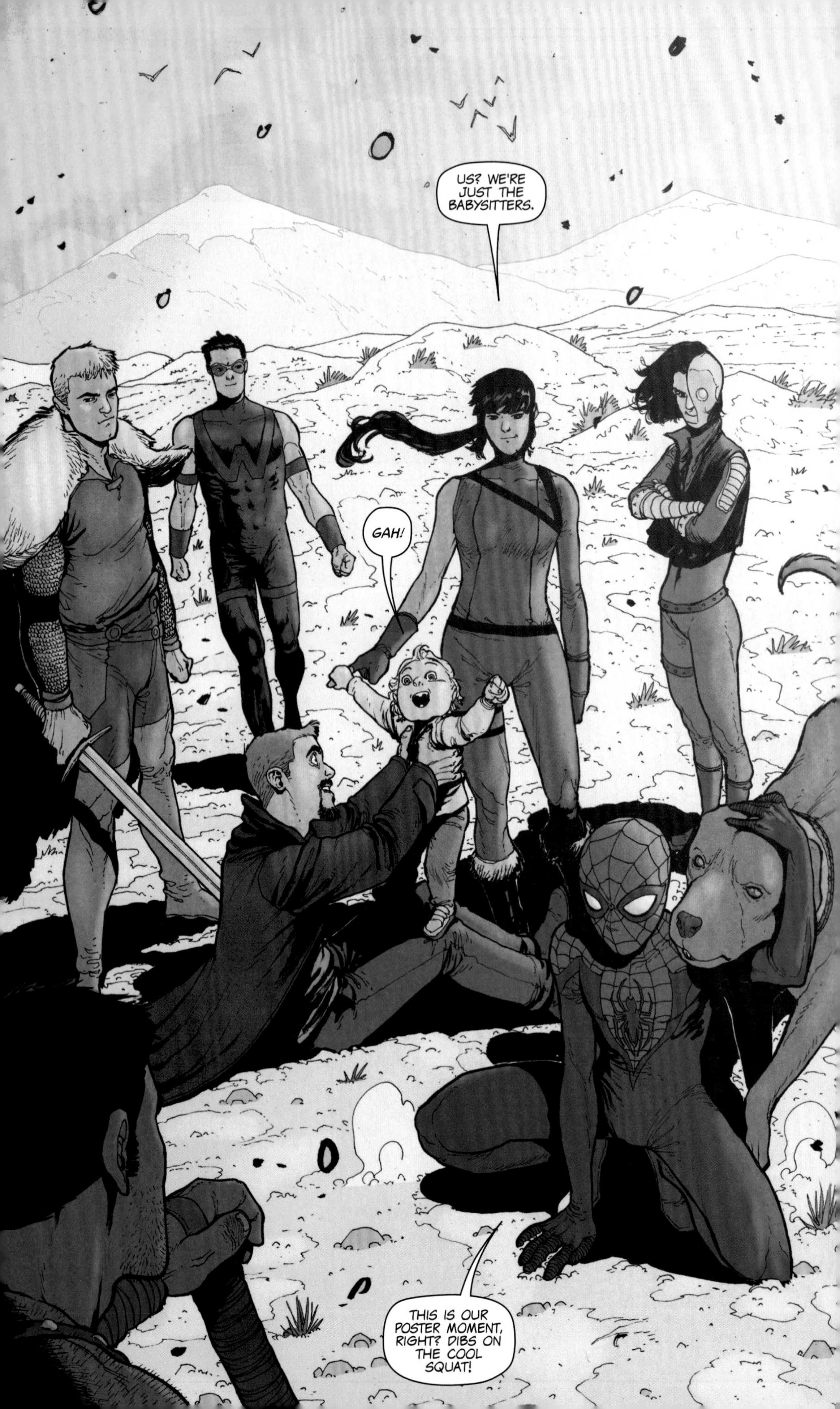
US? WE'RE JUST THE BABYSITTERS.
GAH!
THIS IS OUR POSTER MOMENT, RIGHT? DIBS ON THE COOL SQUAT!

IT MATTERS... NOT...

I WAS GUIDED BY *DIVINE PROVIDENCE* TO THIS PLACE, AT THIS MOMENT, AND PROMISED BY THE QUEEN OF CINDERS--

ACTUALLY...

...THAT WAS *ME!*

MORE DEMONS! THORI IS SO VERY TIRED OF DEMONS.

DEMON *RIDER,* THORI. WE MET THIS ONE, REMEMBER?

HELLO AGAIN, SEBASTIAN DRUID.

HI-HO, KUSHALA.

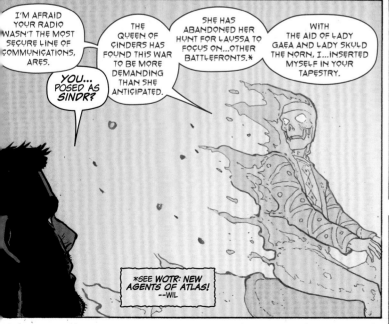

I'M AFRAID YOUR RADIO WASN'T THE MOST SECURE LINE OF COMMUNICATIONS, ARES.

YOU... POSED AS *SINDR?*

THE QUEEN OF CINDERS HAS FOUND THIS WAR TO BE MORE DEMANDING THAN SHE ANTICIPATED.

SHE HAS ABANDONED HER HUNT FOR LAUSSA TO FOCUS ON...OTHER BATTLEFRONTS.*

WITH THE AID OF LADY GAEA AND LADY SKULD THE NORN, I...INSERTED MYSELF IN YOUR TAPESTRY.

*SEE WOTR: NEW AGENTS OF ATLAS! --WIL

BUT WHY?

BECAUSE SHE ASKED ME TO.

SINDR?

NO...

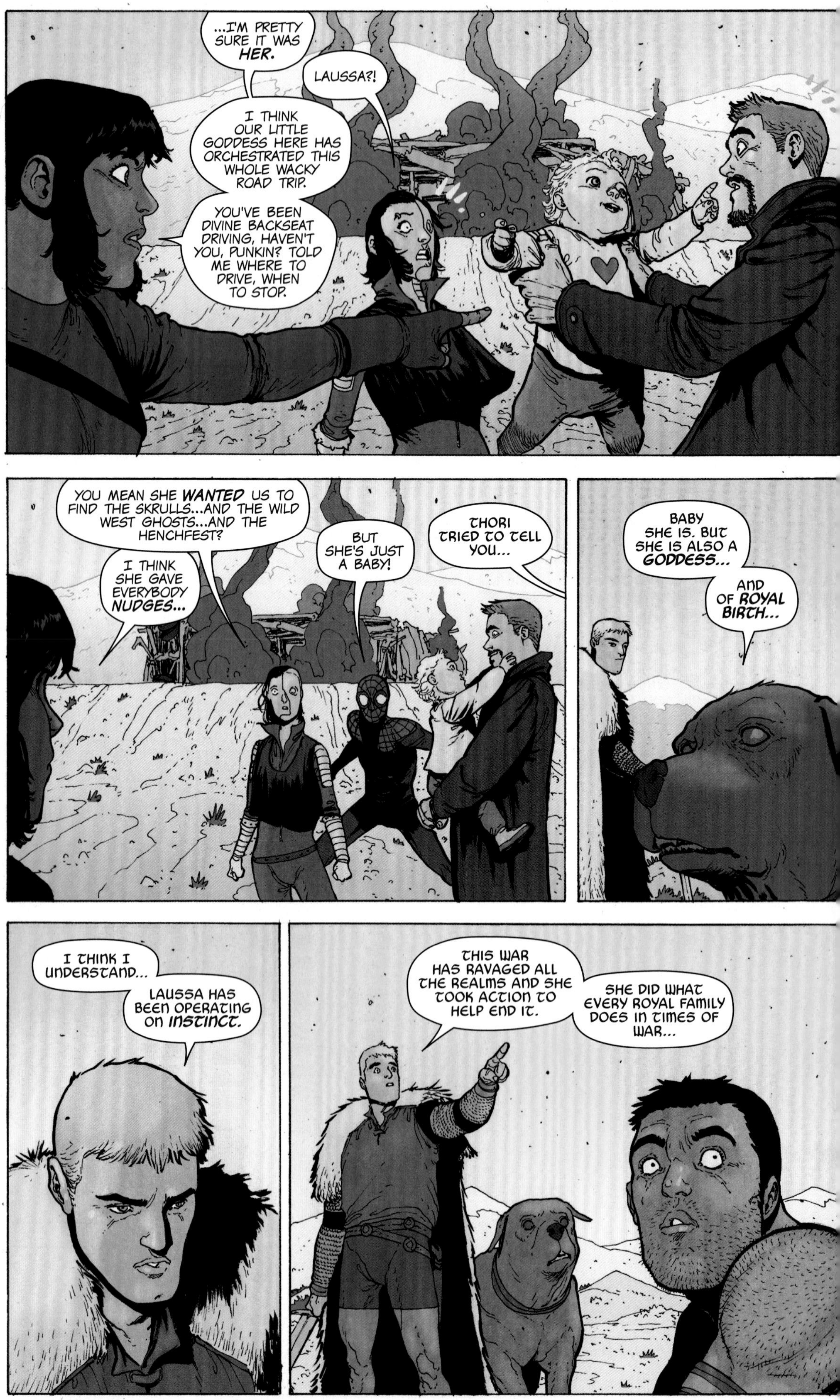
...I'M PRETTY SURE IT WAS HER.
LAUSSA?!
I THINK OUR LITTLE GODDESS HERE HAS ORCHESTRATED THIS WHOLE WACKY ROAD TRIP.
YOU'VE BEEN DIVINE BACKSEAT DRIVING, HAVEN'T YOU, PUNKIN? TOLD ME WHERE TO DRIVE, WHEN TO STOP.
YOU MEAN SHE WANTED US TO FIND THE SKRULLS...AND THE WILD WEST GHOSTS...AND THE HENCHFEST?
I THINK SHE GAVE EVERYBODY NUDGES...
BUT SHE'S JUST A BABY!
THORI TRIED TO TELL YOU...
BABY SHE IS. BUT SHE IS ALSO A GODDESS...
AND OF ROYAL BIRTH...
I THINK I UNDERSTAND...
LAUSSA HAS BEEN OPERATING ON INSTINCT.
THIS WAR HAS RAVAGED ALL THE REALMS AND SHE TOOK ACTION TO HELP END IT.
SHE DID WHAT EVERY ROYAL FAMILY DOES IN TIMES OF WAR...

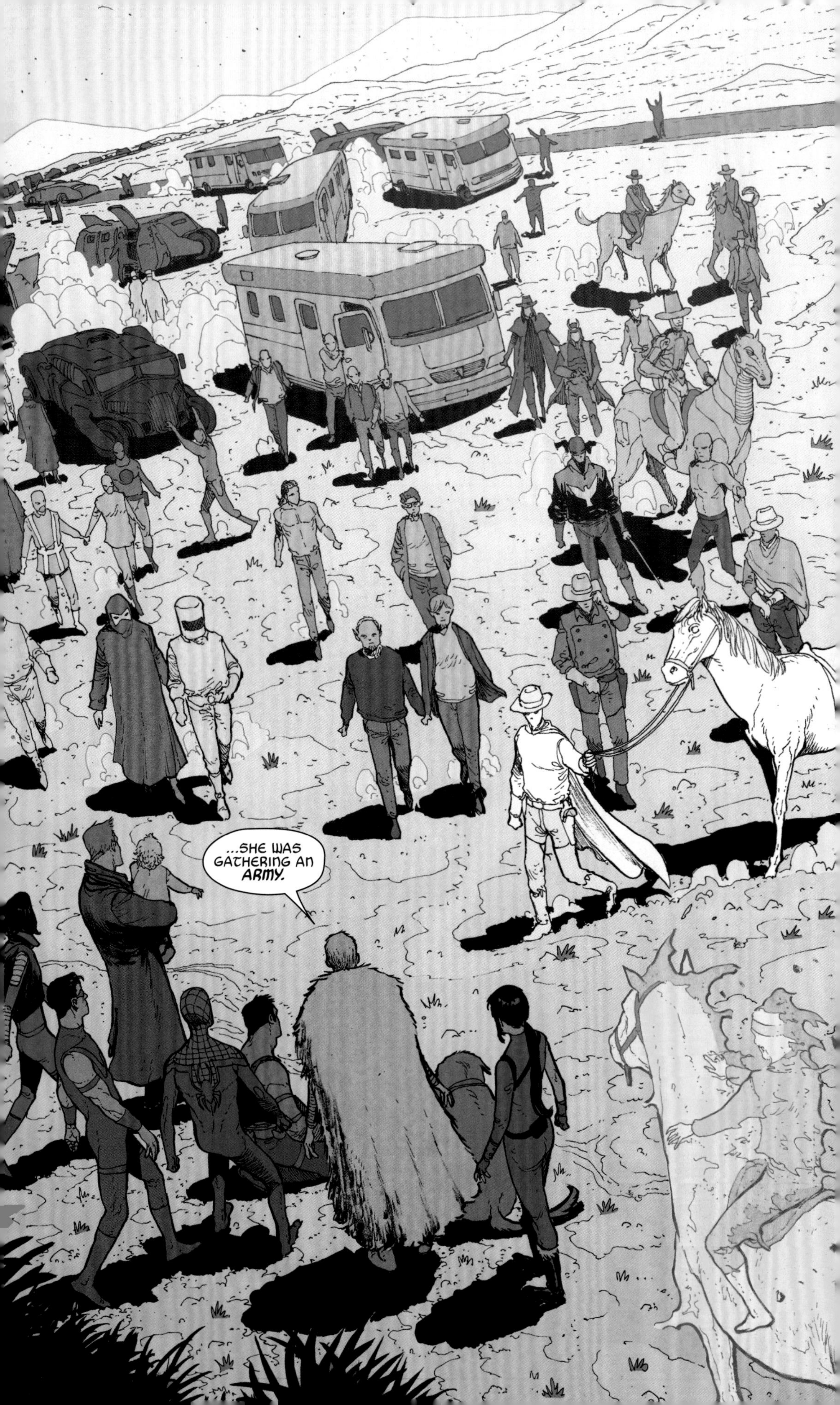
...SHE WAS GATHERING AN ARMY.

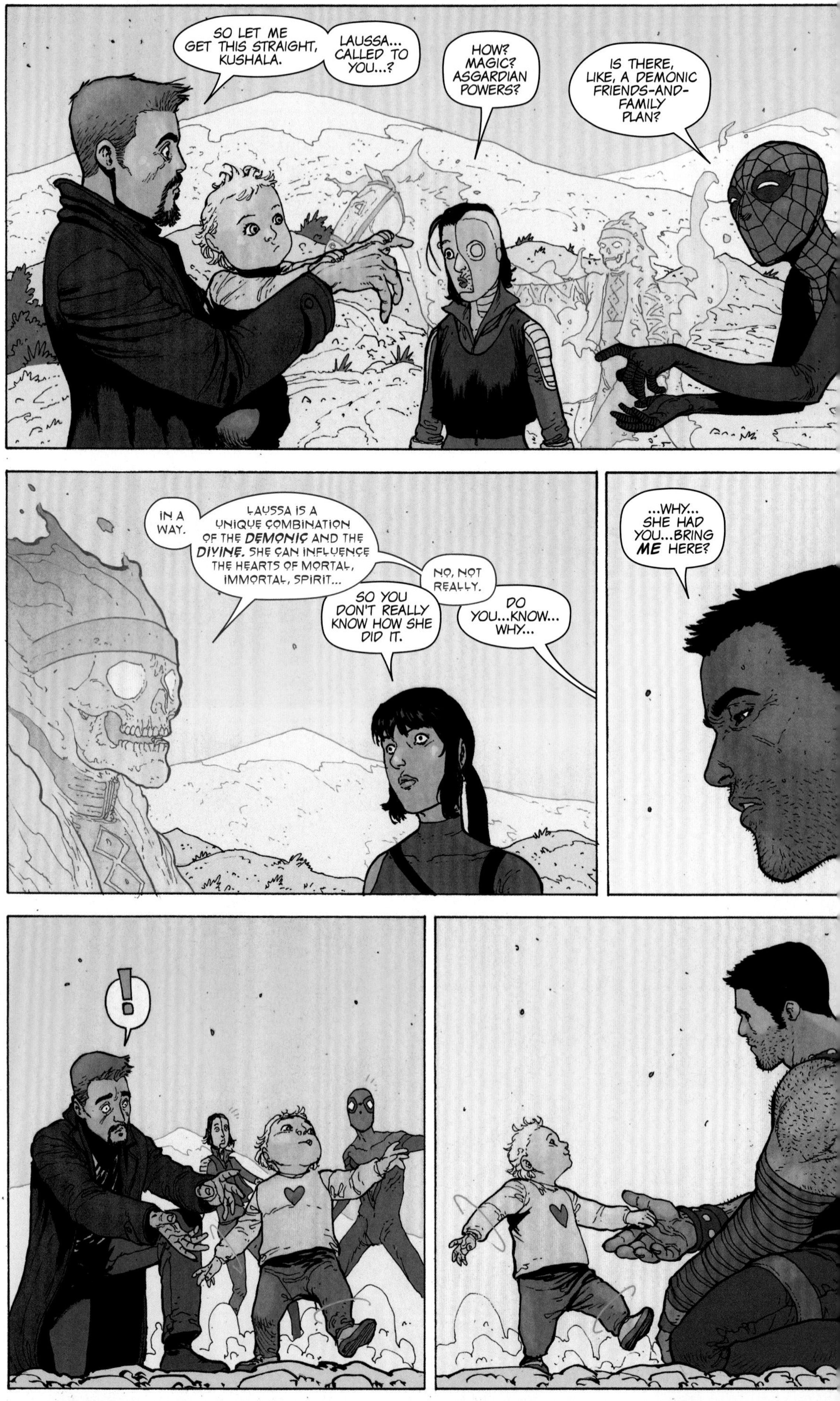

SO LET ME GET THIS STRAIGHT, KUSHALA.
LAUSSA... CALLED TO YOU...?
HOW? MAGIC? ASGARDIAN POWERS?
IS THERE, LIKE, A DEMONIC FRIENDS-AND-FAMILY PLAN?
IN A WAY.
LAUSSA IS A UNIQUE COMBINATION OF THE DEMONIC AND THE DIVINE. SHE CAN INFLUENCE THE HEARTS OF MORTAL, IMMORTAL, SPIRIT...
SO YOU DON'T REALLY KNOW HOW SHE DID IT.
NO, NOT REALLY.
DO YOU...KNOW... WHY...
...WHY... SHE HAD YOU...BRING ME HERE?
!

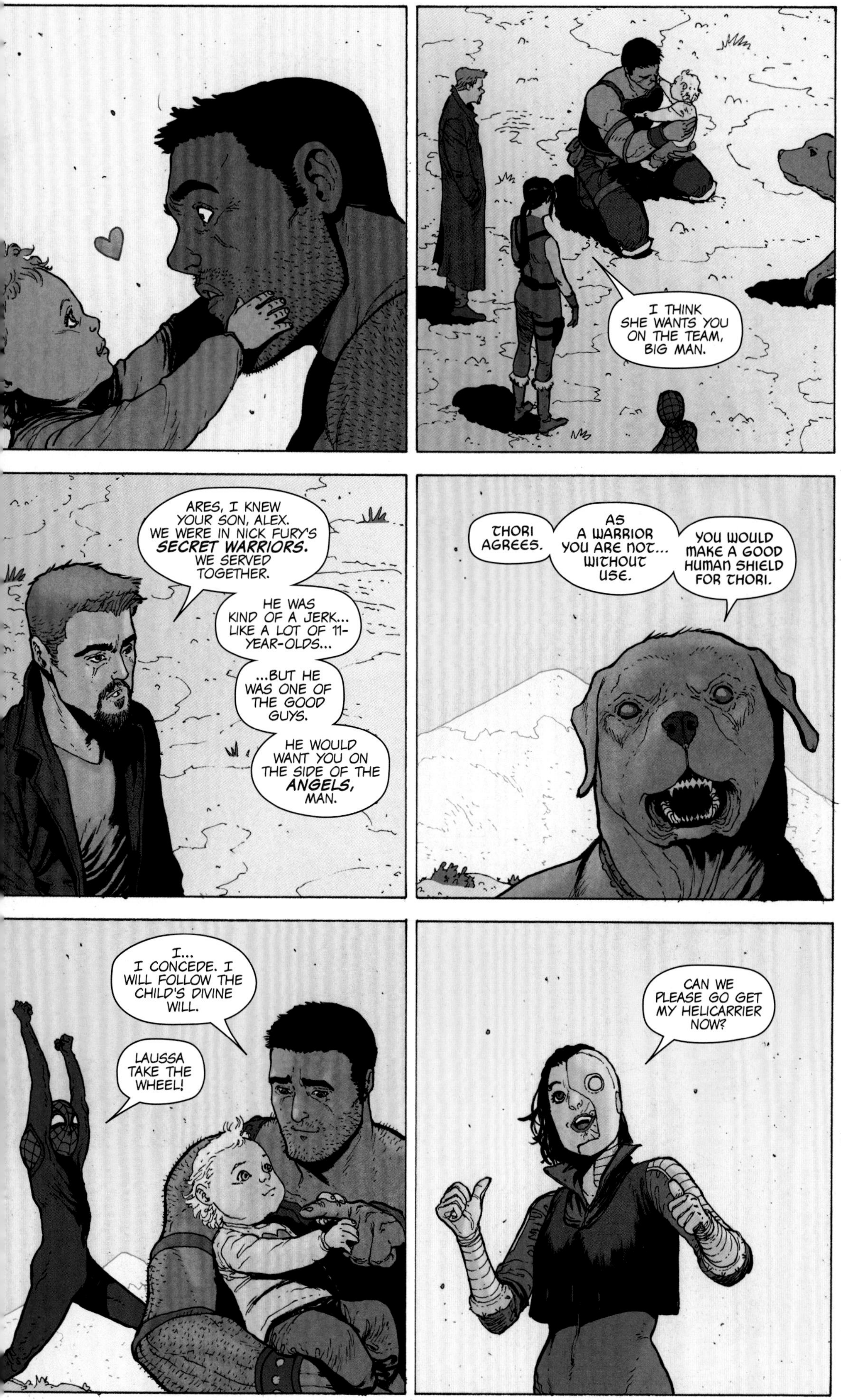

I THINK SHE WANTS YOU ON THE TEAM, BIG MAN.
ARES, I KNEW YOUR SON, ALEX. WE WERE IN NICK FURY'S SECRET WARRIORS. WE SERVED TOGETHER.
HE WAS KIND OF A JERK... LIKE A LOT OF 11-YEAR-OLDS...
...BUT HE WAS ONE OF THE GOOD GUYS.
HE WOULD WANT YOU ON THE SIDE OF THE ANGELS, MAN.
THORI AGREES.
AS A WARRIOR YOU ARE NOT... WITHOUT USE.
YOU WOULD MAKE A GOOD HUMAN SHIELD FOR THORI.
I... I CONCEDE. I WILL FOLLOW THE CHILD'S DIVINE WILL.
LAUSSA TAKE THE WHEEL!
CAN WE PLEASE GO GET MY HELICARRIER NOW?

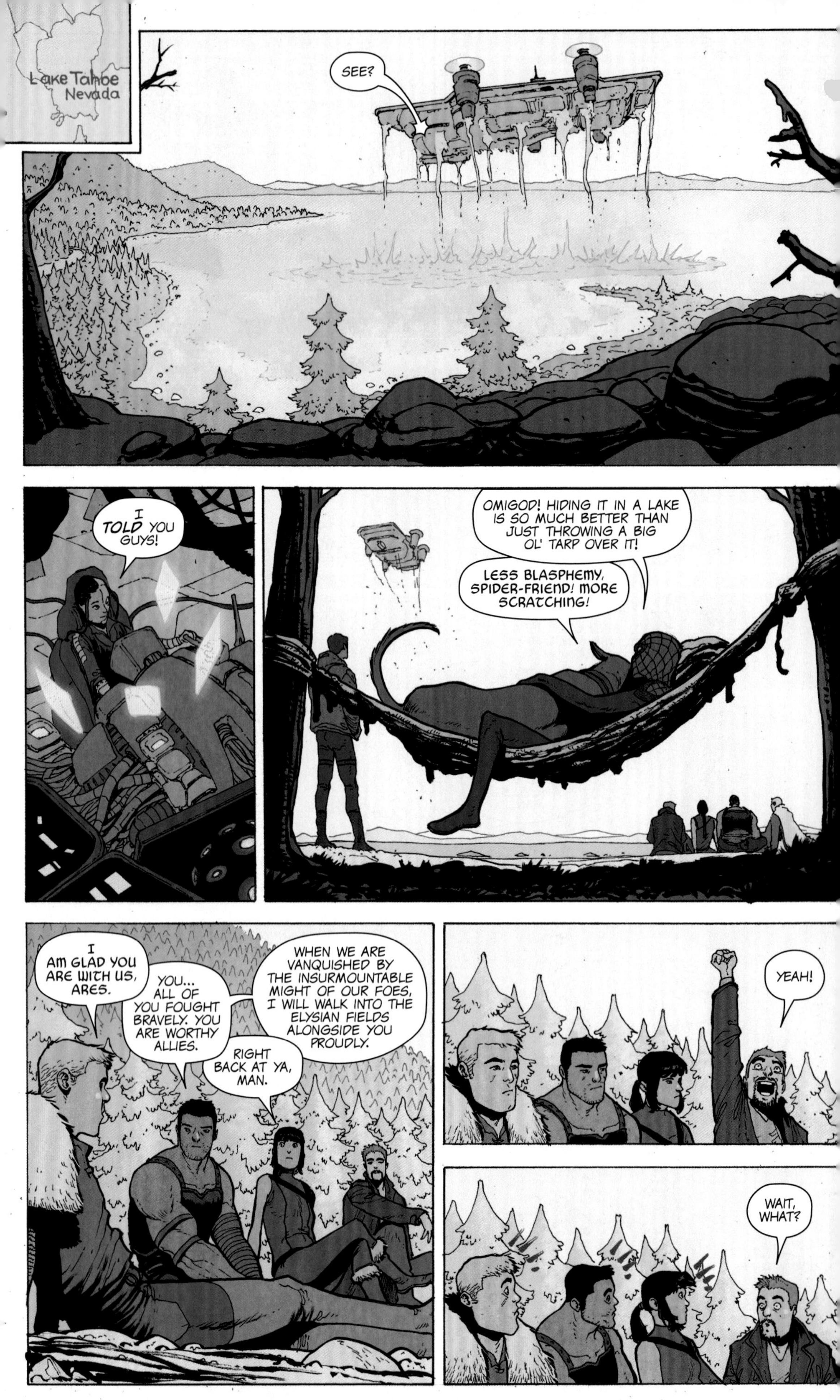
Lake Tahoe
Nevada
SEE?
I TOLD YOU GUYS!
OMIGOD! HIDING IT IN A LAKE IS SO MUCH BETTER THAN JUST THROWING A BIG OL' TARP OVER IT!
LESS BLASPHEMY, SPIDER-FRIEND! MORE SCRATCHING!
I AM GLAD YOU ARE WITH US, ARES.
YOU... ALL OF YOU FOUGHT BRAVELY. YOU ARE WORTHY ALLIES.
RIGHT BACK AT YA, MAN.
WHEN WE ARE VANQUISHED BY THE INSURMOUNTABLE MIGHT OF OUR FOES, I WILL WALK INTO THE ELYSIAN FIELDS ALONGSIDE YOU PROUDLY.
YEAH!
WAIT, WHAT?

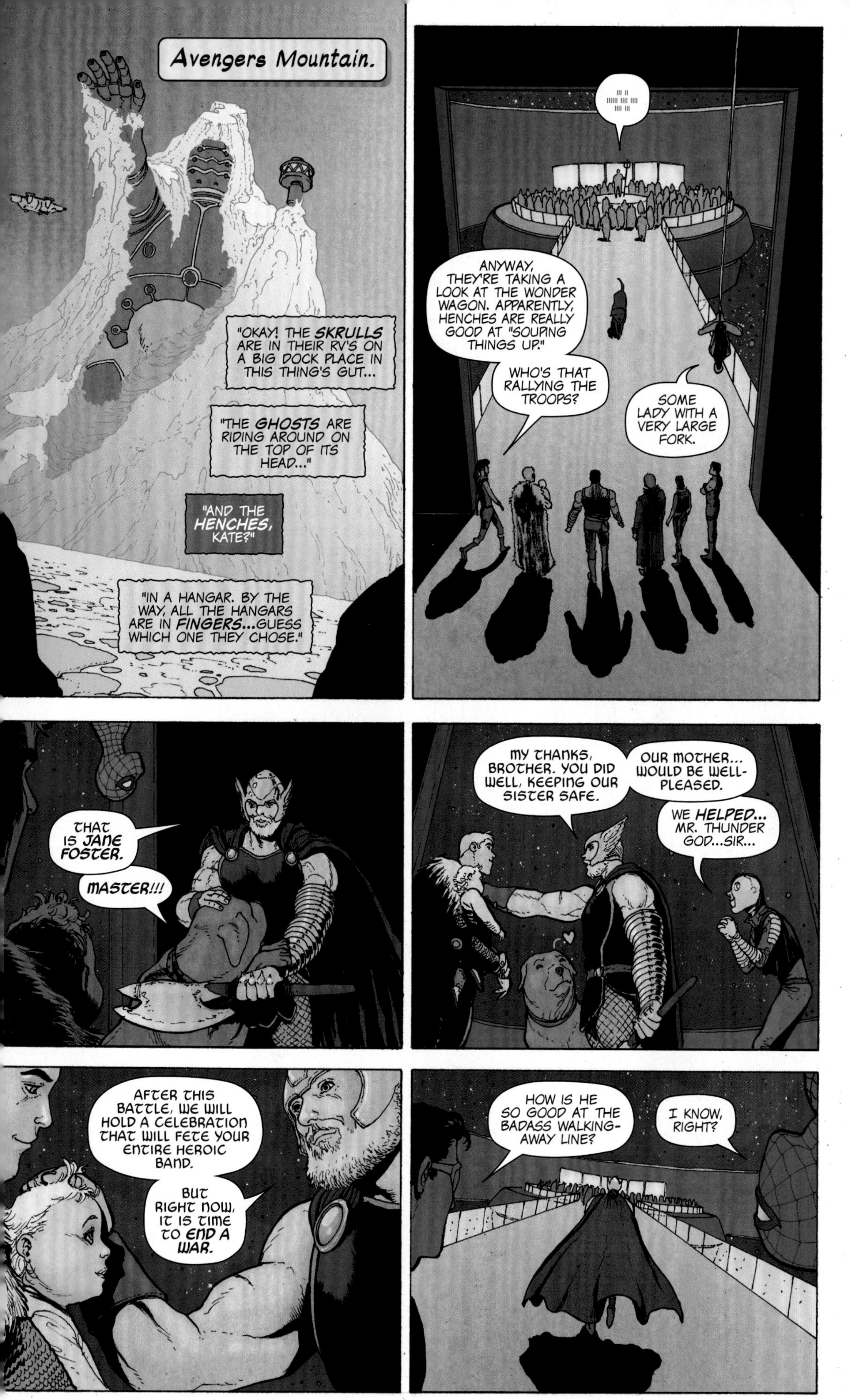
Avengers Mountain.
"OKAY! THE SKRULLS ARE IN THEIR RV'S ON A BIG DOCK PLACE IN THIS THING'S GUT...
"THE GHOSTS ARE RIDING AROUND ON THE TOP OF ITS HEAD..."
"AND THE HENCHES, KATE?"
"IN A HANGAR. BY THE WAY, ALL THE HANGARS ARE IN FINGERS...GUESS WHICH ONE THEY CHOSE."
ANYWAY, THEY'RE TAKING A LOOK AT THE WONDER WAGON. APPARENTLY, HENCHES ARE REALLY GOOD AT "SOUPING THINGS UP."
WHO'S THAT RALLYING THE TROOPS?
SOME LADY WITH A VERY LARGE FORK.
THAT IS JANE FOSTER.
MASTER!!!
MY THANKS, BROTHER. YOU DID WELL, KEEPING OUR SISTER SAFE.
OUR MOTHER... WOULD BE WELL-PLEASED.
WE HELPED... MR. THUNDER GOD...SIR...
AFTER THIS BATTLE, WE WILL HOLD A CELEBRATION THAT WILL FETE YOUR ENTIRE HEROIC BAND.
BUT RIGHT NOW, IT IS TIME TO END A WAR.
HOW IS HE SO GOOD AT THE BADASS WALKING-AWAY LINE?
I KNOW, RIGHT?

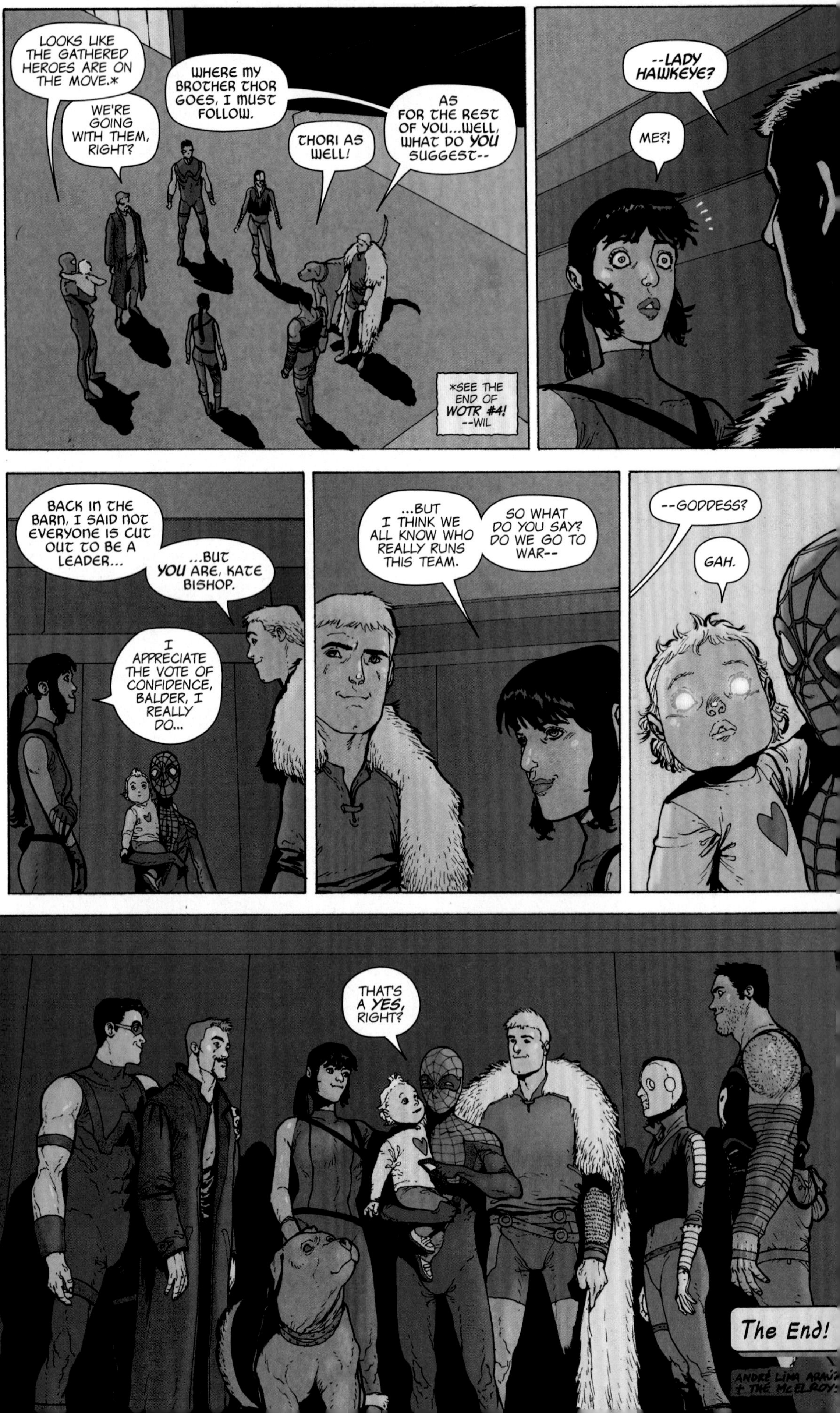
LOOKS LIKE THE GATHERED HEROES ARE ON THE MOVE.*
WE'RE GOING WITH THEM, RIGHT?
WHERE MY BROTHER THOR GOES, I MUST FOLLOW.
THORI AS WELL!
AS FOR THE REST OF YOU...WELL, WHAT DO YOU SUGGEST--
*SEE THE END OF WOTR #4! --WIL
--LADY HAWKEYE?
ME?!
BACK IN THE BARN, I SAID NOT EVERYONE IS CUT OUT TO BE A LEADER...
...BUT YOU ARE, KATE BISHOP.
I APPRECIATE THE VOTE OF CONFIDENCE, BALDER, I REALLY DO...
...BUT I THINK WE ALL KNOW WHO REALLY RUNS THIS TEAM.
SO WHAT DO YOU SAY? DO WE GO TO WAR--
--GODDESS?
GAH.
THAT'S A YES, RIGHT?
The End!
ANDRÉ LIMA ARAÚ
+ THE McELROY

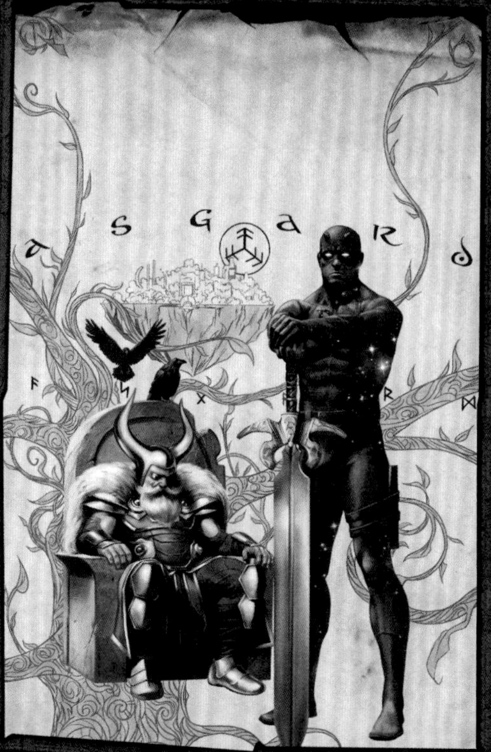
A S G A R D

#1 VARIANT BY
Giuseppe Camuncoli
& Elia Bonetti

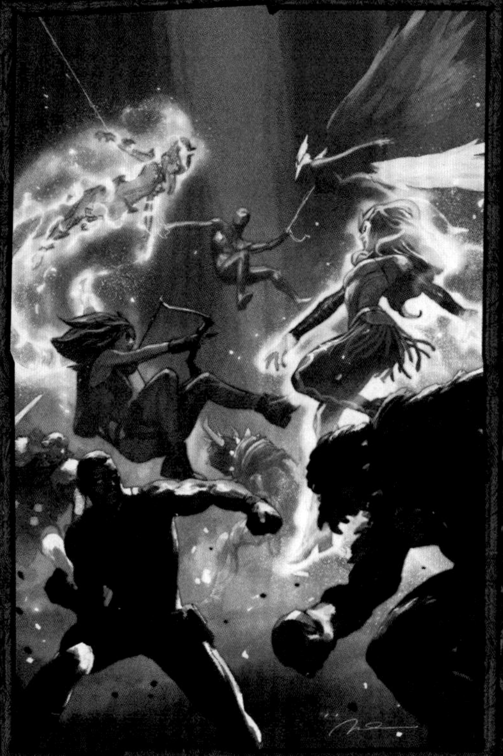

#1 VARIANT BY
Gerald Parel

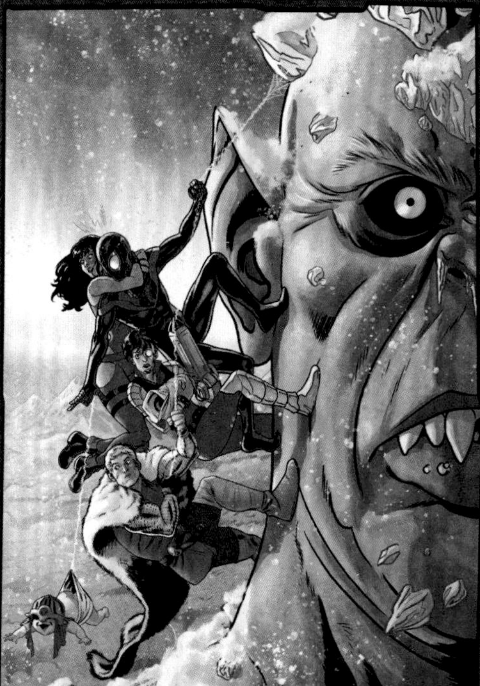

#1 VARIANT BY
Joe Quinones
& Matthew Wilson

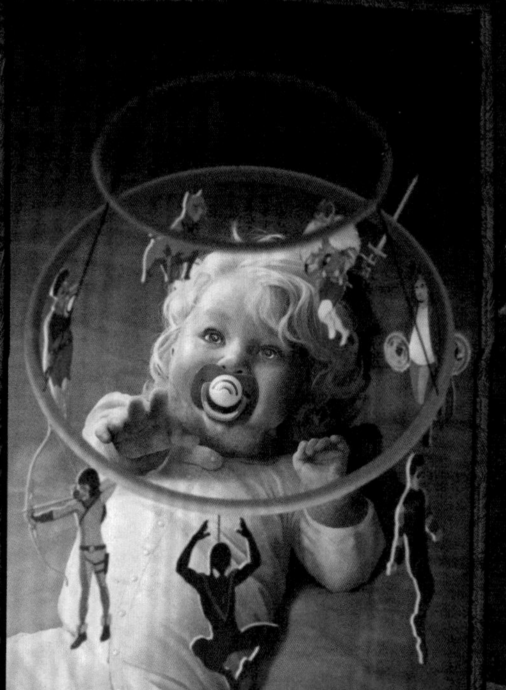

#2 VARIANT BY
Rahzzah

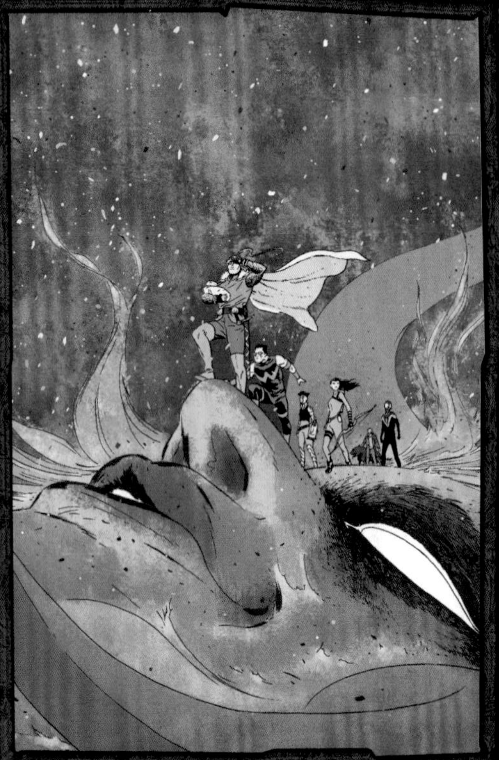

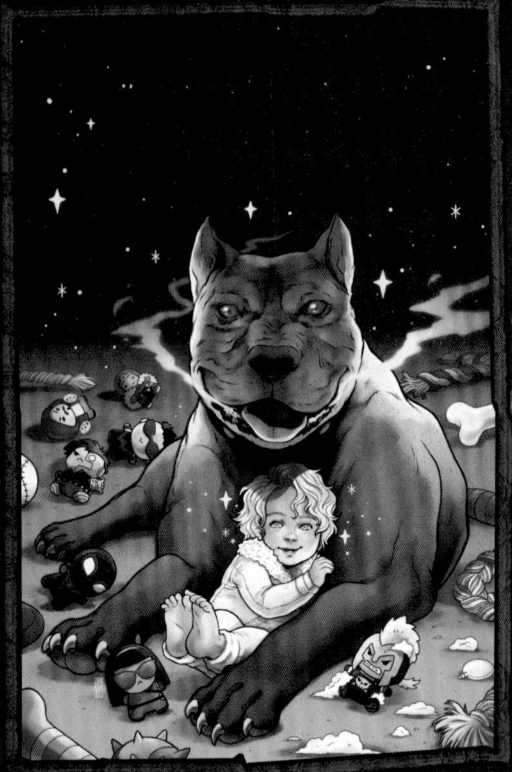

#3 VARIANT BY
Marcos Martin

#4 VARIANT BY
Jen Bartel

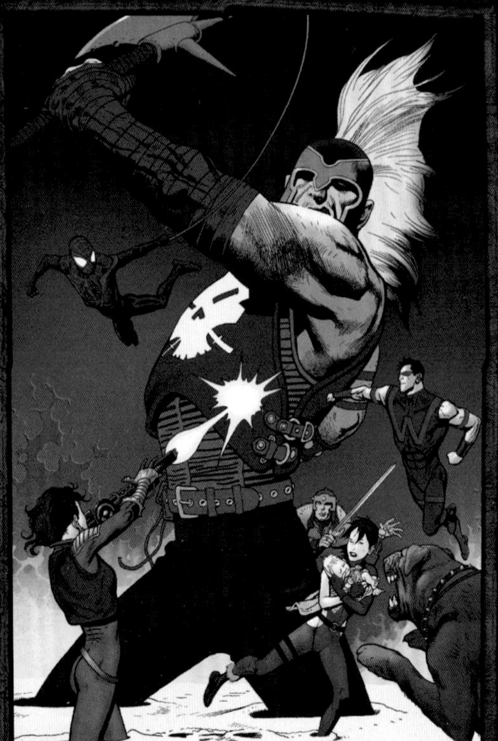

#5 VARIANT BY
Kevin Nowlan